Gleanings from the Writings of Bahá'u'lláh

Gleanings
from the Writings of
Bahá'u'lláh

*Translated
By
Shoghi Effendi*

BAHÁ'Í PUBLISHING TRUST
WILMETTE, ILLINOIS

Bahá'í Publishing Trust, Wilmette, IL 60091

Copyright 1952, © 1976 by the National Spiritual Assembly
of the Bahá'ís of the United States. All rights reserved
Second Edition 1976. First pocket-size edition 1983
Printed in the United States of America
05   10   9

Library of Congress Cataloging in Publication Data

Baha Ullāh, 1817–1892.
  Gleanings from the writings of Bahá'u'lláh.

  Includes index.
  1. Bahaism.   I. Shoghi, effendi.   II. Title.
BP360.B282 1976   297´.892´08   76–45364
ISBN 0–87743–111–6
ISBN 0–87743–112–4 pbk.

INTRODUCTION

This book is a selection from some of the chief writings of Bahá'u'lláh, the Founder of the Bahá'í Faith. Quite literally these are gleanings intended to convey the spirit of Bahá'u'lláh's life and teachings, and not bring together a cross-section of all His writings.

Key sentences may give us a first hint of the spirit of the book. "Let your vision be world-embracing, rather than confined to your own self." "All men have been created to carry forward an ever-advancing civilization." "That one indeed is a man who, today, dedicateth himself to the service of the entire human race."

1

The religion with the universal aims suggested by these sentences had its origin in Persia in the last century. Bahá'u'lláh was born in 1817 and died in 1892. He was the son of a Persian nobleman and born to wealth and luxury. Yet the major part of His life was spent in imprisonment and exile. He knew intimately torture and the dungeon, scorn and hunger, poverty and betrayal. The story of His life and of the Faith which bears His name (for Bahá'í means "a follower of Bahá") is intensely dramatic and, until recent years, was little known in the west.

About the first half of the nineteenth century, many Christians were stirred by the hope of the return of Christ. This expectancy, latent in the teachings of the New Testament, found its most vivid expression in the Millerites but it by no means was limited to humble Christians nor was it limited to America. Europe too was stirred by this phenomenon. A group of German Templars left their native land and settled permanently at the foot of Mount Carmel, to await their Lord.

What most Westerners do not understand at all, is that at the same time a wave of expectancy swept through Islám. Emerson would have understood this, but few other Americans were prepared at the time to consider any other world faith with even a modicum of sympathy. Yet the fact remains that in Islám some students and theologians felt that Islamic prophecies indicated an end of the laws of the Qur'án and a beginning of a new spiritual age. The thinking of these theologians was that the "Lord of the Age", to use the Islamic phrase, would appear.

In 1844 a young merchant of Shíráz named Siyyid 'Alí Muḥammad suddenly began to teach a new faith in Persia. He assumed the title of the Báb, which literally means "the Gate." The force of the Báb's character and utterance was like a bombshell in that backward, priest-ridden land. Pleasant academic discussions as to the meaning of the traditions of Islám were at an end. A flame of interest in the Báb and devoted acceptance of Him swept the country. The astonished priests reacted with orthodox fury. They arrested and imprisoned the Báb and instigated systematic massacres of His followers.

The Báb taught that a new spiritual era was at hand. He criticized vehemently the hypocrisy and intellectual dishonesty of the Muslim clergy. He urged the highest standard of character. And He promised that within nineteen years "Him Whom God would make manifest" would begin to teach and bring to men the basic laws and principles for a new age. The degenerate clergy, long corrupted by their powerful position in the church-state of Persia, feared and hated the movement initiated by the Báb. It was as if a strong, clean wind had suddenly swept through the dank atmosphere of a room long closed. The massacres of the Bábís find their parallel in the bloody holidays of ancient Rome. Hypocrisy and tyranny tried to destroy faith by the sword. The Báb was soon arrested and imprisoned in a remote mountain village. On July 9, 1850 hatred found its climax when the Báb was publicly martyred in the barracks square of the city of Tabríz. An attempt was made to completely exterminate the new faith in Persia. Bloody scenes multiplied throughout the country, and the surviving faithful went underground.

2

The consternation of the priesthood during these years had been deepened by the fact that many of their own outstanding members had accepted the teachings of the Báb. Also outstanding men in other walks of life had accepted Him. Among these was Mírzá Ḥusayn 'Alí, a young man of eminent and wealthy family. Ignoring the jibes of family and class, Mírzá Ḥusayn 'Alí, Who is known to history as Bahá'u'lláh ("the Glory of God"), publicly championed the Báb. In the nation-wide campaign to exterminate the faith, Bahá'u'lláh's position had caused Him to be spared. But in 1852 when two crazed young Bábís made an attempt to kill the Sháh, Bahá'u'lláh was imprisoned for four months in the Siyáh Chál, a dreadful underground prison in Ṭihrán. Bahá'u'lláh's innocence was clearly proven in the courts. But this incident is of great historic significance because during the imprisonment Bahá'u'lláh became aware that He was the Promised One foretold by the Báb.

Immediately after being released from prison, He was exiled to Baghdád by the Persian government, in an effort to remove from the country the last effective leader of the detested new faith. Bahá'u'lláh was an exile in 'Iráq for about ten years. During this time He transformed the outlook and character of the followers of the Báb. His own fame spread to such an extent that scholars and men of renown visited Him in increasing numbers.

To this first exile period belong two of Bahá'u'lláh's most famous books. One is a very small book of penetrating meditations entitled *Hidden Words*. In epigrammatic sentences, each prefaced by a salutation, Bahá'u'lláh restated the essential spiritual truths which have been taught by the Founders of all the world religions. No complicated theology mars the directness of the passages. It is the voice of God speaking directly to the heart of man.

"O Son of Spirit!

"The best beloved of all things in My sight is Justice; turn not away therefrom if thou desirest Me, and neglect it not that I may confide in thee. By its aid thou shalt see with thine own eyes and not through the eyes of others, and shalt know of thine own knowledge and not through the knowledge of thy neighbor. Ponder this in thy heart; how it behoveth thee to be. Verily justice is my gift to thee and the sign of My loving-kindness. Set it then before thine eyes."

The other outstanding work of this period was the *Kitáb-i-Íqán*, the English subtitle of which is the "Book of Certitude." This book is one of the major keys to understanding the teachings of Bahá'u'lláh. The great theme is this: in every age God reveals His will and purpose for human destiny through a chosen individual or Manifestation. Religion thus progressively evolves. The spiritual aspects of man's relation to God are not changed from age to age but restated and clarified. The social part of religion undergoes changes in every age because the conditions of life change. Thus Moses made certain laws which Jesus later changed or ignored, to the horror of the priests and the orthodox. The evolutionary principle in world religion is Bahá'u'lláh's first challenging contribution to the spiritual unity of mankind. A generous selection from the *Íqán* concerning the "City of Certitude" is found on pages 264-270. Other selections from the *Íqán* in this volume are on pages 17-27, 46-49, 50-56, 177, and 179.

The Muslim priests and the Turkish and Persian governments as Islamic church-states could not tolerate the rebirth of the new faith under Bahá'u'lláh. So it was decreed that Bahá'u'lláh be exiled from Baghdád to Constantinople, on the theory that distance would dissipate His influence — a theory repeatedly tried and repeatedly bringing opposite results. In 1863 the exile was ordered. And in the few days while a caravan was being prepared for the long journey, Bahá'u'lláh announced to His followers that He was the One Whose coming the Báb foretold.

After being four months in Constantinople, Bahá'u'lláh was banished to Adrianople. He here publicly proclaimed His message, addressing collectively the temporal and spiritual rulers of the earth. He wrote some of the first of a series of letters known collectively as the "Tablets to the Kings." He addressed the Sultán of Turkey, the Sháh of Persia, and Napoleon III, Emperor of the French. Among the themes in these letters was a call to the rulers "to be just and vigilant, to compose their differences and reduce their armaments." Later He addressed such letters to Queen Victoria, Alexander II of Russia, Pope Pius IX, William I, the Emperor of Germany, and Francis Joseph, the Emperor of Austria. In His book of laws the *Kitáb-i-Aqdas*, Bahá'u'lláh addressed a passage to "the Rulers of America and the Presidents of the Republics therein," asking them to "adorn the temple of dominion with the ornament of justice" and bidding them "bind with the hands of justice the broken." A few selections from this series of Tablets are in this volume, on pages 122-125, 210-212, 219-232, 232-240, and 246-249. (For the full scope of these letters, see *Bahá'í World Faith*, Chapter One, and *The Promised Day Is Come*, by Shoghi Effendi.)

A fourth and final exile was ordered, this time (1868) sending Bahá'u'lláh to the prison-city of 'Akká on the Bay of Haifa in the Holy Land. Bahá'u'lláh was an exile in 'Akká and the surrounding countryside until the end of His life in 1892.

Here He revealed the major portion of His teachings, and despite restrictions His influence increased. Two of His major books in this period were the *Kitáb-i-Aqdas* in which He stated the laws and ordinances of a new dispensation and the *Epistle to the Son of the Wolf*, a summary and defense of His teachings addressed to the son of a fanatic Muslim clergyman whom the Bahá'ís called "the Wolf."

3.

In the teachings of Bahá'u'lláh we find that He "abolishes the institution of priesthood; prohibits slavery, asceticism, mendicancy, monasticism, penance, the use of pulpits and the kissing of hands; prescribes monogamy; condemns cruelty to animals, idleness and sloth, backbiting and calumny; censures divorce; interdicts gambling, the use of opium, wine and other intoxicating drinks ... stresses the importance of marriage and lays down its essential conditions; imposes the obligation of engaging in some trade or profession, exalting such occupation to the rank of worship; emphasizes the necessity of providing the means for the education of children . . ."

The chief principle of Bahá'u'lláh's teachings is "the oneness and wholeness of the human race." This is the pivotal point of all that He taught. The purpose of the Bahá'í Faith is to unite the entire world in one common faith and one common social order. We may perhaps state that Bahá'u'lláh's second challenging contribution to the unity of the human race is a set of principles and a social structure designed to produce justice. He called justice "the best beloved of all things" in the sight of God. He urged moderation and warned against fanaticism and excesses of all kinds. The acquiring of education is essential to everyone. True religion and science are in agreement. Consultation is the key method for the settling of disputes and for developing plans and policies for the common good.

To achieve the unity of the human race was Bahá'u'lláh's compelling life purpose.

The aim of religion is to produce the strong, intangible bonds of unity. Bahá'u'lláh clarifies the historic development of religion as the evolution of one faith, serving different needs in each age. Abraham, Moses, Buddha, Zoroaster, Krishna, Jesus, Muḥammad, the Báb, and Bahá'u'lláh have been successive Manifestations, through Whom God has progressively revealed the purpose of religion. Because of ignorance, the followers of these Manifestations may quarrel, but the open-minded individual can see the pattern of agreement and evolution in what these supreme Educators taught. Stripped of the many layers of theology and custom, the different faiths of the world assume an integrated relationship, each leading to the other in historic development, as links in a chain. And none of the great Founders of the world's religions has ever taught that He was the only or the last Revealor of divine teachings. Instead, Each of them has praised the Prophet Who lived and taught before Him, and also has pointed to the future when another such Educator, or "Spirit of Truth" as Jesus taught, would live.

Bahá'u'lláh claimed to speak with the same divine authority as Moses, Jesus, and Muḥammad. He taught that the time was now ripe for the coming of age of the human race and the beginning of its conscious unity.

To achieve this, He urged the abolition of racial, religious, political, and economic prejudices, the adoption of an international auxiliary language, equal opportunities and privileges for men and women, a universal system of education, the independent investigation of truth, the adoption of a world code of human rights and responsibilities, and the creation of a world federal government. He taught that in each community there should be a House of Justice, this finally culminating in a Universal House of Justice.

4.

And Bahá'u'lláh took decided steps to prevent the corruption of His Faith into sects. He wrote His teachings, and as a result oral tradition was struck a blow. He abolished the authority of a priesthood. He forbade the creation of sacraments. And He appointed 'Abdu'l-Bahá, His eldest Son, as the Center of His Covenant, the point of unity to Whom all should turn on questions of interpretation of the teachings.

'Abdu'l-Bahá had been born in 1844 and shared the series of exiles with His Father. He himself continued a prisoner until in 1908 the revolution of the Young Turks released all religious prisoners. In 1910 'Abdu'l-Bahá began a series of missionary journeys which extended over a period of three years. He visited Egypt, Europe, the United States and Canada. Everywhere He was greeted with respect, scholars and noted men visiting Him. In pulpit, synagogue, and college hall, He freely proclaimed His Father's Faith. The result was a great strengthening of the little group of Bahá'ís in the West.

At the death of 'Abdu'l-Bahá in 1921, the Faith entered a new period of development. 'Abdu'l-Bahá left a Will and Testament in which He appointed Shoghi Effendi Rabbani, His eldest grandson, as Guardian of the Faith. This remarkable document not only made Shoghi Effendi the interpreter of the teachings but it also called upon the believers to arise and teach the Faith and build the World Order of Bahá'u'lláh.

Under the direction of Shoghi Effendi, the Bahá'ís have organized Local Spiritual Assemblies which are prototypes of the future Houses of Justice. Here group effort and consultation are learned and applied to the problems of a fast-evolving world faith. A beautiful House of Worship has been built in Wilmette, Illinois, as a first step in proclaiming Bahá'u'lláh's concept of worship and the unity of religion. Eleven National Spiritual Assemblies, some of them regional in nature, have been elected and they form a band around the earth — Canada; the United States; Central America; South America; the British Isles; Germany and Austria; Egypt and the Sudan; Iraq; Persia; India, Pakistan, and Burma; and Australia and New Zealand. The work of teaching the Faith goes on in dozens of countries where there are not yet enough Bahá'ís to form a National Assembly.

The houses and gardens associated with Bahá'u'lláh's imprisonment and exile in 'Akká and near-by Haifa are now centers of pilgrimage. On Mount Carmel a beautiful Shrine is being erected to fittingly shelter the remains of the Báb, which were hidden secretly by His followers and, after many decades of concealment, brought to the Holy Land. The Guardian of the Faith lives in Haifa, its World Center, and assisting him is the International Bahá'í Council.

Since 1921 the translation and publication of Bahá'u'lláh's teachings have increased with great rapidity. This book is an example of Shoghi Effendi's masterful translations into English. At this writing the teachings of Bahá'u'lláh have been rendered in over eighty languages.

5.

This very briefly summarizes the story which is so intimately associated with the spirit of *Gleanings*. The reader may be further assisted by the fact that the contents of *Gleanings* may be divided into five parts. Part one, pages 1-46, proclaims this age as the "Day of God." "The advent of such a Revelation hath been heralded in all the sacred Scriptures." This is the culminating age when the past dispensations will bear fruit as men and women the world over unite in a common faith. Part two, pages 46-136, concerns the Manifestation of God and the significance of the Manifestation in representing the attributes of God. Part three, pages 136-200, deals with basic questions concerning the soul and its immortality. Part four, pages 200-259, concerns spiritual aspects of World Order and the Most Great Peace. Part five, pages 259-346, deals with the duties of the individual and the spiritual meaning of life. Bahá'u'lláh's teachings may be further studied in *Bahá'í World Faith* and in other translations of His writings. The most detailed history of the Faith is *God Passes By* written by Shoghi Effendi.

Gleanings is a book for meditative study. It is not a book of history and facts, but of love and spiritual power. No one can understand the faith of the thousands of martyred followers of the Báb, unless he catches the spirit of this book. No one can appreciate why thousands of Bahá'ís give up the comfort of settled homes and move into strange countries to tell the people about Bahá'u'lláh, unless he clearly glimpses the spirit of this book.

Bahá'u'lláh has called into being a constantly-growing body of followers in the five continents of the globe. These people come from differing racial and religious backgrounds. In the Faith of Bahá'u'lláh they become united in belief and action. While wars are waged and the moral fabric of modern civilization becomes more and more tattered, Bahá'ís continue to tell the story of Bahá'u'lláh's life, of the reawakening of men to the call of God in our time. For, to Bahá'ís, quite literally, "This is the changeless faith of God, eternal in the past, eternal in the future." While the rot of modern materialism does its deadly work, Bahá'ís continue to patiently sacrifice and work to build the group consciousness and the social institutions which Bahá'u'lláh promised them would, in time, flower into a world civilization. To a Bahá'í, religion encompasses all of life — it is civilization itself. "All men have been created to carry forward an ever-advancing civilization."

"The earth is but one country, and mankind its citizens."

W. KENNETH CHRISTIAN
1952

Editorial Note: Before his passing in 1957, Shoghi Effendi appointed twenty-seven Hands of the Cause of God charged with the propagation and protection of the Faith. Through their efforts the election of the first Universal House of Justice was called in April 1963. At that time this supreme governing and legislative body of the Bahá'í Faith was elected by the fifty-six existing national administrative bodies (National Spiritual Assemblies), in accordance with provisions in the Writings of Bahá'u'lláh. Through a series of global teaching plans, begun in 1953, the Faith has spread to 190 independent countries and 45 dependent territories and overseas departments, with some 179 National Spiritual Assemblies. [1999]

Gleanings from the Writings of Bahá'u'lláh

GLEANINGS FROM THE WRITINGS OF BAHÁ'U'LLÁH

1. Lauded and glorified art Thou, O Lord, my God! How can I make mention of Thee, assured as I am that no tongue, however deep its wisdom, can befittingly magnify Thy name, nor can the bird of the human heart, however great its longing, ever hope to ascend into the heaven of Thy majesty and knowledge.

If I describe Thee, O my God, as Him Who is the All-Perceiving, I find myself compelled to admit that They Who are the highest Embodiments of perception have been created by virtue of Thy behest. And if I extol Thee as Him Who is the All-Wise, I, likewise, am forced to recognize that the Well Springs of wisdom have themselves been generated through the operation of Thy Will. And if I proclaim Thee as the Incomparable One, I soon discover that they Who are the inmost essence of oneness have been sent down by Thee and are but the evidences of Thine handiwork. And if I acclaim Thee as the Knower of all things, I must confess that they Who are the Quintessence of knowledge are but the creation and instruments of Thy Purpose.

Exalted, immeasurably exalted, art Thou above the strivings of mortal man to unravel Thy mystery, to describe Thy glory, or even to hint at the nature of Thine Essence. For whatever such strivings may accomplish, they never can hope to transcend the limitations imposed upon Thy creatures, inasmuch as these efforts are actuated by Thy decree, and are begotten of Thine invention. The loftiest sentiments which the holiest of saints can express in praise of Thee, and the deepest wisdom which the most learned of men can utter in their attempts to comprehend Thy nature, all revolve around that Center Which is wholly subjected to Thy sovereignty, Which adoreth Thy Beauty, and is propelled through the movement of Thy Pen.

Nay, forbid it, O my God, that I should have uttered such words as must of necessity imply the existence of any direct relationship between the Pen of Thy Revelation and the essence of all created things. Far, far are They Who are related to Thee above the conception of such relationship! All comparisons and likenesses fail to do justice to the Tree of Thy Revelation, and every way is barred to the comprehension of the Manifestation of Thy Self and the Day Spring of Thy Beauty.

Far, far from Thy glory be what mortal man can affirm of Thee, or attribute unto Thee, or the praise with which he can glorify Thee! Whatever duty Thou hast prescribed unto Thy servants of extolling to the utmost Thy majesty and glory is but a token of Thy grace unto them, that they may be enabled to ascend unto the station conferred upon their own inmost being, the station of the knowledge of their own selves.

No one else besides Thee hath, at any time, been able to fathom Thy mystery, or befittingly to extol Thy greatness. Unsearchable and high above the praise of men wilt Thou remain for ever. There is none other God but Thee, the Inaccessible, the Omnipotent, the Omniscient, the Holy of Holies.

II.   The beginning of all things is the knowledge of God, and the end of all things is strict observance of whatsoever hath been sent down from the empyrean of the Divine Will that pervadeth all that is in the heavens and all that is on the earth.

III.   The Revelation which, from time immemorial, hath been acclaimed as the Purpose and Promise of all the Prophets of God, and the most cherished Desire of His Messengers, hath now, by virtue of the pervasive Will of the Almighty and at His irresistible bidding, been revealed unto men. The advent of such a Revelation hath been heralded in all the sacred Scriptures. Behold how, notwithstanding such an announcement, mankind hath strayed from its path and shut out itself from its glory.

Say: O ye lovers of the One true God! Strive, that ye may truly recognize and know Him, and observe befittingly His precepts. This is a Revelation, under which, if a man shed for its sake one drop of blood, myriads of oceans will be his recompense. Take heed, O friends, that ye forfeit not so inestimable a benefit, or disregard its transcendent station. Consider the multitude of lives that have been, and are still being, sacrificed in a world deluded by a mere phantom which the vain imaginations of its peoples have conceived. Render thanks unto God, inasmuch as ye have attained unto your heart's Desire, and been united to Him Who is the Promise of all nations. Guard ye, with the aid of the one true God—exalted be His glory—the integrity of the station which ye have attained, and cleave to that which shall promote His Cause. He, verily, enjoineth on you what is right and conducive to the exaltation of man's station. Glorified be the All-Merciful, the Revealer of this wondrous Tablet.

IV.   This is the Day in which God's most excellent favors have been poured out upon men, the Day in which His most mighty grace hath been infused into all created things. It is incumbent upon all the peoples of the world to reconcile their differences, and, with perfect unity and peace, abide beneath the shadow of the Tree of His care and loving-kindness. It behoveth them to cleave to whatsoever will, in this Day, be conducive to the exaltation of their stations, and to the promotion of their best interests. Happy are those whom the all-glorious Pen was moved to remember, and blessed are those men whose names, by virtue of Our inscrutable decree, We have preferred to conceal.

Beseech ye the one true God to grant that all men may be graciously assisted to fulfil that which is acceptable in Our sight. Soon will the present-day order be rolled up, and a new one spread out in its stead. Verily, thy Lord speaketh the truth, and is the Knower of things unseen.

v. This is the Day whereon the Ocean of God's mercy hath been manifested unto men, the Day in which the Day Star of His loving-kindness hath shed its radiance upon them, the Day in which the clouds of His bountiful favor have overshadowed the whole of mankind. Now is the time to cheer and refresh the down-cast through the invigorating breeze of love and fellowship, and the living waters of friendliness and charity.

They who are the beloved of God, in whatever place they gather and whomsoever they may meet, must evince, in their attitude towards God, and in the manner of their celebration of His praise and glory, such humility and submissiveness that every atom of the dust beneath their feet may attest the depth of their devotion. The conversation carried by these holy souls should be informed with such power that these same atoms of dust will be thrilled by its influence. They should conduct themselves in such manner that the earth upon which they tread may never be allowed to address to them such words as these: "I am to be preferred above you. For witness, how patient I am in bearing the burden which the husbandman layeth upon me. I am the instrument that continually imparteth unto all beings the blessings with which He Who is the Source of all grace hath entrusted me. Notwithstanding the honor conferred upon me, and the unnumbered evidences of my wealth—a wealth that supplieth the needs of all creation—behold the measure of my humility, witness with what absolute submissiveness I allow myself to be trodden beneath the feet of men. . . ."

Show forbearance and benevolence and love to one another. Should any one among you be incapable of grasping a certain truth, or be striving to comprehend it, show forth, when conversing with him, a spirit of extreme kindliness and good-will. Help him to see and recognize the truth, without esteeming yourself to be, in the least, superior to him, or to be possessed of greater endowments.

The whole duty of man in this Day is to attain that share of the flood of grace which God poureth forth for him. Let none, therefore, consider the largeness or smallness of the receptacle. The portion of some might lie in the palm of a man's hand, the portion of others might fill a cup, and of others even a gallon-measure.

Every eye, in this Day, should seek what will best

promote the Cause of God. He, Who is the Eternal Truth, beareth Me witness! Nothing whatever can, in this Day, inflict a greater harm upon this Cause than dissension and strife, contention, estrangement and apathy, among the loved ones of God. Flee them, through the power of God and His sovereign aid, and strive ye to knit together the hearts of men, in His Name, the Unifier, the All-Knowing, the All-Wise.

Beseech ye the one true God to grant that ye may taste the savor of such deeds as are performed in His path, and partake of the sweetness of such humility and submissiveness as are shown for His sake. Forget your own selves, and turn your eyes towards your neighbor. Bend your energies to whatever may foster the education of men. Nothing is, or can ever be, hidden from God. If ye follow in His way, His incalculable and imperishable blessings will be showered upon you. This is the luminous Tablet, whose verses have streamed from the moving Pen of Him Who is the Lord of all worlds. Ponder it in your hearts, and be ye of them that observe its precepts.

VI. Behold, how the divers peoples and kindreds of the earth have been waiting for the coming of the Promised One. No sooner had He, Who is the Sun of Truth, been made manifest, than, lo, all turned away from Him, except them whom God was pleased to guide. We dare not, in this Day, lift the veil that concealeth the exalted station which every true believer can attain, for the joy which such a revelation must provoke might well cause a few to faint away and die.

He Who is the Heart and Center of the Bayán hath written: "The germ that holdeth within itself the potentialities of the Revelation that is to come is endowed with a potency superior to the combined forces of all those who follow Me." And, again, He saith: "Of all the tributes I have paid to Him Who is to come after Me, the greatest is this, My written confession, that no words of Mine can adequately describe Him, nor can any reference to Him in My Book, the Bayán, do justice to His Cause."

Whoso hath searched the depths of the oceans that lie hid within these exalted words, and fathomed their import, can be said to have discovered a glimmer of the unspeakable glory with which this mighty, this sublime, and most holy Revelation hath been endowed. From the excellence of so great a Revelation the honor with which its faithful followers must needs be invested can be well imagined. By the righteousness of the one true God! The very breath of these souls is in itself richer than all the treasures of the earth. Happy is the man that hath attained thereunto, and woe betide the heedless.

VII.   Verily I say, this is the Day in which mankind can behold the Face, and hear the Voice, of the Promised One. The Call of God hath been raised, and the light of His countenance hath been lifted up upon men. It behoveth every man to blot out the trace of every idle word from the tablet of his heart, and to gaze, with an open and unbiased mind, on the signs of His Revelation, the proofs of His Mission, and the tokens of His glory.

Great indeed is this Day! The allusions made to it in all the sacred Scriptures as the Day of God attest its greatness. The soul of every Prophet of God, of every Divine Messenger, hath thirsted for this wondrous Day. All the divers kindreds of the earth have, likewise, yearned to attain it. No sooner, however, had the Day Star of His Revelation manifested itself in the heaven of God's Will, than all, except those whom the Almighty was pleased to guide, were found dumbfounded and heedless.

O thou that hast remembered Me! The most grievous veil hath shut out the peoples of the earth from His glory, and hindered them from hearkening to His call. God grant that the light of unity may envelop the whole earth, and that the seal, "the Kingdom is God's", may be stamped upon the brow of all its peoples.

VIII. By the righteousness of God! These are the days in which God hath proved the hearts of the entire company of His Messengers and Prophets, and beyond them those that stand guard over His sacred and inviolable Sanctuary, the inmates of the celestial

Pavilion and dwellers of the Tabernacle of Glory. How severe, therefore, the test to which they who join partners with God must needs be subjected!

IX.   Ḥusayn! Consider the eagerness with which certain peoples and nations have anticipated the return of Imám-Ḥusayn, whose coming, after the appearance of the Qá'im, hath been prophesied, in days past, by the chosen ones of God, exalted be His glory. These holy ones have, moreover, announced that when He Who is the Day Spring of the manifold grace of God manifesteth Himself, all the Prophets and Messengers, including the Qá'im, will gather together beneath the shadow of the sacred Standard which the Promised One will raise. That hour is now come. The world is illumined with the effulgent glory of His countenance. And yet, behold how far its peoples have strayed from His path! None have believed in Him except them who, through the power of the Lord of Names, have shattered the idols of their vain imaginings and corrupt desires and entered the city of certitude. The seal of the choice Wine of His Revelation hath, in this Day and in His Name, the Self-Sufficing, been broken. Its grace is being poured out upon men. Fill thy cup, and drink in, in His Name, the Most Holy, the All-Praised.

X.   The time foreordained unto the peoples and kindreds of the earth is now come. The promises of

God, as recorded in the holy Scriptures, have all been fulfilled. Out of Zion hath gone forth the Law of God, and Jerusalem, and the hills and land thereof, are filled with the glory of His Revelation. Happy is the man that pondereth in his heart that which hath been revealed in the Books of God, the Help in Peril, the Self-Subsisting. Meditate upon this, O ye beloved of God, and let your ears be attentive unto His Word, so that ye may, by His grace and mercy, drink your fill from the crystal waters of constancy, and become as steadfast and immovable as the mountain in His Cause.

In the Book of Isaiah it is written: "Enter into the rock, and hide thee in the dust, for fear of the Lord, and for the glory of His majesty." No man that meditateth upon this verse can fail to recognize the greatness of this Cause, or doubt the exalted character of this Day—the Day of God Himself. This same verse is followed by these words: "And the Lord alone shall be exalted in that Day." This is the Day which the Pen of the Most High hath glorified in all the holy Scriptures. There is no verse in them that doth not declare the glory of His holy Name, and no Book that doth not testify unto the loftiness of this most exalted theme. Were We to make mention of all that hath been revealed in these heavenly Books and holy Scriptures concerning this Revelation, this Tablet would assume impossible dimensions. It is incumbent in this Day, upon every man to place his whole trust in the manifold bounties of God, and arise to disseminate, with the utmost wisdom, the verities of His Cause. Then, and only then, will the whole earth be enveloped with the morning light of His Revelation.

XI.   All glory be to this Day, the Day in which the fragrances of mercy have been wafted over all created things, a Day so blest that past ages and centuries can never hope to rival it, a Day in which the countenance of the Ancient of Days hath turned towards His holy seat. Thereupon the voices of all created things, and beyond them those of the Concourse on high, were heard calling aloud: "Haste thee, O Carmel, for lo, the light of the countenance of God, the Ruler of the Kingdom of Names and Fashioner of the heavens, hath been lifted upon thee."

Seized with transports of joy, and raising high her voice, she thus exclaimed: "May my life be a sacrifice to Thee, inasmuch as Thou hast fixed Thy gaze upon me, hast bestowed upon me Thy bounty, and hast directed towards me Thy steps. Separation from Thee, O Thou Source of everlasting life, hath well nigh consumed me, and my remoteness from Thy presence hath burned away my soul. All praise be to Thee for having enabled me to hearken to Thy call, for having honored me with Thy footsteps, and for having quickened my soul through the vitalizing fragrance of Thy Day and the shrilling voice of Thy

[14]

Pen, a voice Thou didst ordain as Thy trumpet-call amidst Thy people. And when the hour at which Thy resistless Faith was to be made manifest did strike, Thou didst breathe a breath of Thy spirit into Thy Pen, and lo, the entire creation shook to its very foundations, unveiling to mankind such mysteries as lay hidden within the treasuries of Him Who is the Possessor of all created things."

No sooner had her voice reached that most exalted Spot than We made reply: "Render thanks unto thy Lord, O Carmel. The fire of thy separation from Me was fast consuming thee, when the ocean of My presence surged before thy face, cheering thine eyes and those of all creation, and filling with delight all things visible and invisible. Rejoice, for God hath in this Day established upon thee His throne, hath made thee the dawning-place of His signs and the day spring of the evidences of His Revelation. Well is it with him that circleth around thee, that proclaimeth the revelation of thy glory, and recounteth that which the bounty of the Lord thy God hath showered upon thee. Seize thou the Chalice of Immortality in the name of thy Lord, the All-Glorious, and give thanks unto Him, inasmuch as He, in token of His mercy unto thee, hath turned thy sorrow into gladness, and transmuted thy grief into blissful joy. He, verily, loveth the spot which hath been made the seat of His throne, which His footsteps have trodden, which hath been honored by His presence, from which He raised His call, and upon which He shed His tears.

"Call out to Zion, O Carmel, and announce the joyful tidings: He that was hidden from mortal eyes is come! His all-conquering sovereignty is manifest; His all-encompassing splendor is revealed. Beware lest thou hesitate or halt. Hasten forth and circumambulate the City of God that hath descended from heaven, the celestial Kaaba round which have circled in adoration the favored of God, the pure in heart, and the company of the most exalted angels. Oh, how I long to announce unto every spot on the surface of the earth, and to carry to each one of its cities, the glad-tidings of this Revelation—a Revelation to which the heart of Sinai hath been attracted, and in whose name the Burning Bush is calling: 'Unto God, the Lord of Lords, belong the kingdoms of earth and heaven.' Verily this is the Day in which both land and sea rejoice at this announcement, the Day for which have been laid up those things which God, through a bounty beyond the ken of mortal mind or heart, hath destined for revelation. Ere long will God sail His Ark upon thee, and will manifest the people of Bahá who have been mentioned in the Book of Names."

Sanctified be the Lord of all mankind, at the mention of Whose name all the atoms of the earth have been made to vibrate, and the Tongue of Grandeur hath been moved to disclose that which had been

[16]

wrapt in His knowledge and lay concealed within the treasury of His might. He, verily, through the potency of His name, the Mighty, the All-Powerful, the Most High, is the ruler of all that is in the heavens and all that is on earth.

XII. Bestir yourselves, O people, in anticipation of the days of Divine justice, for the promised hour is now come. Beware lest ye fail to apprehend its import and be accounted among the erring.

XIII. Consider the past. How many, both high and low, have, at all times, yearningly awaited the advent of the Manifestations of God in the sanctified persons of His chosen Ones. How often have they expected His coming, how frequently have they prayed that the breeze of Divine mercy might blow, and the promised Beauty step forth from behind the veil of concealment, and be made manifest to all the world. And whensoever the portals of grace did open, and the clouds of divine bounty did rain upon mankind, and the light of the Unseen did shine above the horizon of celestial might, they all denied Him, and turned away from His face—the face of God Himself. . . .

Reflect, what could have been the motive for such deeds? What could have prompted such behavior towards the Revealers of the beauty of the All-Glorious? Whatever in days gone by hath been the cause

[17]

of the denial and opposition of those people hath now led to the perversity of the people of this age. To maintain that the testimony of Providence was incomplete, that it hath therefore been the cause of the denial of the people, is but open blasphemy. How far from the grace of the All-Bountiful and from His loving providence and tender mercies it is to single out a soul from amongst all men for the guidance of His creatures, and, on one hand, to withhold from Him the full measure of His divine testimony, and, on the other, inflict severe retribution on His people for having turned away from His chosen One! Nay, the manifold bounties of the Lord of all beings have, at all times, through the Manifestations of His Divine Essence, encompassed the earth and all that dwell therein. Not for a moment hath His grace been withheld, nor have the showers of His loving-kindness ceased to rain upon mankind. Consequently, such behavior can be attributed to naught save the petty-mindedness of such souls as tread the valley of arrogance and pride, are lost in the wilds of remoteness, walk in the ways of their idle fancy, and follow the dictates of the leaders of their faith. Their chief concern is mere opposition; their sole desire is to ignore the truth. Unto every discerning observer it is evident and manifest that had these people in the days of each of the Manifestations of the Sun of Truth sanctified their eyes, their ears, and their hearts from whatever they had seen, heard, and felt, they surely would not have been deprived of beholding the beauty of God, nor strayed far from the habitations of glory. But having weighed the testimony of God by the standard of their own knowledge, gleaned from the teachings of the leaders of their faith, and found it at variance with their limited understanding, they arose to perpetrate such unseemly acts. . . .

Consider Moses! Armed with the rod of celestial dominion, adorned with the white hand of Divine knowledge, and proceeding from the Párán of the love of God, and wielding the serpent of power and everlasting majesty, He shone forth from the Sinai of light upon the world. He summoned all the peoples and kindreds of the earth to the kingdom of eternity, and invited them to partake of the fruit of the tree of faithfulness. Surely you are aware of the fierce opposition of Pharaoh and his people, and of the stones of idle fancy which the hands of infidels cast upon that blessed Tree. So much so that Pharaoh and his people finally arose and exerted their utmost endeavor to extinguish with the waters of falsehood and denial the fire of that sacred Tree, oblivious of the truth that no earthly water can quench the flames of Divine wisdom, nor mortal blasts extinguish the lamp of everlasting dominion. Nay, rather, such water cannot but intensify the burning of the flame, and such blasts cannot but ensure the preservation of the lamp, were ye to observe with the eye of discernment, and walk in the way of God's holy will and pleasure. . . .

[19]

And when the days of Moses were ended, and the light of Jesus, shining forth from the Day Spring of the Spirit, encompassed the world, all the people of Israel arose in protest against Him. They clamored that He Whose advent the Bible had foretold must needs promulgate and fulfil the laws of Moses, whereas this youthful Nazarene, who laid claim to the station of the divine Messiah, had annulled the laws of divorce and of the sabbath day—the most weighty of all the laws of Moses. Moreover, what of the signs of the Manifestation yet to come? These people of Israel are even unto the present day still expecting that Manifestation which the Bible hath foretold! How many Manifestations of Holiness, how many Revealers of the light everlasting, have appeared since the time of Moses, and yet Israel, wrapt in the densest veils of satanic fancy and false imaginings, is still expectant that the idol of her own handiwork will appear with such signs as she herself hath conceived! Thus hath God laid hold of them for their sins, hath extinguished in them the spirit of faith, and tormented them with the flames of the nethermost fire. And this for no other reason except that Israel refused to apprehend the meaning of such words as have been revealed in the Bible concerning the signs of the coming Revelation. As she never grasped their true significance, and, to outward seeming, such events never came to pass, she, therefore, remained deprived of recognizing the beauty of Jesus

[20]

and of beholding the Face of God. And they still await His coming! From time immemorial even unto this day, all the kindreds and peoples of the earth have clung to such fanciful and unseemly thoughts, and thus have deprived themselves of the clear waters streaming from the springs of purity and holiness. . . .

To them that are endowed with understanding, it is clear and manifest that, when the fire of the love of Jesus consumed the veils of Jewish limitations, and His authority was made apparent and partially enforced, He, the Revealer of the unseen Beauty, addressing one day His disciples, referred unto His passing, and, kindling in their hearts the fire of bereavement, said unto them: "I go away and come again unto you." And in another place He said: "I go and another will come, Who will tell you all that I have not told you, and will fulfil all that I have said." Both these sayings have but one meaning, were ye to ponder upon the Manifestations of the Unity of God with Divine insight.

Every discerning observer will recognize that in the Dispensation of the Qur'án both the Book and the Cause of Jesus were confirmed. As to the matter of names, Muḥammad, Himself, declared: "I am Jesus." He recognized the truth of the signs, prophecies, and words of Jesus, and testified that they were all of God. In this sense, neither the person of Jesus nor His writings hath differed from that of Muḥammad and of His holy Book, inasmuch as both have

[21]

championed the Cause of God, uttered His praise, and revealed His commandments. Thus it is that Jesus, Himself, declared: "I go away and come again unto you." Consider the sun. Were it to say now, "I am the sun of yesterday," it would speak the truth. And should it, bearing the sequence of time in mind, claim to be other than that sun, it still would speak the truth. In like manner, if it be said that all the days are but one and the same, it is correct and true. And if it be said, with respect to their particular names and designations, that they differ, that again is true. For though they are the same, yet one doth recognize in each a separate designation, a specific attribute, a particular character. Conceive accordingly the distinction, variation, and unity characteristic of the various Manifestations of holiness, that thou mayest comprehend the allusions made by the Creator of all names and attributes to the mysteries of distinction and unity, and discover the answer to thy question as to why that everlasting Beauty should have, at sundry times, called Himself by different names and titles. . . .

When the Unseen, the Eternal, the Divine Essence, caused the Day Star of Muḥammad to rise above the horizon of knowledge, among the cavils which the Jewish divines raised against Him was that after Moses no Prophet should be sent of God. Yea, mention hath been made in the Scriptures of a Soul Who must needs be made manifest and Who will advance

the Faith, and promote the interests of the people of
Moses, so that the Law of the Mosaic Dispensation
may encompass the whole earth. Thus hath the King
of eternal glory referred in His Book to the words uttered by those wanderers in the vale of remoteness
and error: " 'The hand of God,' say the Jews, 'is
chained up.' Chained up be their own hands; And
for that which they have said, they were accursed.
Nay, outstretched are both His hands!" "The hand
of God is above their hands." Although the commen-
tators of the Qur'án have related in divers manners
the circumstances attending the revelation of this
verse, yet thou shouldst endeavor to apprehend the
purpose thereof. He saith: How false is that which
the Jews have imagined! How can the hand of Him
Who is the King in truth, Who caused the countenance of Moses to be made manifest, and conferred
upon Him the robe of Prophethood—how can the
hand of such a One be chained and fettered? How
can He be conceived as powerless to raise up yet another Messenger after Moses? Behold the absurdity
of their saying; how far it hath strayed from the path
of knowledge and understanding! Observe how in
this Day also, all these people have occupied themselves with such foolish absurdities. For over a thousand years they have been reciting this verse, and un-
wittingly pronouncing their censure against the Jews,
utterly unaware that they themselves, openly and
privily, are voicing the sentiments and belief of the

Jewish people! Thou art surely aware of their idle contention, that all Revelation is ended, that the portals of Divine mercy are closed, that from the day springs of eternal holiness no Sun shall rise again, that the Ocean of everlasting bounty is forever stilled, and that out of the Tabernacle of ancient glory the Messengers of God have ceased to be made manifest. Such is the measure of the understanding of these small-minded, contemptible people. These people have imagined that the flow of God's all-encompassing grace and plenteous mercies, the cessation of which no mind can contemplate, has been halted. From every side they have risen and girded up the loins of tyranny, and exerted the utmost endeavor to quench with the bitter waters of their vain fancy the flame of God's Burning Bush, oblivious that the globe of power shall, within its own mighty stronghold, protect the Lamp of God. . . .

Behold how the sovereignty of Muḥammad, the Messenger of God, is today apparent and manifest amongst the people. You are well aware of what befell His Faith in the early days of His Dispensation. What woeful sufferings did the hand of the infidel and erring, the divines of that age and their associates, inflict upon that spiritual Essence, that most pure and holy Being! How abundant the thorns and briars which they have strewn over His path! It is evident that that wretched generation, in their wicked and satanic fancy, regarded every injury to that immortal

[24]

Being as a means to the attainment of an abiding felicity; inasmuch as the recognized divines of that age, such as 'Abdu'lláh-i-Ubayy, Abú 'Ámir, the hermit, Ka'b-ibn-i-Ashraf, and Naḍr-ibn-i-Ḥárith, all treated Him as an impostor, and pronounced Him a lunatic and a calumniator. Such sore accusations they brought against Him that in recounting them God forbiddeth the ink to flow, Our pen to move, or the page to bear them. These malicious imputations provoked the people to arise and torment Him. And how fierce that torment, if the divines of the age be its chief instigators, if they denounce Him to their followers, cast Him out from their midst, and declare Him a miscreant! Hath not the same befallen this Servant, and been witnessed by all?

For this reason did Muḥammad cry out: "No Prophet of God hath suffered such harm as I have suffered." And in the Qur'án are recorded all the calumnies and reproaches uttered against Him, as well as all the afflictions which He suffered. Refer ye thereunto, that haply ye may be informed of that which hath befallen His Revelation. So grievous was His plight, that for a time all ceased to hold intercourse with Him and His companions. Whoever associated with Him fell a victim to the relentless cruelty of His enemies. . . .

Consider, how great is the change today! Behold, how many are the Sovereigns who bow the knee before His name! How numerous the nations and kingdoms who have sought the shelter of His shadow, who bear allegiance to His Faith, and pride themselves therein! From the pulpit-top there ascendeth today the words of praise which, in utter lowliness, glorify His blessed name; and from the heights of minarets there resoundeth the call that summoneth the concourse of His people to adore Him. Even those Kings of the earth who have refused to embrace His Faith and to put off the garment of unbelief, none-the-less confess and acknowledge the greatness and overpowering majesty of that Day Star of loving-kindness. Such is His earthly sovereignty, the evidences of which thou dost on every side behold. This sovereignty must needs be revealed and established either in the lifetime of every Manifestation of God or after His ascension unto His true habitation in the realms above. . . .

It is evident that the changes brought about in every Dispensation constitute the dark clouds that intervene between the eye of man's understanding and the Divine Luminary which shineth forth from the day spring of the Divine Essence. Consider how men for generations have been blindly imitating their fathers, and have been trained according to such ways and manners as have been laid down by the dictates of their Faith. Were these men, therefore, to discover suddenly that a Man, Who hath been living in their midst, Who, with respect to every human limitation hath been their equal, had risen to abolish every established principle imposed by their Faith—principles by which for centuries they have been disciplined, and every opposer and denier of which they have come to regard as infidel, profligate and wicked,—they would of a certainty be veiled and hindered from acknowledging His truth. Such things are as "clouds" that veil the eyes of those whose inner being hath not tasted the Salsabíl of detachment, nor drunk from the Kawthar of the knowledge of God. Such men, when acquainted with those circumstances, become so veiled that, without the least question, they pronounce the Manifestation of God as infidel, and sentence Him to death. You must have heard of such things taking place all down the ages, and are now observing them in these days.

It behoveth us, therefore, to make the utmost endeavor, that, by God's invisible assistance, these dark veils, these clouds of Heaven-sent trials, may not hinder us from beholding the beauty of His shining Countenance, and that we may recognize Him only by His own Self.

XIV.   The Divine Springtime is come, O Most Exalted Pen, for the Festival of the All-Merciful is fast approaching. Bestir thyself, and magnify, before the entire creation, the name of God, and celebrate His praise, in such wise that all created things may be regenerated and made new. Speak, and hold not thy peace. The day star of blissfulness shineth above the horizon of Our name, the Blissful, inasmuch as the kingdom of the name of God hath been adorned with the ornament of the name of thy Lord, the Creator of the heavens. Arise before the nations of the earth, and arm thyself with the power of this Most Great Name, and be not of those who tarry.

Methinks that thou hast halted and movest not upon My Tablet. Could the brightness of the Divine Countenance have bewildered thee, or the idle talk of the froward filled thee with grief and paralyzed thy movement? Take heed lest anything deter thee from extolling the greatness of this Day—the Day whereon the Finger of majesty and power hath opened the seal of the Wine of Reunion, and called all who are in the heavens and all who are on the earth. Preferrest thou to tarry when the breeze announcing the Day of God hath already breathed over thee, or art thou of them that are shut out as by a veil from Him?

No veil whatever have I allowed, O Lord of all names and Creator of the heavens, to shut me from the recognition of the glories of Thy Day—the Day which is the lamp of guidance unto the whole world, and the sign of the Ancient of Days unto all them that dwell therein. My silence is by reason of the veils that have blinded Thy creatures' eyes to Thee, and my muteness is because of the impediments that have hindered Thy people from recognizing Thy truth.

Thou knowest what is in me, but I know not what is in Thee. Thou art the All-Knowing, the All-Informed. By Thy name that excelleth all other names! If Thy overruling and all-compelling behest should ever reach me, it would empower me to revive the souls of all men, through Thy most exalted Word, which I have heard uttered by Thy Tongue of power in Thy Kingdom of glory. It would enable me to announce the revelation of Thy effulgent countenance wherethrough that which lay hidden from the eyes of men hath been manifested in Thy name, the Perspicuous, the sovereign Protector, the Self-Subsisting.

Canst thou discover any one but Me, O Pen, in this Day? What hath become of the creation and the manifestations thereof? What of the names and their kingdom? Whither are gone all created things, whether seen or unseen? What of the hidden secrets of the universe and its revelations? Lo, the entire creation hath passed away! Nothing remaineth except My Face, the Ever-Abiding, the Resplendent, the All-Glorious.

This is the Day whereon naught can be seen except the splendors of the Light that shineth from the face of Thy Lord, the Gracious, the Most Bountiful. Verily, We have caused every soul to expire by virtue of Our irresistible and all-subduing sovereignty. We have, then, called into being a new creation, as a token of Our grace unto men. I am, verily, the All-Bountiful, the Ancient of Days.

This is the Day whereon the unseen world crieth out: "Great is thy blessedness, O earth, for thou hast been made the foot-stool of thy God, and been chosen as the seat of His mighty throne." The realm of glory exclaimeth: "Would that my life could be sacrificed for thee, for He Who is the Beloved of the All-Merciful hath established His sovereignty upon thee, through the power of His Name that hath been promised unto all things, whether of the past or of the future." This is the Day whereon every sweet smelling thing hath derived its fragrance from the smell of My garment—a garment that hath shed its perfume upon the whole of creation. This is the Day whereon the rushing waters of everlasting life have gushed out of the Will of the All-Merciful. Haste ye, with your hearts and souls, and quaff your fill, O Concourse of the realms above!

Say: He it is Who is the Manifestation of Him Who is the Unknowable, the Invisible of the Invisibles, could ye but perceive it. He it is Who hath laid bare before you the hidden and treasured Gem, were ye to seek it. He it is Who is the one Beloved of all things, whether of the past or of the future. Would that ye might set your hearts and hopes upon Him!

We have heard the voice of thy pleading, O Pen,

and excuse thy silence. What is it that hath so sorely bewildered thee?

The inebriation of Thy presence, O Well-Beloved of all worlds, hath seized and possessed me.

Arise, and proclaim unto the entire creation the tidings that He Who is the All-Merciful hath directed His steps towards the Riḍván and entered it. Guide, then, the people unto the garden of delight which God hath made the Throne of His Paradise. We have chosen thee to be our most mighty Trumpet, whose blast is to signalize the resurrection of all mankind.

Say: This is the Paradise on whose foliage the wine of utterance hath imprinted the testimony: "He that was hidden from the eyes of men is revealed, girded with sovereignty and power!" This is the Paradise, the rustling of whose leaves proclaims: "O ye that inhabit the heavens and the earth! There hath appeared what hath never previously appeared. He Who, from everlasting, had concealed His Face from the sight of creation is now come." From the whispering breeze that wafteth amidst its branches there cometh the cry: "He Who is the sovereign Lord of all is made manifest. The Kingdom is God's," while from its streaming waters can be heard the murmur: "All eyes are gladdened, for He Whom none hath beheld, Whose secret no one hath discovered, hath lifted the veil of glory, and uncovered the countenance of Beauty."

Within this Paradise, and from the heights of its loftiest chambers, the Maids of Heaven have cried out and shouted: "Rejoice, ye dwellers of the realms above, for the fingers of Him Who is the Ancient of Days are ringing, in the name of the All-Glorious, the Most Great Bell, in the midmost heart of the heavens. The hands of bounty have borne round the cup of everlasting life. Approach, and quaff your fill. Drink with healthy relish, O ye that are the very incarnations of longing, ye who are the embodiments of vehement desire!"

This is the Day whereon He Who is the Revealer of the names of God hath stepped out of the Tabernacle of glory, and proclaimed unto all who are in the heavens and all who are on the earth: "Put away the cups of Paradise and all the life-giving waters they contain, for lo, the people of Bahá have entered the blissful abode of the Divine Presence, and quaffed the wine of reunion, from the chalice of the beauty of their Lord, the All-Possessing, the Most High."

Forget the world of creation, O Pen, and turn thou towards the face of thy Lord, the Lord of all names. Adorn, then, the world with the ornament of the favors of thy Lord, the King of everlasting days. For We perceive the fragrance of the Day whereon He Who is the Desire of all nations hath shed upon the kingdoms of the unseen and of the seen the splendor of the light of His most excellent names, and enveloped them with the radiance of the luminaries

[32]

of His most gracious favors—favors which none can reckon except Him, Who is the omnipotent Protector of the entire creation.

Look not upon the creatures of God except with the eye of kindliness and of mercy, for Our loving providence hath pervaded all created things, and Our grace encompassed the earth and the heavens. This is the Day whereon the true servants of God partake of the life-giving waters of reunion, the Day whereon those that are nigh unto Him are able to drink of the soft-flowing river of immortality, and they who believe in His unity, the wine of His Presence, through their recognition of Him Who is the Highest and Last End of all, in Whom the Tongue of Majesty and Glory voiceth the call: "The Kingdom is Mine. I, Myself, am, of Mine own right, its Ruler."

Attract the hearts of men, through the call of Him, the one alone Beloved. Say: This is the Voice of God, if ye do but hearken. This is the Day Spring of the Revelation of God, did ye but know it. This is the Dawning-Place of the Cause of God, were ye to recognize it. This is the Source of the commandment of God, did ye but judge it fairly. This is the manifest and hidden Secret; would that ye might perceive it. O peoples of the world! Cast away, in My name that transcendeth all other names, the things ye possess, and immerse yourselves in this Ocean in whose depths lay hidden the pearls of wisdom and of utterance, an ocean that surgeth in My name, the All-Merciful.

Thus instructeth you He with Whom is the Mother Book.

The Best-Beloved is come. In His right hand is the sealed Wine of His name. Happy is the man that turneth unto Him, and drinketh his fill, and exclaimeth: "Praise be to Thee, O Revealer of the signs of God!" By the righteousness of the Almighty! Every hidden thing hath been manifested through the power of truth. All the favors of God have been sent down, as a token of His grace. The waters of everlasting life have, in their fullness, been proffered unto men. Every single cup hath been borne round by the hand of the Well-Beloved. Draw near, and tarry not, though it be for one short moment.

Blessed are they that have soared on the wings of detachment and attained the station which, as ordained by God, overshadoweth the entire creation, whom neither the vain imaginations of the learned, nor the multitude of the hosts of the earth have succeeded in deflecting from His Cause. Who is there among you, O people, who will renounce the world, and draw nigh unto God, the Lord of all names? Where is he to be found who, through the power of My name that transcendeth all created things, will cast away the things that men possess, and cling, with all his might, to the things which God, the Knower of the unseen and of the seen, hath bidden him observe? Thus hath His bounty been sent down unto men, His testimony fulfilled, and His proof shone

[34]

forth above the Horizon of mercy. Rich is the prize that shall be won by him who hath believed and exclaimed: "Lauded art Thou, O Beloved of all worlds! Magnified be Thy name, O Thou the Desire of every understanding heart!"

Rejoice with exceeding gladness, O people of Bahá, as ye call to remembrance the Day of supreme felicity, the Day whereon the Tongue of the Ancient of Days hath spoken, as He departed from His House, proceeding to the Spot from which He shed upon the whole of creation the splendors of His name, the All-Merciful. God is Our witness. Were We to reveal the hidden secrets of that Day, all they that dwell on earth and in the heavens would swoon away and die, except such as will be preserved by God, the Almighty, the All-Knowing, the All-Wise.

Such is the inebriating effect of the words of God upon Him Who is the Revealer of His undoubted proofs, that His Pen can move no longer. With these words He concludeth His Tablet: "No God is there but Me, the Most Exalted, the Most Powerful, the Most Excellent, the All-Knowing."

xv. The Pen of Revelation exclaimeth: "On this Day the Kingdom is God's!" The Tongue of Power is calling: "On this Day all sovereignty is, in very deed, with God!" The Phœnix of the realms above crieth out from the immortal Branch: "The glory of all greatness belongeth to God, the Incomparable, the

[35]

All-Compelling!" The Mystic Dove proclaimeth from its blissful bower, in the everlasting Paradise: "The source of all bounty is derived, in this Day, from God, the One, the Forgiving!" The Bird of the Throne warbleth its melody in its retreats of holiness: "Supreme ascendancy is to be attributed, this Day, to none except God, Him Who hath no peer nor equal, Who is the Most Powerful, the All-Subduing!" The inmost essence of all things voiceth in all things the testimony: "All forgiveness floweth, in this Day, from God, Him to Whom none can compare, with Whom no partners can be joined, the Sovereign Protector of all men, and the Concealer of their sins!" The Quintessence of Glory hath lifted up its voice above My head, and crieth from such heights as neither pen nor tongue can in any degree describe: "God is my witness! He, the Ancient of everlasting days is come, girded with majesty and power. There is none other God but Him, the All-Glorious, the Almighty, the All-Highest, the All-Wise, the All-Pervading, the All-Seeing, the All-Informed, the Sovereign Protector, the Source of eternal light!"

O My servant, who hast sought the good-pleasure of God and clung to His love on the Day when all except a few who were endued with insight have broken away from Him! May God, through His grace, recompense thee with a generous, an incorruptible and everlasting reward, inasmuch as thou hast sought Him on the Day when eyes were blinded.

Know thou that if We reveal to thee but a sprinkling of the showers which, through God's decree, and at the hands of the envious and the malicious, have rained upon Us, thou wouldst weep with a great weeping, and wouldst bewail day and night Our plight. Oh, would that a discerning and fair-minded soul could be found who would recognize the wonders of this Revelation—wonders that proclaim the sovereignty of God and the greatness of its power. Would that such a man might arise and, wholly for the sake of God, admonish, privately and openly, the people, that haply they may bestir themselves and aid this wronged One Whom the workers of iniquity have so sorely afflicted.

Methinks that I hear the Voice of the Holy Spirit calling from behind Me saying: Vary Thou Thy theme, and alter Thy tone, lest the heart of him who hath fixed his gaze upon Thy face be saddened. Say: I have through the grace of God and His might besought the help of no one in the past, neither will I seek the help of any one in the future. He it is Who aided Me, through the power of truth, during the days of My banishment in 'Iráq. He it is Who overshadowed Me with His protection at a time when the kindreds of the earth were contending with Me. He it is Who enabled Me to depart out of the city, clothed with such majesty as none, except the denier and the malicious, can fail to admit.

Say: My army is My reliance on God; My people, the force of My confidence in Him. My love is My standard, and My companion the remembrance of God, the Sovereign Lord of all, the Most Powerful, the All-Glorious, the Unconditioned.

Arise, O wayfarer in the path of the Love of God, and aid thou His Cause. Say: Barter not away this Youth, O people, for the vanities of this world or the delights of heaven. By the righteousness of the one true God! One hair of Him excelleth all that is in the heavens and all that is on the earth. Beware, O men, lest ye be tempted to part with Him in exchange for the gold and silver ye possess. Let His love be a storehouse of treasure for your souls, on the Day when naught else but Him shall profit you, the Day when every pillar shall tremble, when the very skins of men shall creep, when all eyes shall stare up with terror. Say: O people! Fear ye God, and turn not away disdainfully from His Revelation. Fall prostrate on your faces before God, and celebrate His praise in the daytime and in the night season.

Let thy soul glow with the flame of this undying Fire that burneth in the midmost heart of the world, in such wise that the waters of the universe shall be powerless to cool down its ardor. Make, then, mention of thy Lord, that haply the heedless among Our servants may be admonished through thy words, and the hearts of the righteous be gladdened.

[38]

XVI. Say: O men! This is a matchless Day. Matchless must, likewise, be the tongue that celebrateth the praise of the Desire of all nations, and matchless the deed that aspireth to be acceptable in His sight. The whole human race hath longed for this Day, that perchance it may fulfil that which well beseemeth its station, and is worthy of its destiny. Blessed is the man whom the affairs of the world have failed to deter from recognizing Him Who is the Lord of all things.

So blind hath become the human heart that neither the disruption of the city, nor the reduction of the mountain in dust, nor even the cleaving of the earth, can shake off its torpor. The allusions made in the Scriptures have been unfolded, and the signs recorded therein have been revealed, and the prophetic cry is continually being raised. And yet all, except such as God was pleased to guide, are bewildered in the drunkenness of their heedlessness!

Witness how the world is being afflicted with a fresh calamity every day. Its tribulation is continually deepening. From the moment the Súriy-i-Ra'ís (Tablet to Ra'ís) was revealed until the present day, neither hath the world been tranquillized, nor have the hearts of its peoples been at rest. At one time it hath been agitated by contentions and disputes, at another it hath been convulsed by wars, and fallen a victim to inveterate diseases. Its sickness is approaching the stage of utter hopelessness, inasmuch as the true Physician is debarred from administering the remedy, whilst unskilled practitioners are regarded with favor, and are accorded full freedom to act. . . . The dust of sedition hath clouded the hearts of men, and blinded their eyes. Erelong, they will perceive the consequences of what their hands have wrought in the Day of God. Thus warneth you He Who is the All-Informed, as bidden by One Who is the Most Powerful, the Almighty.

XVII.   By Him Who is the Great Announcement! The All-Merciful is come invested with undoubted sovereignty. The Balance hath been appointed, and all them that dwell on earth have been gathered together. The Trumpet hath been blown, and lo, all eyes have stared up with terror, and the hearts of all who are in the heavens and on the earth have trembled, except them whom the breath of the verses of God hath quickened, and who have detached themselves from all things.

This is the Day whereon the earth shall tell out her tidings. The workers of iniquity are her burdens, could ye but perceive it. The moon of idle fancy hath been cleft, and the heaven hath given out a palpable smoke. We see the people laid low, awed with the dread of thy Lord, the Almighty, the Most Powerful. The Crier hath cried out, and men have been torn away, so great hath been the fury of His wrath. The people of the left hand sigh and bemoan. The people of the right abide in noble habitations: they quaff the Wine that is life indeed, from the hands of the All-Merciful, and are, verily, the blissful.

The earth hath been shaken, and the mountains have passed away, and the angels have appeared, rank on rank, before Us. Most of the people are bewildered in their drunkenness and wear on their faces the evidences of anger. Thus have We gathered together the workers of iniquity. We see them rushing on towards their idol. Say: None shall be secure this Day from the decree of God. This indeed is a grievous Day. We point out to them those that led them astray. They see them, and yet recognize them not. Their eyes are drunken; they are indeed a blind people. Their proofs are the calumnies they uttered; condemned are their calumnies by God, the Help in Peril, the Self-Subsisting. The Evil One hath stirred up mischief in their hearts, and they are afflicted with a torment that none can avert. They hasten to the wicked, bearing the register of the workers of iniquity. Such are their doings.

Say: The heavens have been folded together, and the earth is held within His grasp, and the corrupt doers have been held by their forelock, and still they understand not. They drink of the tainted water, and know it not. Say: The shout hath been raised, and the people have come forth from their graves, and arising, are gazing around them. Some have made haste to attain the court of the God of Mercy, others have fallen down on their faces in the fire of Hell, while still others are lost in bewilderment. The verses of God have been revealed, and yet they have turned away from them. His proof hath been manifested, and yet they are unaware of it. And when they behold the face of the All-Merciful, their own faces are saddened, while they are disporting themselves. They hasten forward to Hell Fire, and mistake it for light. Far from God be what they fondly imagine! Say: Whether ye rejoice or whether ye burst for fury, the heavens are cleft asunder, and God hath come down, invested with radiant sovereignty. All created things are heard exclaiming: "The Kingdom is God's, the Almighty, the All-Knowing, the All-Wise."

Know thou, moreover, that We have been cast into an afflictive Prison, and are encompassed with the hosts of tyranny, as a result of what the hands of the infidels have wrought. Such is the gladness, however, which the Youth hath tasted that no earthly joy can compare unto it. By God! The harm He suffereth at the hands of the oppressor can never grieve His heart, nor can He be saddened by the ascendancy of such as have repudiated His truth.

Say: Tribulation is a horizon unto My Revelation. The day star of grace shineth above it, and sheddeth a light which neither the clouds of men's idle fancy nor the vain imaginations of the aggressor can obscure.

Follow thou the footsteps of thy Lord, and remember His servants even as He doth remember thee, undeterred by either the clamor of the heedless ones or the sword of the enemy. . . . Spread abroad the sweet savors of thy Lord, and hesitate not, though it be for less than a moment, in the service of His Cause. The day is approaching when the victory of thy Lord, the Ever-Forgiving, the Most Bountiful, will be proclaimed.

xviii. Say: We have caused the rivers of Divine utterance to proceed out of Our throne, that the tender herbs of wisdom and understanding may spring forth from the soil of your hearts. Will ye not be thankful? They who disdain to worship their Lord shall be of those who are cast off. And oft as Our verses are rehearsed unto them, they persist in proud disdain, and in their gross violation of His law, and know it not. As for them who have disbelieved in Him, they shall be in the shadow of a black smoke. "The Hour" hath come upon them, while they are disporting themselves. They have been seized by their forelock, and yet know it not.

The thing that must come hath come suddenly; behold how they flee from it! The inevitable hath come to pass; witness how they have cast it behind their backs! This is the Day whereon every man will fly from himself, how much more from his kindred, could ye but perceive it. Say: By God! The blast hath been blown on the trumpet, and lo, mankind hath swooned away before us! The Herald hath cried out, and the Summoner raised His voice saying: "The Kingdom is God's, the Most Powerful, the Help in Peril, the Self-Subsisting."

This is the Day on which all eyes shall stare up with terror, the Day in which the hearts of them that dwell on earth shall tremble, save them whom thy Lord, the All-Knowing, the All-Wise, pleaseth to deliver. All faces have turned black except those to whom the God of Mercy hath vouchsafed a radiant heart. Drunken are the eyes of those men that have openly refused to behold the face of God, the All-Glorious, the All-Praised.

Say: Perused ye not the Qur'án? Read it, that haply ye may find the Truth, for this Book is verily the Straight Path. This is the Way of God unto all who are in the heavens and all who are on the earth. If ye have been careless of the Qur'án, the Bayán cannot be regarded to be remote from you. Behold it open before your eyes. Read ye its verses, that perchance ye desist from committing that which will cause the Messengers of God to mourn and lament.

Speed out of your sepulchers. How long will ye sleep? The second blast hath been blown on the trumpet. On whom are ye gazing? This is your Lord, the God of Mercy. Witness how ye gainsay His signs! The earth hath quaked with a great quaking, and cast forth her burdens. Will ye not admit it? Say: Will ye not recognize how the mountains have become like flocks of wool, how the people are sore vexed at the awful majesty of the Cause of God? Witness how their houses are empty ruins, and they themselves a drowned host.

This is the Day whereon the All-Merciful hath come down in the clouds of knowledge, clothed with manifest sovereignty. He well knoweth the actions of men. He it is Whose glory none can mistake, could ye but comprehend it. The heaven of every religion hath been rent, and the earth of human understanding been cleft asunder, and the angels of God are seen descending. Say: This is the Day of mutual deceit; whither do ye flee? The mountains have passed away, and the heavens have been folded together, and the whole earth is held within His grasp, could ye but understand it. Who is it that can protect you? None, by Him Who is the All-Merciful! None, except God, the Almighty, the All-Glorious, the Beneficent. Every woman that hath had a burden in her womb hath cast her burden. We see men drunken in this Day, the Day in which men and angels have been gathered together.

Say: Is there any doubt concerning God? Behold how He hath come down from the heaven of His grace, girded with power and invested with sovereignty. Is there any doubt concerning His signs? Open ye your eyes, and consider His clear evidence. Paradise is on your right hand, and hath been brought nigh unto you, while Hell hath been made to blaze. Witness its devouring flame. Haste ye to enter into

[45]

Paradise, as a token of Our mercy unto you, and drink ye from the hands of the All-Merciful the Wine that is life indeed.

Drink with healthy relish, O people of Bahá. Ye are indeed they with whom it shall be well. This is what they who have near access to God have attained. This is the flowing water ye were promised in the Qur'án, and later in the Bayán, as a recompense from your Lord, the God of Mercy. Blessed are they that quaff it.

O My servant that hath turned thy face towards Me! Render thanks unto God for having sent down unto thee this Tablet in this Prison, that thou mayest remind the people of the days of thy Lord, the All-Glorious, the All-Knowing. Thus have We established for thee, through the waters of Our wisdom and utterance, the foundations of thy belief. This, verily, is the water whereon the Throne of thy Lord hath been raised. "His Throne had stood upon the waters." Ponder this in thine heart, that thou mayest comprehend its meaning. Say: Praise be to God, the Lord of all worlds.

XIX. To every discerning and illuminated heart it is evident that God, the unknowable Essence, the Divine Being, is immensely exalted beyond every human attribute, such as corporeal existence, ascent and descent, egress and regress. Far be it from His glory that human tongue should adequately recount

His praise, or that human heart comprehend His fathomless mystery. He is, and hath ever been, veiled in the ancient eternity of His Essence, and will remain in His Reality everlastingly hidden from the sight of men. "No vision taketh in Him, but He taketh in all vision; He is the Subtle, the All-Perceiving." . . .

The door of the knowledge of the Ancient of Days being thus closed in the face of all beings, the Source of infinite grace, according to His saying, "His grace hath transcended all things; My grace hath encompassed them all," hath caused those luminous Gems of Holiness to appear out of the realm of the spirit, in the noble form of the human temple, and be made manifest unto all men, that they may impart unto the world the mysteries of the unchangeable Being, and tell of the subtleties of His imperishable Essence.

These sanctified Mirrors, these Day Springs of ancient glory, are, one and all, the Exponents on earth of Him Who is the central Orb of the universe, its Essence and ultimate Purpose. From Him proceed their knowledge and power; from Him is derived their sovereignty. The beauty of their countenance is but a reflection of His image, and their revelation a sign of His deathless glory. They are the Treasuries of Divine knowledge, and the Repositories of celestial wisdom. Through them is transmitted a grace that is infinite, and by them is revealed the Light that can never fade. . . . These Tabernacles of Holiness, these Primal Mirrors which reflect the light of unfading glory, are but expressions of Him Who is the Invisible of the Invisibles. By the revelation of these Gems of Divine virtue all the names and attributes of God, such as knowledge and power, sovereignty and dominion, mercy and wisdom, glory, bounty, and grace, are made manifest.

These attributes of God are not, and have never been, vouchsafed specially unto certain Prophets, and withheld from others. Nay, all the Prophets of God, His well-favored, His holy and chosen Messengers are, without exception, the bearers of His names, and the embodiments of His attributes. They only differ in the intensity of their revelation, and the comparative potency of their light. Even as He hath revealed: "Some of the Apostles We have caused to excel the others."

It hath, therefore, become manifest and evident that within the tabernacles of these Prophets and chosen Ones of God the light of His infinite names and exalted attributes hath been reflected, even though the light of some of these attributes may or may not be outwardly revealed from these luminous Temples to the eyes of men. That a certain attribute of God hath not been outwardly manifested by these Essences of Detachment doth in no wise imply that they who are the Day Springs of God's attributes and the Treasuries of His holy names did not actually possess it. Therefore, these illuminated Souls, these beauteous Countenances have, each and every one of them, been endowed with all the attributes of God, such as sovereignty, dominion, and the like, even though to outward seeming they be shorn of all earthly majesty. . . .

XX. Know thou of a certainty that the Unseen can in no wise incarnate His Essence and reveal it unto men. He is, and hath ever been, immensely exalted beyond all that can either be recounted or perceived. From His retreat of glory His voice is ever proclaiming: "Verily, I am God; there is none other God besides Me, the All-Knowing, the All-Wise. I have manifested Myself unto men, and have sent down Him Who is the Day Spring of the signs of My Revelation. Through Him I have caused all creation to testify that there is none other God except Him, the Incomparable, the All-Informed, the All-Wise." He Who is everlastingly hidden from the eyes of men can never be known except through His Manifestation, and His Manifestation can adduce no greater proof of the truth of His Mission than the proof of His own Person.

XXI. O Salmán! The door of the knowledge of the Ancient Being hath ever been, and will continue for ever to be, closed in the face of men. No man's understanding shall ever gain access unto His holy court. As a token of His mercy, however, and as a proof of His loving-kindness, He hath manifested unto men the Day Stars of His divine guidance, the Symbols of His divine unity, and hath ordained the knowledge of these sanctified Beings to be identical with the knowledge of His own Self. Whoso recognizeth them hath recognized God. Whoso hearkeneth to their call, hath hearkened to the Voice of God, and whoso testifieth to the truth of their Revelation, hath testified to the truth of God Himself. Whoso turneth away from them, hath turned away from God, and whoso disbelieveth in them, hath disbelieved in God. Every one of them is the Way of God that connecteth this world with the realms above, and the Standard of His Truth unto every one in the kingdoms of earth and heaven. They are the Manifestations of God amidst men, the evidences of His Truth, and the signs of His glory.

XXII. The Bearers of the Trust of God are made manifest unto the peoples of the earth as the Exponents of a new Cause and the Revealers of a new Message. Inasmuch as these Birds of the celestial Throne are all sent down from the heaven of the Will of God, and as they all arise to proclaim His irresistible Faith, they, therefore, are regarded as one soul and the same person. For they all drink from the one Cup of the love of God, and all partake of the fruit of the same Tree of Oneness.

These Manifestations of God have each a twofold

station. One is the station of pure abstraction and essential unity. In this respect, if thou callest them all by one name, and dost ascribe to them the same attributes, thou hast not erred from the truth. Even as He hath revealed: "No distinction do We make between any of His Messengers." For they, one and all, summon the people of the earth to acknowledge the unity of God, and herald unto them the Kawthar of an infinite grace and bounty. They are all invested with the robe of prophethood, and are honored with the mantle of glory. Thus hath Muḥammad, the Point of the Qur'án, revealed: "I am all the Prophets." Likewise, He saith: "I am the first Adam, Noah, Moses, and Jesus." Similar statements have been made by Imám 'Alí. Sayings such as these, which indicate the essential unity of those Exponents of Oneness, have also emanated from the Channels of God's immortal utterance, and the Treasuries of the gems of Divine knowledge, and have been recorded in the Scriptures. These Countenances are the recipients of the Divine Command, and the Day Springs of His Revelation. This Revelation is exalted above the veils of plurality and the exigencies of number. Thus He saith: "Our Cause is but One." Inasmuch as the Cause is one and the same, the Exponents thereof also must needs be one and the same. Likewise, the Imáms of the Muḥammadan Faith, those lamps of certitude, have said: "Muḥammad is our first, Muḥammad is our last, Muḥammad our all."

[51]

It is clear and evident to thee that all the Prophets are the Temples of the Cause of God, Who have appeared clothed in divers attire. If thou wilt observe with discriminating eyes, thou wilt behold Them all abiding in the same tabernacle, soaring in the same heaven, seated upon the same throne, uttering the same speech, and proclaiming the same Faith. Such is the unity of those Essences of Being, those Luminaries of infinite and immeasurable splendor! Wherefore, should one of these Manifestations of Holiness proclaim saying: "I am the return of all the Prophets," He, verily, speaketh the truth. In like manner, in every subsequent Revelation, the return of the former Revelation is a fact, the truth of which is firmly established. . . .

The other station is the station of distinction, and pertaineth to the world of creation, and to the limitations thereof. In this respect, each Manifestation of God hath a distinct individuality, a definitely prescribed mission, a predestined revelation, and specially designated limitations. Each one of them is known by a different name, is characterized by a special attribute, fulfils a definite mission, and is entrusted with a particular Revelation. Even as He saith: "Some of the Apostles We have caused to excel the others. To some God hath spoken, some He hath raised and exalted. And to Jesus, Son of Mary, We gave manifest signs, and We strengthened Him with the Holy Spirit."

It is because of this difference in their station and mission that the words and utterances flowing from these Well Springs of Divine knowledge appear to diverge and differ. Otherwise, in the eyes of them that are initiated into the mysteries of Divine wisdom, all their utterances are, in reality, but the expressions of one Truth. As most of the people have failed to appreciate those stations to which We have referred, they, therefore, feel perplexed and dismayed at the varying utterances pronounced by Manifestations that are essentially one and the same.

It hath ever been evident that all these divergencies of utterance are attributable to differences of station. Thus, viewed from the standpoint of their oneness and sublime detachment, the attributes of Godhead, Divinity, Supreme Singleness, and Inmost Essence, have been, and are applicable to those Essences of Being, inasmuch as they all abide on the throne of Divine Revelation, and are established upon the seat of Divine Concealment. Through their appearance the Revelation of God is made manifest, and by their countenance the Beauty of God is revealed. Thus it is that the accents of God Himself have been heard uttered by these Manifestations of the Divine Being.

Viewed in the light of their second station—the station of distinction, differentiation, temporal limitations, characteristics and standards—they manifest absolute servitude, utter destitution, and complete

[53]

self-effacement. Even as He saith: "I am the servant of God. I am but a man like you." . . .

Were any of the all-embracing Manifestations of God to declare: "I am God!" He, verily, speaketh the truth, and no doubt attacheth thereto. For it hath been repeatedly demonstrated that through their Revelation, their attributes and names, the Revelation of God, His names and His attributes, are made manifest in the world. Thus, He hath revealed: "Those shafts were God's, not Thine." And also He saith: "In truth, they who plighted fealty unto Thee, really plighted that fealty unto God." And were any of them to voice the utterance, "I am the Messenger of God," He, also, speaketh the truth, the indubitable truth. Even as He saith: "Muḥammad is not the father of any man among you, but He is the Messenger of God." Viewed in this light, they are all but Messengers of that ideal King, that unchangeable Essence. And were they all to proclaim, "I am the Seal of the Prophets," they, verily, utter but the truth, beyond the faintest shadow of doubt. For they are all but one person, one soul, one spirit, one being, one revelation. They are all the manifestation of the "Beginning" and the "End," the "First" and the "Last," the "Seen" and "Hidden"—all of which pertain to Him Who is the Innermost Spirit of Spirits and Eternal Essence of Essences. And were they to say, "We are the Servants of God," this also is a manifest and indisputable fact. For they have been made manifest in the uttermost state of servitude, a servitude the like of which no man can possibly attain. Thus in moments in which these Essences of Being were deep immersed beneath the oceans of ancient and everlasting holiness, or when they soared to the loftiest summits of Divine mysteries, they claimed their utterances to be the Voice of Divinity, the Call of God Himself.

Were the eye of discernment to be opened, it would recognize that in this very state, they have considered themselves utterly effaced and non-existent in the face of Him Who is the All-Pervading, the Incorruptible. Methinks, they have regarded themselves as utter nothingness, and deemed their mention in that Court an act of blasphemy. For the slightest whispering of self within such a Court is an evidence of self-assertion and independent existence. In the eyes of them that have attained unto that Court, such a suggestion is itself a grievous transgression. How much more grievous would it be, were aught else to be mentioned in that Presence, were man's heart, his tongue, his mind, or his soul, to be busied with any one but the Well-Beloved, were his eyes to behold any countenance other than His beauty, were his ear to be inclined to any melody but His Voice, and were his feet to tread any way but His way. . . .

By virtue of this station they have claimed for themselves the Voice of Divinity and the like, whilst

[55]

by virtue of their station of Messengership, they have declared themselves the Messengers of God. In every instance they have voiced an utterance that would conform to the requirements of the occasion, and have ascribed all these declarations to Themselves, declarations ranging from the realm of Divine Revelation to the realm of creation, and from the domain of Divinity even unto the domain of earthly existence. Thus it is that whatsoever be their utterance, whether it pertain to the realm of Divinity, Lordship, Prophethood, Messengership, Guardianship, Apostleship, or Servitude, all is true, beyond the shadow of a doubt. Therefore these sayings which We have quoted in support of Our argument must be attentively considered, that the divergent utterances of the Manifestations of the Unseen and Day Springs of Holiness may cease to agitate the soul and perplex the mind.

XXIII. Consider the former generations. Witness how every time the Day Star of Divine bounty hath shed the light of His Revelation upon the world, the people of His Day have arisen against Him, and repudiated His truth. They who were regarded as the leaders of men have invariably striven to hinder their followers from turning unto Him Who is the Ocean of God's limitless bounty.

Behold how the people, as a result of the verdict pronounced by the divines of His age, have cast

Abraham, the Friend of God, into fire; how Moses, He Who held converse with the Almighty, was denounced as liar and slanderer. Reflect how Jesus, the Spirit of God, was, notwithstanding His extreme meekness and perfect tender-heartedness, treated by His enemies. So fierce was the opposition which He, the Essence of Being and Lord of the visible and invisible, had to face, that He had nowhere to lay His head. He wandered continually from place to place, deprived of a permanent abode. Ponder that which befell Muḥammad, the Seal of the Prophets, may the life of all else be a sacrifice unto Him. How severe the afflictions which the leaders of the Jewish people and of the idol-worshipers caused to rain upon Him, Who is the sovereign Lord of all, in consequence of His proclamation of the unity of God and of the truth of His Message! By the righteousness of My Cause! My Pen groaneth, and all created things weep with a great weeping, as a result of the woes He suffered at the hands of them that have broken the Covenant of God, violated His Testament, rejected His proofs, and disputed His signs. Thus recount We unto thee the tale of that which happened in days past, haply thou mayest comprehend.

Thou hast known how grievously the Prophets of God, His Messengers and Chosen Ones, have been afflicted. Meditate a while on the motive and reason which have been responsible for such a persecution. At no time, in no Dispensation, have the Prophets of

God escaped the blasphemy of their enemies, the cruelty of their oppressors, the denunciation of the learned of their age, who appeared in the guise of uprightness and piety. Day and night they passed through such agonies as none can ever measure, except the knowledge of the one true God, exalted be His glory.

Consider this wronged One. Though the clearest proofs attest the truth of His Cause; though the prophecies He, in an unmistakable language, hath made have been fulfilled; though, in spite of His not being accounted among the learned, His being unschooled and inexperienced in the disputations current among the divines, He hath rained upon men the showers of His manifold and Divinely-inspired knowledge; yet, behold how this generation hath rejected His authority, and rebelled against Him! He hath, during the greater part of His life, been sore-tried in the clutches of His enemies. His sufferings have now reached their culmination in this afflictive Prison, into which His oppressors have so unjustly thrown Him. God grant that, with a penetrating vision and radiant heart, thou mayest observe the things that have come to pass and are now happening, and, pondering them in thine heart, mayest recognize that which most men have, in this Day, failed to perceive. Please God, He may enable thee to inhale the sweet fragrance of His Day, to partake of the limitless effusions of His grace, to quaff thy fill, through His gracious favor, from the most great Ocean that surgeth in this Day in the name of the Ancient King, and to remain firm and immovable as the mountain in His Cause.

Say: Glory be to Thee Who hast caused all the holy Ones to confess their helplessness before the manifold revelations of Thy might, and every Prophet to acknowledge His nothingness at the effulgence of Thine abiding glory. I beseech Thee, by Thy name that hath unlocked the gates of Heaven and filled with ecstasy the Concourse on high, to enable me to serve Thee, in this Day, and to strengthen me to observe that which Thou didst prescribe in Thy Book. Thou knowest, O my Lord, what is in me; but I know not what is in Thee. Thou art the All-Knowing, the All-Informed.

XXIV. Beware, O believers in the Unity of God, lest ye be tempted to make any distinction between any of the Manifestations of His Cause, or to discriminate against the signs that have accompanied and proclaimed their Revelation. This indeed is the true meaning of Divine Unity, if ye be of them that apprehend and believe this truth. Be ye assured, moreover, that the works and acts of each and every one of these Manifestations of God, nay whatever pertaineth unto them, and whatsoever they may manifest in the future, are all ordained by God, and are a reflection of His Will and Purpose. Whoso

[59]

maketh the slightest possible difference between their persons, their words, their messages, their acts and manners, hath indeed disbelieved in God, hath repudiated His signs, and betrayed the Cause of His Messengers.

xxv. It is evident that every age in which a Manifestation of God hath lived is divinely ordained, and may, in a sense, be characterized as God's appointed Day. This Day, however, is unique, and is to be distinguished from those that have preceded it. The designation "Seal of the Prophets" fully revealeth its high station. The Prophetic Cycle hath, verily, ended. The Eternal Truth is now come. He hath lifted up the Ensign of Power, and is now shedding upon the world the unclouded splendor of His Revelation.

xxvi. Praise be to God, the All-Possessing, the King of incomparable glory, a praise which is immeasurably above the understanding of all created things, and is exalted beyond the grasp of the minds of men. None else besides Him hath ever been able to sing adequately His praise, nor will any man succeed at any time in describing the full measure of His glory. Who is it that can claim to have attained the heights of His exalted Essence, and what mind can measure the depths of His unfathomable mystery? From each and every revelation emanating from the Source of His glory, holy and never-ending evidences of unimaginable splendor have appeared, and out of every manifestation of His invincible power oceans of eternal light have outpoured. How immensely exalted are the wondrous testimonies of His almighty sovereignty, a glimmer of which, if it but touched them, would utterly consume all that are in the heavens and in the earth! How indescribably lofty are the tokens of His consummate power, a single sign of which, however inconsiderable, must transcend the comprehension of whatsoever hath, from the beginning that hath no beginning, been brought into being, or will be created in the future till the end that hath no end. All the Embodiments of His Names wander in the wilderness of search, athirst and eager to discover His Essence, and all the Manifestations of His Attributes implore Him, from the Sinai of Holiness, to unravel His mystery.

A drop of the billowing ocean of His endless mercy hath adorned all creation with the ornament of existence, and a breath wafted from His peerless Paradise hath invested all beings with the robe of His sanctity and glory. A sprinkling from the unfathomed deep of His sovereign and all-pervasive Will hath, out of utter nothingness, called into being a creation which is infinite in its range and deathless in its duration. The wonders of His bounty can never cease, and the stream of His merciful grace can never be arrested. The process of His creation hath had no beginning, and can have no end.

[61]

In every age and cycle He hath, through the splendorous light shed by the Manifestations of His wondrous Essence, recreated all things, so that whatsoever reflecteth in the heavens and on the earth the signs of His glory may not be deprived of the outpourings of His mercy, nor despair of the showers of His favors. How all-encompassing are the wonders of His boundless grace! Behold how they have pervaded the whole of creation. Such is their virtue that not a single atom in the entire universe can be found which doth not declare the evidences of His might, which doth not glorify His holy Name, or is not expressive of the effulgent light of His unity. So perfect and comprehensive is His creation that no mind nor heart, however keen or pure, can ever grasp the nature of the most insignificant of His creatures; much less fathom the mystery of Him Who is the Day Star of Truth, Who is the invisible and unknowable Essence. The conceptions of the devoutest of mystics, the attainments of the most accomplished amongst men, the highest praise which human tongue or pen can render are all the product of man's finite mind and are conditioned by its limitations. Ten thousand Prophets, each a Moses, are thunderstruck upon the Sinai of their search at His forbidding voice, "Thou shalt never behold Me!"; whilst a myriad Messengers, each as great as Jesus, stand dismayed upon their heavenly thrones by the interdiction, "Mine Essence thou shalt never apprehend!"

From time immemorial He hath been veiled in the ineffable sanctity of His exalted Self, and will everlastingly continue to be wrapt in the impenetrable mystery of His unknowable Essence. Every attempt to attain to an understanding of His inaccessible Reality hath ended in complete bewilderment, and every effort to approach His exalted Self and envisage His Essence hath resulted in hopelessness and failure.

How bewildering to me, insignificant as I am, is the attempt to fathom the sacred depths of Thy knowledge! How futile my efforts to visualize the magnitude of the power inherent in Thine handiwork—the revelation of Thy creative power! How can mine eye, which hath no faculty to perceive itself, claim to have discerned Thine Essence, and how can mine heart, already powerless to apprehend the significance of its own potentialities, pretend to have comprehended Thy nature? How can I claim to have known Thee, when the entire creation is bewildered by Thy mystery, and how can I confess not to have known Thee, when, lo, the whole universe proclaimeth Thy Presence and testifieth to Thy truth? The portals of Thy grace have throughout eternity been open, and the means of access unto Thy Presence made available, unto all created things, and the revelations of Thy matchless Beauty have at all times been imprinted upon the realities of all beings, visible and invisible. Yet, notwithstanding this most gracious favor, this perfect and consummate bestowal, I am moved to testify that Thy court of holiness and glory is immeasurably exalted above the knowledge of all else besides Thee, and the mystery of Thy Presence is inscrutable to every mind except Thine own. No one except Thyself can unravel the secret of Thy nature, and naught else but Thy transcendental Essence can grasp the reality of Thy unsearchable being. How vast the number of those heavenly and all-glorious beings who, in the wilderness of their separation from Thee, have wandered all the days of their lives, and failed in the end to find Thee! How great the multitude of the sanctified and immortal souls who were lost and bewildered while seeking in the desert of search to behold Thy face! Myriad are Thine ardent lovers whom the consuming flame of remoteness from Thee hath caused to sink and perish, and numberless are the faithful souls who have willingly laid down their lives in the hope of gazing on the light of Thy countenance. The sighs and moans of these longing hearts that pant after Thee can never reach Thy holy court, neither can the lamentations of the wayfarers that thirst to appear before Thy face attain Thy seat of glory.

XXVII. All praise to the unity of God, and all honor to Him, the sovereign Lord, the incomparable and all-glorious Ruler of the universe, Who, out of utter nothingness, hath created the reality of all things, Who, from naught, hath brought into being the most refined and subtle elements of His creation, and Who, rescuing His creatures from the abasement of remoteness and the perils of ultimate extinction, hath received them into His kingdom of incorruptible glory. Nothing short of His all-encompassing grace, His all-pervading mercy, could have possibly achieved it. How could it, otherwise, have been possible for sheer nothingness to have acquired by itself the worthiness and capacity to emerge from its state of non-existence into the realm of being?

Having created the world and all that liveth and moveth therein, He, through the direct operation of His unconstrained and sovereign Will, chose to confer upon man the unique distinction and capacity to know Him and to love Him—a capacity that must needs be regarded as the generating impulse and the primary purpose underlying the whole of creation. . . .*Upon the inmost reality of each and every created thing He hath shed the light of one of His names, and made it a recipient of the glory of one of His attributes. Upon the reality of man, however, He hath focused the radiance of all of His names and attributes, and made it a mirror of His own Self. Alone of all created things man hath been singled out for so great a favor, so enduring a bounty.*

These energies with which the Day Star of Divine bounty and Source of heavenly guidance hath endowed the reality of man lie, however, latent within him, even as the flame is hidden within the candle and the rays of light are potentially present in the lamp. The radiance of these energies may be obscured by worldly desires even as the light of the sun can be concealed beneath the dust and dross which cover the mirror. Neither the candle nor the lamp can be lighted through their own unaided efforts, nor can it ever be possible for the mirror to free itself from its dross. It is clear and evident that until a fire is kindled the lamp will never be ignited, and unless the dross is blotted out from the face of the mirror it can never represent the image of the sun nor reflect its light and glory.

And since there can be no tie of direct intercourse to bind the one true God with His creation, and no resemblance whatever can exist between the transient and the Eternal, the contingent and the Absolute, He hath ordained that in every age and dispensation a pure and stainless Soul be made manifest in the kingdoms of earth and heaven. Unto this subtle, this mysterious and ethereal Being He hath assigned a twofold nature; the physical, pertaining to the world of matter, and the spiritual, which is born of the substance of God Himself. He hath, moreover, conferred upon Him a double station. The first station, which is related to His innermost reality, representeth Him as One Whose voice is the voice of God Himself. To this testifieth the tradition: "Manifold and mysterious is My relationship with God. I am He, Him-

[66]

self, and He is I, Myself, except that I am that I am, and He is that He is." And in like manner, the words: "Arise, O Muḥammad, for lo, the Lover and the Beloved are joined together and made one in Thee." He similarly saith: "There is no distinction whatsoever between Thee and Them, except that They are Thy Servants." The second station is the human station, exemplified by the following verses: "I am but a man like you." "Say, praise be to my Lord! Am I more than a man, an apostle?" These Essences of Detachment, these resplendent Realities are the channels of God's all-pervasive grace. Led by the light of unfailing guidance, and invested with supreme sovereignty, They are commissioned to use the inspiration of Their words, the effusions of Their infallible grace and the sanctifying breeze of Their Revelation for the cleansing of every longing heart and receptive spirit from the dross and dust of earthly cares and limitations. Then, and only then, will the Trust of God, latent in the reality of man, emerge, as resplendent as the rising Orb of Divine Revelation, from behind the veil of concealment, and implant the ensign of its revealed glory upon the summits of men's hearts.

From the foregoing passages and allusions it hath been made indubitably clear that in the kingdoms of earth and heaven there must needs be manifested a Being, an Essence Who shall act as a Manifestation and Vehicle for the transmission of the grace of the

Divinity Itself, the Sovereign Lord of all. Through the Teachings of this Day Star of Truth every man will advance and develop until he attaineth the station at which he can manifest all the potential forces with which his inmost true self hath been endowed. It is for this very purpose that in every age and dispensation the Prophets of God and His chosen Ones have appeared amongst men, and have evinced such power as is born of God and such might as only the Eternal can reveal. ✶

Can one of sane mind ever seriously imagine that, in view of certain words the meaning of which he cannot comprehend, the portal of God's infinite guidance can ever be closed in the face of men? Can he ever conceive for these Divine Luminaries, these resplendent Lights either a beginning or an end? What outpouring flood can compare with the stream of His all-embracing grace, and what blessing can excel the evidences of so great and pervasive a mercy? There can be no doubt whatever that if for one moment the tide of His mercy and grace were to be withheld from the world, it would completely perish. For this reason, from the beginning that hath no beginning the portals of Divine mercy have been flung open to the face of all created things, and the clouds of Truth will continue to the end that hath no end to rain on the soil of human capacity, reality and personality their favors and bounties. Such hath been God's method continued from everlasting to everlasting.

XXVIII.   Happy is the man who will arise to serve My Cause, and glorify My beauteous Name. Take hold of My Book with the power of My might, and cleave tenaciously to whatsoever commandment thy Lord, the Ordainer, the All-Wise, hath prescribed therein. Behold, O Muḥammad, how the sayings and doings of the followers of S͟hí'ih Islám have dulled the joy and fervor of its early days, and tarnished the pristine brilliancy of its light. In its primitive days, whilst they still adhered to the precepts associated with the name of their Prophet, the Lord of mankind, their career was marked by an unbroken chain of victories and triumphs. As they gradually strayed from the path of their Ideal Leader and Master, as they turned away from the Light of God and corrupted the principle of His Divine unity, and as they increasingly centered their attention upon them who were only the revealers of the potency of His Word, their power was turned into weakness, their glory into shame, their courage into fear. Thou dost witness to what a pass they have come. Behold, how they have joined partners with Him Who is the Focal-Point of Divine unity. Behold how their evil doings have hindered them from recognizing, in the Day of Resurrection, the Word of Truth, exalted be His glory. We cherish the hope that this people will henceforth shield themselves from vain hopes and idle fancies, and will attain to a true understanding of the meaning of Divine unity.

The Person of the Manifestation hath ever been the representative and mouthpiece of God. He, in truth, is the Day Spring of God's most excellent Titles, and the Dawning-Place of His exalted Attributes. If any be set up by His side as peers, if they be regarded as identical with His Person, how can it, then, be maintained that the Divine Being is One and Incomparable, that His Essence is indivisible and peerless? Meditate on that which We have, through the power of truth, revealed unto thee, and be thou of them that comprehend its meaning.

XXIX. The purpose of God in creating man hath been, and will ever be, to enable him to know his Creator and to attain His Presence. To this most excellent aim, this supreme objective, all the heavenly Books and the divinely-revealed and weighty Scriptures unequivocally bear witness. Whoso hath recognized the Day Spring of Divine guidance and entered His holy court hath drawn nigh unto God and attained His Presence, a Presence which is the real Paradise, and of which the loftiest mansions of heaven are but a symbol. Such a man hath attained the knowledge of the station of Him Who is "at the distance of two bows," Who standeth beyond the Sadratu'l-Muntahá. Whoso hath failed to recognize

Him will have condemned himself to the misery of remoteness, a remoteness which is naught but utter nothingness and the essence of the nethermost fire. Such will be his fate, though to outward seeming he may occupy the earth's loftiest seats and be established upon its most exalted throne.

He Who is the Day Spring of Truth is, no doubt, fully capable of rescuing from such remoteness wayward souls and of causing them to draw nigh unto His court and attain His Presence. "If God had pleased He had surely made all men one people." His purpose, however, is to enable the pure in spirit and the detached in heart to ascend, by virtue of their own innate powers, unto the shores of the Most Great Ocean, that thereby they who seek the Beauty of the All-Glorious may be distinguished and separated from the wayward and perverse. Thus hath it been ordained by the all-glorious and resplendent Pen. . . .

That the Manifestations of Divine justice, the Day Springs of heavenly grace, have when they appeared amongst men always been destitute of all earthly dominion and shorn of the means of worldly ascendancy, should be attributed to this same principle of separation and distinction which animateth the Divine Purpose. Were the Eternal Essence to manifest all that is latent within Him, were He to shine in the plentitude of His glory, none would be found to question His power or repudiate His truth. Nay, all created things would be so dazzled and thunderstruck by the evidences of His light as to be reduced to utter nothingness. How, then, can the godly be differentiated under such circumstances from the froward?

This principle hath operated in each of the previous Dispensations and been abundantly demonstrated. . . . It is for this reason that, in every age, when a new Manifestation hath appeared and a fresh revelation of God's transcendent power was vouchsafed unto men, they that misbelieved in Him, deluded by the appearance of the peerless and everlasting Beauty in the garb of mortal men, have failed to recognize Him. They have erred from His path and eschewed His company—the company of Him Who is the Symbol of nearness to God. They have even arisen to decimate the ranks of the faithful and to exterminate such as believed in Him.

Behold how in this Dispensation the worthless and foolish have fondly imagined that by such instruments as massacre, plunder and banishment they can extinguish the Lamp which the Hand of Divine power hath lit, or eclipse the Day Star of everlasting splendor. How utterly unaware they seem to be of the truth that such adversity is the oil that feedeth the flame of this Lamp! Such is God's transforming power. He changeth whatsoever He willeth; He verily hath power over all things. . . .

Consider at all times the sovereignty exercised by the Ideal King, and behold the evidences of His power and paramount influence. Sanctify your ears from the idle talk of them that are the symbols of denial and the exponents of violence and anger. The hour is approaching when ye will witness the power of the one true God triumphing over all created things and the signs of His sovereignty encompassing all creation. On that day ye will discover how all else besides Him will have been forgotten and come to be regarded as utter nothingness.

It should, however, be borne in mind that God and His Manifestation can, under no circumstances, be dissociated from the loftiness and sublimity which They inherently possess. Nay, loftiness and sublimity are themselves the creations of His Word, if ye choose to see with My sight not with yours.

xxx.   God witnesseth that there is no God but Him, the Gracious, the Best-Beloved. All grace and bounty are His. To whomsoever He will He giveth whatsoever is His wish. He, verily, is the All-Powerful, the Almighty, the Help in Peril, the Self-Subsisting. We, verily, believe in Him Who, in the person of the Báb, hath been sent down by the Will of the one true God, the King of Kings, the All-Praised. We, moreover, swear fealty to the One Who, in the time of Mustagháth, is destined to be made manifest, as well as to those Who shall come after Him till the end that hath no end. We recognize in the manifestation of each one of them, whether outwardly or inwardly, the manifestation of none but God Himself, if ye be of those that comprehend. Every one of them is a mirror of God, reflecting naught else but His Self, His Beauty, His Might and Glory, if ye will understand. All else besides them are to be regarded as mirrors capable of reflecting the glory of these Manifestations Who are themselves the Primary Mirrors of the Divine Being, if ye be not devoid of understanding. No one hath ever escaped them, neither are they to be hindered from achieving their purpose. These Mirrors will everlastingly succeed each other, and will continue to reflect the light of the Ancient of Days. They that reflect their glory will, in like manner, continue to exist for evermore, for the Grace of God can never cease from flowing. This is a truth that none can disprove.

XXXI. Contemplate with thine inward eye the chain of successive Revelations that hath linked the Manifestation of Adam with that of the Báb. I testify before God that each one of these Manifestations hath been sent down through the operation of the Divine Will and Purpose, that each hath been the bearer of a specific Message, that each hath been entrusted with a divinely-revealed Book and been commissioned to unravel the mysteries of a mighty Tablet. The measure of the Revelation with which every one of them hath been identified had been definitely fore-ordained. This, verily, is a token of

Our favor unto them, if ye be of those that comprehend this truth. . . . And when this process of progressive Revelation culminated in the stage at which His peerless, His most sacred, and exalted Countenance was to be unveiled to men's eyes, He chose to hide His own Self behind a thousand veils, lest profane and mortal eyes discover His glory. This He did at a time when the signs and tokens of a divinely-appointed Revelation were being showered upon Him —signs and tokens which none can reckon except the Lord, your God, the Lord of all worlds. And when the set time of concealment was fulfilled, We sent forth, whilst still wrapt within a myriad veils, an infinitesimal glimmer of the effulgent Glory enveloping the Face of the Youth, and lo, the entire company of the dwellers of the Realms above were seized with violent commotion and the favored of God fell down in adoration before Him. He hath, verily, manifested a glory such as none in the whole creation hath witnessed, inasmuch as He hath arisen to proclaim in person His Cause unto all who are in the heavens and all who are on the earth.

XXXII. That which thou hast heard concerning Abraham, the Friend of the All-Merciful, is the truth, and no doubt is there about it. The Voice of God commanded Him to offer up Ishmael as a sacrifice, so that His steadfastness in the Faith of God and His detachment from all else but Him may be demonstrated unto men. The purpose of God, moreover, was to sacrifice him as a ransom for the sins and iniquities of all the peoples of the earth. This same honor, Jesus, the Son of Mary, besought the one true God, exalted be His name and glory, to confer upon Him. For the same reason was Ḥusayn offered up as a sacrifice by Muḥammad, the Apostle of God.

No man can ever claim to have comprehended the nature of the hidden and manifold grace of God; none can fathom His all-embracing mercy. Such hath been the perversity of men and their transgressions, so grievous have been the trials that have afflicted the Prophets of God and their chosen ones, that all mankind deserveth to be tormented and to perish. God's hidden and most loving providence, however, hath, through both visible and invisible agencies, protected and will continue to protect it from the penalty of its wickedness. Ponder this in thine heart, that the truth may be revealed unto thee, and be thou steadfast in His path.

XXXIII. It hath been decreed by Us that the Word of God and all the potentialities thereof shall be manifested unto men in strict conformity with such conditions as have been foreordained by Him Who is the All-Knowing, the All-Wise. We have, moreover, ordained that its veil of concealment be none other except its own Self. Such indeed is Our Power to achieve Our Purpose. Should the Word be allowed to release suddenly all the energies latent within it, no man could sustain the weight of so mighty a Revelation. Nay, all that is in heaven and on earth would flee in consternation before it.

Consider that which hath been sent down unto Muḥammad, the Apostle of God. The measure of the Revelation of which He was the bearer had been clearly foreordained by Him Who is the Almighty, the All-Powerful. They that heard Him, however, could apprehend His purpose only to the extent of their station and spiritual capacity. He, in like manner, uncovered the Face of Wisdom in proportion to their ability to sustain the burden of His Message. No sooner had mankind attained the stage of maturity, than the Word revealed to men's eyes the latent energies with which it had been endowed —energies which manifested themselves in the plenitude of their glory when the Ancient Beauty appeared, in the year sixty, in the person of 'Alí-Muḥammad, the Báb.

XXXIV. All praise and glory be to God Who, through the power of His might, hath delivered His creation from the nakedness of non-existence, and clothed it with the mantle of life. From among all created things He hath singled out for His special favor the pure, the gem-like reality of man, and invested it with a unique capacity of knowing Him and of reflecting the greatness of His glory.

This twofold distinction conferred upon him hath cleansed away from his heart the rust of every vain desire, and made him worthy of the vesture with which his Creator hath deigned to clothe him. It hath served to rescue his soul from the wretchedness of ignorance.

This robe with which the body and soul of man hath been adorned is the very foundation of his well-being and development. Oh, how blessed the day when, aided by the grace and might of the one true God, man will have freed himself from the bondage and corruption of the world and all that is therein, and will have attained unto true and abiding rest beneath the shadow of the Tree of Knowledge!

The songs which the bird of thine heart had uttered in its great love for its friends have reached their ears, and moved Me to answer thy questions, and reveal to thee such secrets as I am allowed to unfold. In thine esteemed letter thou hadst inquired which of the Prophets of God should be regarded as superior to others. Know thou assuredly that the essence of all the Prophets of God is one and the same. Their unity is absolute. God, the Creator, saith: There is no distinction whatsoever among the Bearers of My Message. They all have but one purpose; their secret is the same secret. To prefer one in honor to another, to exalt certain ones above the rest, is in no wise to be permitted. Every true Prophet hath regarded His Message as fundamentally the same as the

Revelation of every other Prophet gone before Him. If any man, therefore, should fail to comprehend this truth, and should consequently indulge in vain and unseemly language, no one whose sight is keen and whose understanding is enlightened would ever allow such idle talk to cause him to waver in his belief.

The measure of the revelation of the Prophets of God in this world, however, must differ. Each and every one of them hath been the Bearer of a distinct Message, and hath been commissioned to reveal Himself through specific acts. It is for this reason that they appear to vary in their greatness. Their Revelation may be likened unto the light of the moon that sheddeth its radiance upon the earth. Though every time it appeareth, it revealeth a fresh measure of its brightness, yet its inherent splendor can never diminish, nor can its light suffer extinction.

It is clear and evident, therefore, that any apparent variation in the intensity of their light is not inherent in the light itself, but should rather be attributed to the varying receptivity of an ever-changing world. Every Prophet Whom the Almighty and Peerless Creator hath purposed to send to the peoples of the earth hath been entrusted with a Message, and charged to act in a manner that would best meet the requirements of the age in which He appeared. God's purpose in sending His Prophets unto men is twofold. The first is to liberate the children of men from the darkness of ignorance, and guide them to the light of true understanding. The second is to ensure the peace and tranquillity of mankind, and provide all the means by which they can be established. ✗

The Prophets of God should be regarded as physicians whose task is to foster the well-being of the world and its peoples, that, through the spirit of oneness, they may heal the sickness of a divided humanity. To none is given the right to question their words or disparage their conduct, for they are the only ones who can claim to have understood the patient and to have correctly diagnosed its ailments. No man, however acute his perception, can ever hope to reach the heights which the wisdom and understanding of the Divine Physician have attained. Little wonder, then, if the treatment prescribed by the physician in this day should not be found to be identical with that which he prescribed before. How could it be otherwise when the ills affecting the sufferer necessitate at every stage of his sickness a special remedy? In like manner, every time the Prophets of God have illumined the world with the resplendent radiance of the Day Star of Divine knowledge, they have invariably summoned its peoples to embrace the light of God through such means as best befitted the exigencies of the age in which they appeared. They were thus able to scatter the darkness of ignorance, and to shed upon the world the glory of their own knowledge. It is towards the inmost essence of these Prophets, therefore, that the eye of every man of discernment must be directed, inasmuch as their one and only purpose hath always been to guide the erring, and give peace to the afflicted. . . . These are not days of prosperity and triumph. The whole of mankind is in the grip of manifold ills. Strive, therefore, to save its life through the wholesome medicine which the almighty hand of the unerring Physician hath prepared.

And now concerning thy question regarding the nature of religion. Know thou that they who are truly wise have likened the world unto the human temple. As the body of man needeth a garment to clothe it, so the body of mankind must needs be adorned with the mantle of justice and wisdom. Its robe is the Revelation vouchsafed unto it by God. Whenever this robe hath fulfilled its purpose, the Almighty will assuredly renew it. For every age requireth a fresh measure of the light of God. Every Divine Revelation hath been sent down in a manner that befitted the circumstances of the age in which it hath appeared.

As to thy question regarding the sayings of the leaders of past religions. Every wise and praiseworthy man will no doubt eschew such vain and profitless talk. The incomparable Creator hath created all men from one same substance, and hath exalted their reality above the rest of His creatures. Success or failure, gain or loss, must, therefore, depend upon man's own exertions. The more he striveth, the greater will be his progress. We fain would hope that the vernal showers of the bounty of God may cause the flowers of true understanding to spring from the soil of men's hearts, and may wash them from all earthly defilements.

xxxv.   Ponder a while. What is it that prompted, in every Dispensation, the peoples of the earth to shun the Manifestation of the All-Merciful? What could have impelled them to turn away from Him and to challenge His authority? Were men to meditate on these words which have flowed from the Pen of the Divine Ordainer, they would, one and all, hasten to embrace the truth of this God-given, and ever-enduring Revelation, and would testify to that which He Himself hath solemnly affirmed.   It is the veil of idle imaginations which, in the days of the Manifestations of the Unity of God and the Day Springs of His everlasting glory, hath intervened, and will continue to intervene, between them and the rest of mankind. For in those days, He Who is the Eternal Truth manifesteth Himself in conformity with that which He Himself hath purposed, and not according to the desires and expectations of men. Even as He hath revealed: "So oft, then, as an Apostle cometh to you with that which your souls desire not, do ye swell with pride, and treat some as impostors, and slay others."

There can be no doubt whatever that had these

[82]

Apostles appeared, in bygone ages and cycles, in accordance with the vain imaginations which the hearts of men had devised, no one would have repudiated the truth of these sanctified Beings. Though such men have been, night and day, remembering the one true God, and have been devoutly engaged in the exercise of their devotions, yet they failed in the end to recognize, and partake of the grace of, the Day Springs of the signs of God and the Manifestations of His irrefutable evidences. To this the Scriptures bear witness. Thou hast, no doubt, heard about it.

Consider the Dispensation of Jesus Christ. Behold, how all the learned men of that generation, though eagerly anticipating the coming of the Promised One, have nevertheless denied Him. Both Annas, the most learned among the divines of His day, and Caiaphas, the high priest, denounced Him and pronounced the sentence of His death.

In like manner, when Muḥammad, the Prophet of God—may all men be a sacrifice unto Him—appeared, the learned men of Mecca and Medina arose, in the early days of His Revelation, against Him and rejected His Message, while they who were destitute of all learning recognized and embraced His Faith. Ponder a while. Consider how Balál, the Ethiopian, unlettered though he was, ascended into the heaven of faith and certitude, whilst 'Abdu'lláh Ubayy, a leader among the learned, maliciously strove to oppose Him. Behold, how a mere shepherd was so

[83]

carried away by the ecstasy of the words of God that he was able to gain admittance into the habitation of his Best-Beloved, and was united to Him Who is the Lord of Mankind, whilst they who prided themselves on their knowledge and wisdom strayed far from His path and remained deprived of His grace. For this reason He hath written: "He that is exalted among you shall be abased, and he that is abased shall be exalted." References to this theme are to be found in most of the heavenly Books, as well as in the sayings of the Prophets and Messengers of God.

Verily I say, such is the greatness of this Cause that the father flieth from his son, and the son flieth from his father. Call ye to mind the story of Noah and Canaan. God grant that, in these days of heavenly delight, ye may not deprive yourselves of the sweet savors of the All-Glorious God, and may partake, in this spiritual Springtime, of the outpourings of His grace. Arise in the name of Him Who is the Object of all knowledge, and, with absolute detachment from the learning of men, lift up your voices and proclaim His Cause. I swear by the Day Star of Divine Revelation! The very moment ye arise, ye will witness how a flood of Divine knowledge will gush out of your hearts, and will behold the wonders of His heavenly wisdom manifested in all their glory before you. Were ye to taste of the sweetness of the sayings of the All-Merciful, ye would unhesitatingly

[84]

forsake your selves, and would lay down your lives for the Well-Beloved.

Who can ever believe that this Servant of God hath at any time cherished in His heart a desire for any earthly honor or benefit? The Cause associated with His Name is far above the transitory things of this world. Behold Him, an exile, a victim of tyranny, in this Most Great Prison. His enemies have assailed Him on every side, and will continue to do so till the end of His life. Whatever, therefore, He saith unto you is wholly for the sake of God, that haply the peoples of the earth may cleanse their hearts from the stain of evil desire, may rend its veil asunder, and attain unto the knowledge of the one true God—the most exalted station to which any man can aspire. Their belief or disbelief in My Cause can neither profit nor harm Me. We summon them wholly for the sake of God. He, verily, can afford to dispense with all creatures.

XXXVI. Know thou that when the Son of Man yielded up His breath to God, the whole creation wept with a great weeping. By sacrificing Himself, however, a fresh capacity was infused into all created things. Its evidences, as witnessed in all the peoples of the earth, are now manifest before thee. The deepest wisdom which the sages have uttered, the profoundest learning which any mind hath unfolded, the arts which the ablest hands have produced, the influence exerted by the most potent of rulers, are but manifestations of the quickening power released by His transcendent, His all-pervasive, and resplendent Spirit.

We testify that when He came into the world, He shed the splendor of His glory upon all created things. Through Him the leper recovered from the leprosy of perversity and ignorance. Through Him, the unchaste and wayward were healed. Through His power, born of Almighty God, the eyes of the blind were opened, and the soul of the sinner sanctified.

Leprosy may be interpreted as any veil that interveneth between man and the recognition of the Lord, his God. Whoso alloweth himself to be shut out from Him is indeed a leper, who shall not be remembered in the Kingdom of God, the Mighty, the All-Praised. We bear witness that through the power of the Word of God every leper was cleansed, every sickness was healed, every human infirmity was banished. He it is Who purified the world. Blessed is the man who, with a face beaming with light, hath turned towards Him.

XXXVII. Blessed is the man that hath acknowledged his belief in God and in His signs, and recognized that "He shall not be asked of His doings." Such a recognition hath been made by God the ornament of every belief and its very foundation. Upon it must depend the acceptance of every goodly deed.

[86]

Fasten your eyes upon it, that haply the whisperings of the rebellious may not cause you to slip.

Were He to decree as lawful the thing which from time immemorial had been forbidden, and forbid that which had, at all times, been regarded as lawful, to none is given the right to question His authority. Whoso will hesitate, though it be for less than a moment, should be regarded as a transgressor.

Whoso hath not recognized this sublime and fundamental verity, and hath failed to attain this most exalted station, the winds of doubt will agitate him, and the sayings of the infidels will distract his soul. He that hath acknowledged this principle will be endowed with the most perfect constancy. All honor to this all-glorious station, the remembrance of which adorneth every exalted Tablet. Such is the teaching which God bestoweth on you, a teaching that will deliver you from all manner of doubt and perplexity, and enable you to attain unto salvation both in this world and in the next. He, verily, is the Ever-Forgiving, the Most Bountiful.

XXXVIII. Know of a certainty that in every Dispensation the light of Divine Revelation hath been vouchsafed unto men in direct proportion to their spiritual capacity. Consider the sun. How feeble its rays the moment it appeareth above the horizon. How gradually its warmth and potency increase as it approacheth its zenith, enabling meanwhile all created things to adapt themselves to the growing intensity of its light. How steadily it declineth until it reacheth its setting point. Were it, all of a sudden, to manifest the energies latent within it, it would, no doubt, cause injury to all created things. . . . In like manner, if the Sun of Truth were suddenly to reveal, at the earliest stages of its manifestation, the full measure of the potencies which the providence of the Almighty hath bestowed upon it, the earth of human understanding would waste away and be consumed; for men's hearts would neither sustain the intensity of its revelation, nor be able to mirror forth the radiance of its light. Dismayed and overpowered, they would cease to exist.

XXXIX.   Praise be to Thee, O Lord My God, for the wondrous revelations of Thy inscrutable decree and the manifold woes and trials Thou hast destined for Myself. At one time Thou didst deliver Me into the hands of Nimrod; at another Thou hast allowed Pharaoh's rod to persecute Me. Thou, alone, canst estimate, through Thine all-encompassing knowledge and the operation of Thy Will, the incalculable afflictions I have suffered at their hands. Again Thou didst cast Me into the prison-cell of the ungodly, for no reason except that I was moved to whisper into the ears of the well-favored denizens of Thy Kingdom an intimation of the vision with which Thou hadst, through Thy knowledge, inspired Me, and revealed to Me its meaning through the potency of Thy might. And again Thou didst decree that I be beheaded by the sword of the infidel. Again I was crucified for having unveiled to men's eyes the hidden gems of Thy glorious unity, for having revealed to them the wondrous signs of Thy sovereign and everlasting power. How bitter the humiliations heaped upon Me, in a subsequent age, on the plain of Karbilá! How lonely did I feel amidst Thy people! To what a state of helplessness I was reduced in that land! Unsatisfied with such indignities, My persecutors decapitated Me, and, carrying aloft My head from land to land paraded it before the gaze of the unbelieving multitude, and deposited it on the seats of the perverse and faithless. In a later age, I was suspended, and My breast was made a target to the darts of the malicious cruelty of My foes. My limbs were riddled with bullets, and My body was torn asunder. Finally, behold how, in this Day, My treacherous enemies have leagued themselves against Me, and are continually plotting to instill the venom of hate and malice into the souls of Thy servants. With all their might they are scheming to accomplish their purpose. . . . Grievous as is My plight, O God, My Well-Beloved, I render thanks unto Thee, and My Spirit is grateful for whatsoever hath befallen me in the path of Thy good-pleasure. I am well pleased with that which Thou didst ordain for Me, and welcome, however calamitous, the pains and sorrows I am made to suffer.

XL.   O My Well-Beloved! Thou hast breathed Thy Breath into Me, and divorced Me from Mine own Self. Thou didst, subsequently, decree that no more than a faint reflection, a mere emblem of Thy Reality within Me be left among the perverse and envious. Behold, how, deluded by this emblem, they have risen against Me, and heaped upon Me their denials! Uncover Thy Self, therefore, O My Best-Beloved, and deliver Me from My plight.

Thereupon a Voice replied: "I love, I dearly cherish this emblem. How can I consent that Mine eyes, alone, gaze upon this emblem, and that no heart except Mine heart recognize it? By My Beauty, which is the same as Thy Beauty! My wish is to hide Thee from Mine own eyes: how much more from the eyes of men!"

I was preparing to make reply, when lo, the Tablet was suddenly ended, leaving My theme unfinished, and the pearl of Mine utterance unstrung.

XLI.   God is My witness, O people! I was asleep on My couch, when lo, the Breeze of God wafting over Me roused Me from My slumber. His quickening Spirit revived Me, and My tongue was unloosed to voice His Call. Accuse Me not of having transgressed against God. Behold Me, not with your eyes but with Mine. Thus admonisheth you He Who is the Gracious, the All-Knowing. Think ye, O people, that I hold within My grasp the control of God's ultimate Will and Purpose? Far be it from Me to advance such claim. To this I testify before God, the Almighty, the Exalted, the All-Knowing, the All-Wise. Had the ultimate destiny of God's Faith been in Mine hands, I would have never consented, even though for one moment, to manifest Myself unto you, nor would I have allowed one word to fall from My lips. Of this God Himself is, verily, a witness.

XLII. O Son of Justice! In the night season the beauty of the immortal Being hath repaired from the emerald height of fidelity unto the Sadratu'l-Muntahá, and wept with such a weeping that the Concourse on high and the dwellers of the realms above wailed at His lamenting. Whereupon there was asked, Why the wailing and weeping? He made reply: As bidden I waited expectant upon the hill of faithfulness, yet inhaled not from them that dwell on earth the fragrance of fidelity. Then summoned to return I beheld, and lo! certain doves of holiness were sore tried within the claws of the dogs of earth. Thereupon the Maid of Heaven hastened forth unveiled and resplendent from Her mystic mansion, and asked of their names, and all were told but one. And when urged, the first letter thereof was uttered, whereupon the dwellers of the celestial chambers

[91]

rushed forth out of their habitation of glory. And whilst the second letter was pronounced they fell down, one and all, upon the dust. At that moment a voice was heard from the inmost shrine: "Thus far and no farther." Verily, We bear witness unto that which they have done, and now are doing.

XLIII. O Afnán, O thou that hast branched from Mine ancient Stock! My glory and My loving-kindness rest upon thee. How vast is the tabernacle of the Cause of God! It hath overshadowed all the peoples and kindreds of the earth, and will, erelong, gather together the whole of mankind beneath its shelter. Thy day of service is now come. Countless Tablets bear the testimony of the bounties vouchsafed unto thee. Arise for the triumph of My Cause, and, through the power of thine utterance, subdue the hearts of men. Thou must show forth that which will ensure the peace and the well-being of the miserable and the down-trodden. Gird up the loins of thine endeavor, that perchance thou mayest release the captive from his chains, and enable him to attain unto true liberty.

Justice is, in this day, bewailing its plight, and Equity groaneth beneath the yoke of oppression. The thick clouds of tyranny have darkened the face of the earth, and enveloped its peoples. Through the movement of Our Pen of glory We have, at the bidding of the omnipotent Ordainer, breathed a new life into every human frame, and instilled into every word a fresh potency. All created things proclaim the evidences of this world-wide regeneration. This is the most great, the most joyful tidings imparted by the Pen of this wronged One to mankind. Wherefore fear ye, O My well-beloved ones? Who is it that can dismay you? A touch of moisture sufficeth to dissolve the hardened clay out of which this perverse generation is molded. The mere act of your gathering together is enough to scatter the forces of these vain and worthless people. . . .

Every man of insight will, in this day, readily admit that the counsels which the Pen of this wronged One hath revealed constitute the supreme animating power for the advancement of the world and the exaltation of its peoples. Arise, O people, and, by the power of God's might, resolve to gain the victory over your own selves, that haply the whole earth may be freed and sanctified from its servitude to the gods of its idle fancies—gods that have inflicted such loss upon, and are responsible for the misery of, their wretched worshipers. These idols form the obstacle that impedeth man in his efforts to advance in the path of perfection. We cherish the hope that the Hand of Divine power may lend its assistance to mankind, and deliver it from its state of grievous abasement.

In one of the Tablets these words have been revealed: O people of God! Do not busy yourselves in your own concerns; let your thoughts be fixed upon that which will rehabilitate the fortunes of mankind and sanctify the hearts and souls of men. This can best be achieved through pure and holy deeds, through a virtuous life and a goodly behavior. Valiant acts will ensure the triumph of this Cause, and a saintly character will reinforce its power. Cleave unto righteousness, O people of Bahá! This, verily, is the commandment which this wronged One hath given unto you, and the first choice of His unrestrained Will for every one of you.

O friends! It behoveth you to refresh and revive your souls through the gracious favors which in this Divine, this soul-stirring Springtime are being showered upon you. The Day Star of His great glory hath shed its radiance upon you, and the clouds of His limitless grace have overshadowed you. How high the reward of him that hath not deprived himself of so great a bounty, nor failed to recognize the beauty of his Best-Beloved in this, His new attire. Watch over yourselves, for the Evil One is lying in wait, ready to entrap you. Gird yourselves against his wicked devices, and, led by the light of the name of the All-Seeing God, make your escape from the darkness that surroundeth you. Let your vision be world-embracing, rather than confined to your own self. The Evil One is he that hindereth the rise and obstructeth the spiritual progress of the children of men.

It is incumbent upon every man, in this Day, to hold fast unto whatsoever will promote the interests, and exalt the station, of all nations and just governments. Through each and every one of the verses which the Pen of the Most High hath revealed, the doors of love and unity have been unlocked and flung open to the face of men. We have erewhile declared —and Our Word is the truth—: "Consort with the followers of all religions in a spirit of friendliness and fellowship." Whatsoever hath led the children of men to shun one another, and hath caused dissensions and divisions amongst them, hath, through the revelation of these words, been nullified and abolished. From the heaven of God's Will, and for the purpose of ennobling the world of being and of elevating the minds and souls of men, hath been sent down that which is the most effective instrument for the education of the whole human race. The highest essence and most perfect expression of whatsoever the peoples of old have either said or written hath, through this most potent Revelation, been sent down from the heaven of the Will of the All-Possessing, the Ever-Abiding God. Of old it hath been revealed: "Love of one's country is an element of the Faith of God." The Tongue of Grandeur hath, however, in the day of His manifestation proclaimed: "It is not his to boast who loveth his country, but it is his who loveth the world." Through the power released by these exalted words He hath lent a fresh impulse, and set a new direction, to the birds of men's hearts, and hath obliterated every trace of restriction and limitation from God's holy Book. . . .

O people of Justice! Be as brilliant as the light, and as splendid as the fire that blazed in the Burning Bush. The brightness of the fire of your love will no doubt fuse and unify the contending peoples and kindreds of the earth, whilst the fierceness of the flame of enmity and hatred cannot but result in strife and ruin. We beseech God that He may shield His creatures from the evil designs of His enemies. He verily hath power over all things.

All praise be to the one true God—exalted be His glory—inasmuch as He hath, through the Pen of the Most High, unlocked the doors of men's hearts. Every verse which this Pen hath revealed is a bright and shining portal that discloseth the glories of a saintly and pious life, of pure and stainless deeds. The summons and the message which We gave were never intended to reach or to benefit one land or one people only. Mankind in its entirety must firmly adhere to whatsoever hath been revealed and vouchsafed unto it. Then and only then will it attain unto true liberty. The whole earth is illuminated with the resplendent glory of God's Revelation. In the year sixty He Who heralded the light of Divine Guidance —may all creation be a sacrifice unto Him—arose to announce a fresh revelation of the Divine Spirit, and was followed, twenty years later, by Him through Whose coming the world was made the recipient of this promised glory, this wondrous favor. Behold how the generality of mankind hath been endued with the capacity to hearken unto God's most exalted Word—the Word upon which must depend the gathering together and spiritual resurrection of all men. . . .

Incline your hearts, O people of God, unto the counsels of your true, your incomparable Friend. The Word of God may be likened unto a sapling, whose roots have been implanted in the hearts of men. It is incumbent upon you to foster its growth through the living waters of wisdom, of sanctified and holy words, so that its root may become firmly fixed and its branches may spread out as high as the heavens and beyond.

O ye that dwell on earth! The distinguishing feature that marketh the preeminent character of this Supreme Revelation consisteth in that We have, on the one hand, blotted out from the pages of God's holy Book whatsoever hath been the cause of strife, of malice and mischief amongst the children of men, and have, on the other, laid down the essential prerequisites of concord, of understanding, of complete and enduring unity. Well is it with them that keep My statutes.

Time and again have We admonished Our beloved ones to avoid, nay to flee from, anything whatsoever from which the odor of mischief can be detected. The world is in great turmoil, and the minds of its people are in a state of utter confusion. We entreat the Almighty that He may graciously illuminate them with the glory of His Justice, and enable them to discover that which will be profitable unto them at all times and under all conditions. He, verily is the All-Possessing, the Most High.

XLIV. Lay not aside the fear of God, O ye the learned of the world, and judge fairly the Cause of this unlettered One to Whom all the Books of God, the Protector, the Self-Subsisting, have testified. . . . Will not the dread of Divine displeasure, the fear of Him Who hath no peer or equal, arouse you? He Whom the world hath wronged hath, at no time, associated with you, hath never studied your writings, nor participated in any of your disputations. The garb He weareth, His flowing locks, His headdress, attest the truth of His words. How long will ye persist in your injustice? Witness the habitation in which He, Who is the incarnation of justice, hath been forced to dwell. Open your eyes, and, beholding His plight, meditate diligently upon that which your hands have wrought, that haply ye may not be deprived of the light of His Divine utterance, nor remain bereft of your share of the ocean of His knowledge.

Certain ones among both commoners and nobles have objected that this wronged One is neither a member of the ecclesiastical order nor a descendant of the Prophet. Say: O ye that claim to be just! Reflect a little while, and ye shall recognize how infinitely exalted is His present state above the station ye claim He should possess. The Will of the Almighty hath decreed that out of a house wholly devoid of all that the divines, the doctors, the sages, and scholars commonly possess His Cause should proceed and be made manifest.

The Breathings of the Divine Spirit awoke Him, and bade Him arise and proclaim His Revelation. No sooner was He roused from His slumber than He lifted up His voice and summoned the whole of mankind unto God, the Lord of all worlds. We have been moved to reveal these words in consideration of the weakness and frailty of men; otherwise, the Cause We have proclaimed is such as no pen can ever describe, nor any mind conceive its greatness. To this beareth witness He with Whom is the Mother Book.

XLV. The Ancient Beauty hath consented to be bound with chains that mankind may be released from its bondage, and hath accepted to be made a prisoner within this most mighty Stronghold that the whole world may attain unto true liberty. He hath drained to its dregs the cup of sorrow, that all the peoples of the earth may attain unto abiding joy, and be filled with gladness. This is of the mercy of your Lord, the Compassionate, the Most Merciful. We have accepted to be abased, O believers in the Unity of God, that ye may be exalted, and have suffered manifold afflictions, that ye might prosper and flourish. He Who hath come to build anew the whole world, behold, how they that have joined partners with God have forced Him to dwell within the most desolate of cities!

XLVI.   I sorrow not for the burden of My imprisonment. Neither do I grieve over My abasement, or the tribulation I suffer at the hands of Mine enemies By My life! They are My glory, a glory wherewith God hath adorned His own Self. Would that ye know it!

The shame I was made to bear hath uncovered the glory with which the whole of creation had been invested, and through the cruelties I have endured, the Day Star of Justice hath manifested itself, and shed its splendor upon men.

My sorrows are for those who have involved themselves in their corrupt passions, and claim to be associated with the Faith of God, the Gracious, the All-Praised.

It behoveth the people of Bahá to die to the world and all that is therein, to be so detached from all earthly things that the inmates of Paradise may inhale from their garment the sweet smelling savor of sanctity, that all the peoples of the earth may recognize in their faces the brightness of the All-Merciful, and that through them may be spread abroad the signs and tokens of God, the Almighty, the All-Wise.

They that have tarnished the fair name of the Cause of God, by following the things of the flesh—these are in palpable error!

XLVII. O Jews! If ye be intent on crucifying once again Jesus, the Spirit of God, put Me to death, for He hath once more, in My person, been made manifest unto you. Deal with Me as ye wish, for I have vowed to lay down My life in the path of God. I will fear no one, though the powers of earth and heaven be leagued against Me. Followers of the Gospel! If ye cherish the desire to slay Muḥammad, the Apostle of God, seize Me and put an end to My life, for I am He, and My Self is His Self. Do unto Me as ye like, for the deepest longing of Mine heart is to attain the presence of My Best-Beloved in His Kingdom of Glory. Such is the Divine decree, if ye know it. Followers of Muḥammad! If it be your wish to riddle with your shafts the breast of Him Who hath caused His Book the Bayán to be sent down unto you, lay hands on Me and persecute Me, for I am His Well-Beloved, the revelation of His own Self, though My name be not His name. I have come in the shadows of the clouds of glory, and am invested by God with invincible sovereignty. He, verily, is the Truth, the Knower of things unseen. I, verily, anticipate from you the treatment ye have accorded unto Him that came before Me. To this all things, verily, witness, if ye be of those who hearken.

O people of the Bayán! If ye have resolved to shed the blood of Him Whose coming the Báb hath proclaimed, Whose advent Muḥammad hath prophesied, and Whose Revelation Jesus Christ Himself hath announced, behold Me standing, ready and defenseless, before you. Deal with Me after your own desires.

XLVIII. God is my witness! Had it not been in conflict with that which the Tablets of God have decreed, I would have gladly kissed the hands of whosoever attempted to shed my blood in the path of the Well-Beloved. I would, moreover, have bestowed upon him a share of such worldly goods as God had allowed me to possess, even though he who perpetrated this act would have provoked the wrath of the Almighty, incurred His malediction, and deserved to be tormented throughout the eternity of God, the All-Possessing, the Equitable, the All-Wise.

XLIX. Know verily that whenever this Youth turneth His eyes towards His own self, he findeth it the most insignificant of all creation. When He contemplates, however, the bright effulgences He hath been empowered to manifest, lo, that self is transfigured before Him into a sovereign Potency permeating the essence of all things visible and invisible. Glory be to Him Who, through the power of truth, hath sent down the Manifestation of His own Self and entrusted Him with His message unto all mankind.

L. Shake off, O heedless ones, the slumber of negligence, that ye may behold the radiance which His glory hath spread through the world. How foolish are those who murmur against the premature birth of His light. O ye who are inly blind! Whether too soon or too late, the evidences of His effulgent glory are now actually manifest. It behoveth you to ascertain whether or not such a light hath appeared. It is neither within your power nor mine to set the time at which it should be made manifest. God's inscrutable Wisdom hath fixed its hour beforehand. Be content, O people, with that which God hath desired for you and predestined unto you. . . . O my ill-wishers! The Day Star of eternal Guidance beareth me witness: Had it been in my power, I would have, under no circumstances, consented to distinguish myself amongst men, for the Name I bear utterly disdaineth to associate itself with this generation whose tongues are sullied and whose hearts are false. And whenever I chose to hold my peace and be still, lo, the voice of the Holy Ghost, standing on my right hand, aroused me, and the Supreme Spirit appeared before my face, and Gabriel overshadowed me, and the Spirit of Glory stirred within my bosom, bidding me arise and break my silence. If your hearing be purged and your ears be attentive, ye will assuredly perceive that every limb of my body, nay all the atoms of my being, proclaim and bear witness to this call: "God, besides Whom is none other God, and He,

Whose beauty is now manifest, is the reflection of His glory unto all that are in heaven and on earth."

LI.   O people! I swear by the one true God! This is the Ocean out of which all seas have proceeded, and with which every one of them will ultimately be united. From Him all the Suns have been generated, and unto Him they will all return. Through His potency the Trees of Divine Revelation have yielded their fruits, every one of which hath been sent down in the form of a Prophet, bearing a Message to God's creatures in each of the worlds whose number God, alone, in His all-encompassing Knowledge, can reckon. This He hath accomplished through the agency of but one Letter of His Word, revealed by His Pen—a Pen moved by His directing Finger— His Finger itself sustained by the power of God's Truth.

LII.   Say: O people! Withhold not from yourselves the grace of God and His mercy. Whoso withholdeth himself therefrom is indeed in grievous loss. What, O people! Do ye worship the dust, and turn away from your Lord, the Gracious, the All-Bountiful? Fear ye God, and be not of those who perish. Say: The Book of God hath been sent down in the form of this Youth. Hallowed, therefore, be God, the most excellent of makers! Take ye good heed, O peoples of the world, lest ye flee from His face. Nay, make haste to attain His presence, and be of them that have returned unto Him. Pray to be forgiven, O people, for having failed in your duty towards God, and for having trespassed against His Cause, and be not of the foolish. He it is Who hath created you; He it is Who hath nourished your souls through His Cause, and enabled you to recognize Him Who is the Almighty, the Most Exalted, the All-Knowing. He it is Who hath unveiled to your eyes the treasures of His knowledge, and caused you to ascend unto the heaven of certitude—the certitude of His resistless, His irrefutable, and most exalted Faith. Beware that ye do not deprive yourselves of the grace of God, that ye do not bring to naught your works, and do not repudiate the truth of this most manifest, this lofty, this shining, and glorious Revelation. Judge ye fairly the Cause of God, your Creator, and behold that which hath been sent down from the Throne on high, and meditate thereon with innocent and sanctified hearts. Then will the truth of this Cause appear unto you as manifest as the sun in its noon-tide glory. Then will ye be of them that have believed in Him.

Say: The first and foremost testimony establishing His truth is His own Self. Next to this testimony is His Revelation. For whoso faileth to recognize either the one or the other He hath established the words He hath revealed as proof of His reality and truth. This is, verily, an evidence of His tender mercy unto men. He hath endowed every soul with the capacity to recognize the signs of God. How could He, otherwise, have fulfilled His testimony unto men, if ye be of them that ponder His Cause in their hearts. He will never deal unjustly with any one, neither will He task a soul beyond its power. He, verily, is the Compassionate, the All-Merciful.

Say: So great is the glory of the Cause of God that even the blind can perceive it, how much more they whose sight is sharp, whose vision is pure. The blind, though unable to perceive the light of the sun, are, nevertheless, capable of experiencing its continual heat. The blind in heart, however, among the people of the Bayán—and to this God is My witness—are impotent, no matter how long the Sun may shine upon them, either to perceive the radiance of its glory, or to appreciate the warmth of its rays.

Say: O people of the Bayán! We have chosen you out of the world to know and recognize Our Self. We have caused you to draw nigh unto the right side of Paradise—the Spot out of which the undying Fire crieth in manifold accents: "There is none other God besides Me, the All-Powerful, the Most High!" Take heed lest ye allow yourselves to be shut out as by a veil from this Day Star that shineth above the day-spring of the Will of your Lord, the All-Merciful, and whose light hath encompassed both the small and the great. Purge your sight, that ye may perceive its glory with your own eyes, and depend not on the sight of any one except your self, for God hath never burdened any soul beyond its power. Thus hath it been sent down unto the Prophets and Messengers of old, and been recorded in all the Scriptures.

Strive, O people, to gain admittance into this vast Immensity for which God ordained neither beginning nor end, in which His voice hath been raised, and over which have been wafted the sweet savors of holiness and glory. Divest not yourselves of the Robe of grandeur, neither suffer your hearts to be deprived of remembering your Lord, nor your ears of hearkening unto the sweet melodies of His wondrous, His sublime, His all-compelling, His clear, and most eloquent voice.

LIII. O Naṣír, O My servant! God, the Eternal Truth, beareth Me witness. The Celestial Youth hath, in this Day, raised above the heads of men the glorious Chalice of Immortality, and is standing expectant upon His seat, wondering what eye will recognize His glory, and what arm will, unhesitatingly, be stretched forth to seize the Cup from His snow-white Hand and drain it. Only a few have as yet quaffed from this peerless, this soft-flowing grace of the Ancient King. These occupy the loftiest mansions of Paradise, and are firmly established upon the seats of authority. By the righteousness of God! Neither the mirrors of His glory, nor the revealers of His names, nor any created thing, that hath been or will ever be, can ever excel them, if ye be of them that comprehend this truth.

O Naṣír! The excellence of this Day is immensely exalted above the comprehension of men, however extensive their knowledge, however profound their understanding. How much more must it transcend the imaginations of them that have strayed from its light, and been shut out from its glory! Shouldst thou rend asunder the grievous veil that blindeth thy vision, thou wouldst behold such a bounty as naught, from the beginning that hath no beginning till the end that hath no end, can either resemble or equal. What language should He Who is the Mouthpiece of God choose to speak, so that they who are shut out as by a veil from Him can recognize His glory? The righteous, inmates of the Kingdom on high, shall drink deep from the Wine of Holiness, in My name, the all-glorious. None other besides them will share such benefits.

LIV. By the righteousness of God, my Well-Beloved! I have never aspired after worldly leadership. My sole purpose hath been to hand down unto men that which I was bidden to deliver by God, the Gracious, the Incomparable, that it may detach them from all that pertaineth to this world, and cause them to attain such heights as neither the ungodly can conceive, nor the froward imagine.

LV. Call thou to remembrance, O Land of Ṭá (Ṭihrán), the former days in which thy Lord had made thee the seat of His throne, and had enveloped thee with the effulgence of His glory. How vast the number of those sanctified beings, those symbols of certitude, who, in their great love for thee, have laid down their lives and sacrificed their all for thy sake! Joy be to thee, and blissfulness to them that inhabit thee. I testify that out of thee, as every discerning heart knoweth, proceedeth the living breath of Him Who is the Desire of the world. In thee the Unseen hath been revealed, and out of thee hath gone forth that which lay hid from the eyes of men. Which one of the multitude of thy sincere lovers shall We remember, whose blood hath been shed within thy gates, and whose dust is now concealed beneath thy soil? The sweet savors of God have unceasingly been wafted, and shall everlastingly continue to be wafted upon thee. Our Pen is moved to commemorate thee, and to extol the victims of tyranny, those men and women that sleep beneath thy dust.

Among them is Our own sister, whom We now call to mind as a token of Our fidelity, and as proof of Our loving-kindness, unto her. How piteous was her plight! In what a state of resignation she returned to her God! We, alone, in Our all-encompassing knowledge, have known it.

O Land of Ṭá! Thou art still, through the grace of God, a center around which His beloved ones have gathered. Happy are they; happy every refugee that seeketh thy shelter, in his sufferings in the path of God, the Lord of this wondrous Day! Blessed are they that remember the one true God, that magnify His Name, and seek diligently to serve His Cause. It is to these men that the sacred Books of old have referred. On them hath the Commander of the Faithful lavished his praise, saying: "The blessedness awaiting them excelleth the blessedness we now enjoy." He, verily, hath spoken the truth, and to this We now testify. The glory of their station, however, is as yet undisclosed. The Hand of Divine power will, assuredly, lift up the veil, and expose to the sight of men that which shall cheer and lighten the eye of the world.

Render thanks unto God, the Eternal Truth, exalted be His glory, inasmuch as ye have attained so wondrous a favor, and been adorned with the ornament of His praise. Appreciate the value of these days, and cleave to whatsoever beseemeth this Revelation. He, verily, is the Counsellor, the Compassionate, the All-Knowing.

LVI. Let nothing grieve thee, O Land of Ṭá (Ṭihrán), for God hath chosen thee to be the source of the joy of all mankind. He shall, if it be His Will, bless thy throne with one who will rule with justice, who will gather together the flock of God which the wolves have scattered. Such a ruler will, with joy and gladness, turn his face towards, and extend his favors unto, the people of Bahá. He indeed is accounted in the sight of God as a jewel among men. Upon him rest forever the glory of God, and the glory of all that dwell in the kingdom of His revelation.

Rejoice with great joy, for God hath made thee "the Dayspring of His light," inasmuch as within thee was born the Manifestation of His Glory. Be thou glad for this name that hath been conferred upon thee—a name through which the Day Star of grace hath shed its splendor, through which both earth and heaven have been illumined.

Erelong will the state of affairs within thee be changed, and the reins of power fall into the hands of the people. Verily, thy Lord is the All-Knowing. His authority embraceth all things. Rest thou assured in the gracious favor of thy Lord. The eye of His loving-kindness shall everlastingly be directed towards thee. The day is approaching when thy agitation will have been transmuted into peace and quiet calm. Thus hath it been decreed in the wondrous Book.

LVII. When thou art departed out of the court of My presence, O Muḥammad, direct thy steps towards My House (Baghdád House), and visit it on behalf of thy Lord. When thou reachest its door, stand thou before it and say: Whither is the Ancient Beauty gone, O most great House of God, He through

[111]

Whom God hath made thee the cynosure of an adoring world, and proclaimed thee to be the sign of His remembrance unto all who are in the heavens and all who are on the earth? Oh! for the former days when thou, O House of God, wert made His footstool, the days when in ceaseless strains the melody of the All-Merciful poured forth from thee! What hath become of thy jewel whose glory hath irradiated all creation? Whither are gone the days in which He, the Ancient King, had made thee the throne of His glory, the days in which He had chosen thee alone to be the lamp of salvation between earth and heaven, and caused thee to diffuse, at dawn and at eventide, the sweet fragrance of the All-Glorious?

Where, O House of God, is the Sun of majesty and power Who had enveloped thee with the brightness of His presence? Where is He, the Day Spring of the tender mercies of thy Lord, the Unconstrained, Who had established His seat within thy walls? What is it, O throne of God, that hath altered thy countenance, and made thy pillars to tremble? What could have closed thy door to the face of them that eagerly seek thee? What hath made thee so desolate? Couldst thou have been told that the Beloved of the world is pursued by the swords of His enemies? The Lord bless thee, and bless thy fidelity unto Him, inasmuch as thou hast remained His companion through all His sorrows and His sufferings.

I testify that thou art the scene of His transcendent glory, His most holy habitation. Out of thee hath gone forth the Breath of the All-Glorious, a Breath that hath breathed over all created things, and filled with joy the breasts of the devout that dwell in the mansions of Paradise. The Concourse on high, and they that inhabit the Cities of the Names of God, weep over thee, and bewail the things that have befallen thee.

Thou art still the symbol of the names and attributes of the Almighty, the Point towards which the eyes of the Lord of earth and heaven are directed. There hath befallen thee what hath befallen the Ark in which God's pledge of security had been made to dwell. Well is it with him that apprehendeth the intent of these words, and recognizeth the purpose of Him Who is the Lord of all creation.

Happy are those that inhale from thee the sweet savors of the Merciful, that acknowledge thine exaltation, that safeguard thy sanctity, that reverence, at all times, thy station. We implore the Almighty to grant that the eyes of those who have turned away from thee, and failed to appreciate thy worth, may be opened, that they may truly recognize thee, and Him Who, through the power of truth, hath raised thee up on high. Blind, indeed, are they about thee, and utterly unaware of thee in this day. Thy Lord is, verily, the Gracious, the Forgiving.

I bear witness that through thee God hath proved the hearts of His servants. Blessed be the man that directeth his steps toward thee, and visiteth thee. Woe to him that denieth thy right, that turneth away from thee, that dishonoreth thy name, and profaneth thy holiness.

Grieve not, O House of God, if the veil of thy sanctity be rent asunder by the infidels. God hath, in the world of creation, adorned thee with the jewel of His remembrance. Such an ornament no man can, at any time, profane. Towards thee the eyes of thy Lord shall, under all conditions, remain directed. He, verily, will incline His ear to the prayer of every one that visiteth thee, who will circle around thee, and calleth upon Him in thy name. He, in truth, is the Forgiving, the All-Merciful.

I beseech Thee, O my God, by this House that hath suffered such change in its separation from Thee, that bewaileth its remoteness from Thy presence, and lamenteth Thy tribulation, to forgive me, and my parents, and my kindred, and such of my brethren as have believed in Thee. Grant that all my needs be satisfied, through Thy bounty, O Thou Who art the King of Names. Thou art the most Bountiful of the bountiful, the Lord of all worlds.

LVIII. Call thou to mind that which hath been revealed unto Mihdí, Our servant, in the first year of Our banishment to the Land of Mystery (Adrianople). Unto him have We predicted that which must befall Our House (Baghdád House), in the days to come, lest he grieve over the acts of robbery and violence already perpetrated against it. Verily, the Lord, thy God, knoweth all that is in the heavens and all that is on the earth.

To him We have written: This is not the first humiliation inflicted upon My House. In days gone by the hand of the oppressor hath heaped indignities upon it. Verily, it shall be so abased in the days to come as to cause tears to flow from every discerning eye. Thus have We unfolded to thee things hidden beyond the veil, inscrutable to all save God, the Almighty, the All-Praised. In the fullness of time, the Lord shall, by the power of truth, exalt it in the eyes of all men. He shall cause it to become the Standard of His Kingdom, the Shrine round which will circle the concourse of the faithful. Thus hath spoken the Lord, thy God, ere the day of lamentation arriveth. This revelation have We given thee in Our holy Tablet, lest thou sorrow for what hath befallen Our House through the assaults of the enemy. All praise be to God, the All-Knowing, the All-Wise.

LIX. Every unbiased observer will readily admit that, ever since the dawn of His Revelation, this wronged One hath invited all mankind to turn their faces towards the Day Spring of Glory, and hath forbidden corruption, hatred, oppression, and wickedness. And yet, behold what the hand of the oppressor hath wrought! No pen dare describe his tyranny.

[115]

Though the purpose of Him Who is the Eternal Truth hath been to confer everlasting life upon all men, and ensure their security and peace, yet witness how they have arisen to shed the blood of His loved ones, and have pronounced on Him the sentence of death.

The instigators of this oppression are those very persons who, though so foolish, are reputed the wisest of the wise. Such is their blindness that, with unfeigned severity, they have cast into this fortified and afflictive Prison Him, for the servants of Whose Threshold the world hath been created. The Almighty, however, in spite of them and those that have repudiated the truth of this "Great Announcement," hath transformed this Prison House into the Most Exalted Paradise, the Heaven of Heavens.

We did not refuse such material benefits as could relieve Us from Our afflictions. Every one of Our companions, however, will bear Us witness that Our holy court is sanctified from, and far above, such material benefits. We have nevertheless accepted, while confined in this Prison, those things of which the infidels have striven to deprive Us. If a man be found willing to rear, in Our name, an edifice of pure gold or silver, or a house begemmed with stones of inestimable value, such a wish will no doubt be granted. He, verily, doeth what He willeth, and ordaineth that which He pleaseth. Leave hath, moreover, been given to whosoever may desire to raise,

[116]

throughout the length and breadth of this land, noble and imposing structures, and dedicate the rich and sacred territories adjoining the Jordan and its vicinity to the worship and service of the one true God, magnified be His glory, that the prophecies recorded by the Pen of the Most High in the sacred Scriptures may be fulfilled, and that which God, the Lord of all worlds, hath purposed in this most exalted, this most holy, this mighty, and wondrous Revelation may be made manifest.

We have, of old, uttered these words: Spread thy skirt, O Jerusalem! Ponder this in your hearts, O people of Bahá, and render thanks unto your Lord, the Expounder, the Most Manifest.

Were the mysteries, that are known to none except God, to be unraveled, the whole of mankind would witness the evidences of perfect and consummate justice. With a certitude that none can question, all men would cleave to His commandments, and would scrupulously observe them. We, verily, have decreed in Our Book a goodly and bountiful reward to whosoever will turn away from wickedness and lead a chaste and godly life. He, in truth, is the Great Giver, the All-Bountiful.

LX. My captivity can bring on Me no shame. Nay, by My life, it conferreth on Me glory. That which can make Me ashamed is the conduct of such

[117]

of My followers as profess to love Me, yet in fact follow the Evil One. They, indeed, are of the lost.

When the time set for this Revelation was fulfilled, and He Who is the Day Star of the world appeared in 'Iráq, He bade His followers observe that which would sanctify them from all earthly defilements. Some preferred to follow the desires of a corrupt inclination, while others walked in the way of righteousness and truth, and were rightly guided.

Say: He is not to be numbered with the people of Bahá who followeth his mundane desires, or fixeth his heart on things of the earth. He is My true follower who, if he come to a valley of pure gold, will pass straight through it aloof as a cloud, and will neither turn back, nor pause. Such a man is, assuredly, of Me. From his garment the Concourse on high can inhale the fragrance of sanctity. . . . And if he met the fairest and most comely of women, he would not feel his heart seduced by the least shadow of desire for her beauty. Such an one, indeed, is the creation of spotless chastity. Thus instructeth you the Pen of the Ancient of Days, as bidden by your Lord, the Almighty, the All-Bountiful.

LXI. The world is in travail, and its agitation waxeth day by day. Its face is turned towards waywardness and unbelief. Such shall be its plight, that to disclose it now would not be meet and seemly. Its perversity will long continue. And when the appointed hour is come, there shall suddenly appear that which shall cause the limbs of mankind to quake. Then, and only then, will the Divine Standard be unfurled, and the Nightingale of Paradise warble its melody.

LXII.   Recall thou to mind My sorrows, My cares and anxieties, My woes and trials, the state of My captivity, the tears that I have shed, the bitterness of Mine anguish, and now My imprisonment in this far-off land. God, O Muṣṭafá, beareth Me witness. Couldst thou be told what hath befallen the Ancient Beauty, thou wouldst flee into the wilderness, and weep with a great weeping. In thy grief, thou wouldst smite thyself on the head, and cry out as one stung by the sting of the adder. Be thou grateful to God, that We have refused to divulge unto thee the secrets of those unsearchable decrees that have been sent down unto Us from the heaven of the Will of thy Lord, the Most Powerful, the Almighty.

By the righteousness of God! Every morning I arose from My bed, I discovered the hosts of countless afflictions massed behind My door; and every night when I lay down, lo! My heart was torn with agony at what it had suffered from the fiendish cruelty of its foes. With every piece of bread the Ancient Beauty breaketh is coupled the assault of a fresh affliction, and with every drop He drinketh is mixed the bitterness of the most woeful of trials. He

[119]

is preceded in every step He taketh by an army of unforeseen calamities, while in His rear follow legions of agonizing sorrows.

Such is My plight, wert thou to ponder it in thine heart. Let not, however, thy soul grieve over that which God hath rained down upon Us. Merge thy will in His pleasure, for We have, at no time, desired anything whatsoever except His Will, and have welcomed each one of His irrevocable decrees. Let thine heart be patient, and be thou not dismayed. Follow not in the way of them that are sorely agitated.

LXIII.   O thou whose face is turned towards Me! As soon as thine eyes behold from afar My native city (Ṭihrán), stand thou and say: I am come to thee out of the Prison, O Land of Ṭá, with tidings from God, the Help in Peril, the Self-Subsisting. I announce unto thee, O mother of the world and fountain of light unto all its peoples, the tender mercies of thy Lord, and greet thee in the name of Him Who is the Eternal Truth, the Knower of things unseen. I testify that within thee He Who is the Hidden Name was revealed, and the Unseen Treasure uncovered. Through thee the secret of all things, be they of the past or of the future, hath been unfolded.

O Land of Ṭá! He Who is the Lord of Names remembereth thee in His glorious station. Thou wert the Day Spring of the Cause of God, the fountain of

His Revelation, the manifestation of His Most Great Name—a Name that hath caused the hearts and souls of men to tremble. How vast the number of those men and women, those victims of tyranny, that have, within thy walls, laid down their lives in the path of God, and been buried beneath thy dust with such cruelty as to cause every honored servant of God to bemoan their plight.

LXIV. It is Our wish to remember the Abode of supreme blissfulness (Ṭihrán), the holy and shining city—the city wherein the fragrance of the Well-Beloved hath been shed, wherein His signs have been diffused, wherein the evidences of His glory have been revealed, wherein His standards have been raised, wherein His tabernacle hath been pitched, wherein each of His wise decrees hath been unfolded.

It is the city in which the sweet savors of reunion have breathed, which have caused the sincere lovers of God to draw nigh unto Him, and to gain access to the Habitation of holiness and beauty. Happy is the wayfarer that directeth his steps towards this city, that gaineth admittance into it, and quaffeth the wine of reunion, through the outpouring grace of his Lord, the Gracious, the All-Praised.

I am come to thee, O land of the heart's desire, with tidings from God, and announce to thee His gracious favor and mercy, and greet and magnify thee in His name. He, in truth, is of immense bounteousness and goodness. Blessed be the man that turneth his face towards thee, that perceiveth from thee the fragrance of God's Presence, the Lord of all worlds. His glory be on thee, and the brightness of His light envelop thee, inasmuch as God hath made thee a paradise unto His servants, and proclaimed thee to be the blest and sacred land of which He, Himself, hath made mention in the Books which His Prophets and Messengers have revealed.

Through thee, O land of resplendent glory, the ensign, "There is none other God but Him," hath been unfurled, and the standard, "Verily I am the Truth, the Knower of things unseen," been hoisted. It behoveth every one that visiteth thee to glory in thee and in them that inhabit thee, that have branched from My Tree, who are the leaves thereof, who are the signs of My glory, who follow Me and are My lovers, and who, with the most mighty determination, have turned their faces in the direction of My glorious station.

LXV. Call Thou to remembrance Thine arrival in the City (Constantinople), how the Ministers of the Sultán thought Thee to be unacquainted with their laws and regulations, and believed Thee to be one of the ignorant. Say: Yes, by My Lord! I am ignorant of all things except what God hath, through His bountiful favor, been pleased to teach Me. To this We assuredly testify, and unhesitatingly confess it.

Say: If the laws and regulations to which ye cleave be of your own making, We will, in no wise, follow them. Thus have I been instructed by Him Who is the All-Wise, the All-Informed. Such hath been My way in the past, and such will it remain in the future, through the power of God and His might. This, indeed, is the true and right way. If they be ordained by God, bring forth, then, your proofs, if ye be of them that speak the truth. Say: We have written down in a Book which leaveth not unrecorded the work of any man, however insignificant, all that they have imputed to Thee, and all that they have done unto Thee.

Say: It behoveth you, O Ministers of State, to keep the precepts of God, and to forsake your own laws and regulations, and to be of them who are guided aright. Better is this for you than all ye possess, did ye but know it. If ye transgress the commandment of God, not one jot or one tittle of all your works shall be acceptable in His sight. Ye shall, erelong, discover the consequences of that which ye shall have done in this vain life, and shall be repaid for them. This, verily, is the truth, the undoubted truth.

How great the number of those who, in bygone ages, have committed the things ye have committed, and who, though superior to you in rank, have, in the end, returned unto dust, and been consigned to their inevitable doom! Would that ye might ponder the Cause of God in your hearts! Ye shall follow in their wake, and shall be made to enter a habitation wherein none shall be found to befriend or help you. Ye shall, of a truth, be asked of your doings, shall be called to account for your failure in duty with regard to the Cause of God, and for having disdainfully rejected His loved ones who, with manifest sincerity, have come unto you.

It is ye who have taken counsel together regarding them, ye that have preferred to follow the promptings of your own desires, and forsaken the commandment of God, the Help in Peril, the Almighty.

Say: What! Cleave ye to your own devices, and cast behind your backs the precepts of God? Ye, indeed, have wronged your own selves and others. Would that ye could perceive it! Say: If your rules and principles be founded on justice, why is it, then, that ye follow those which accord with your corrupt inclinations and reject such as conflict with your desires? By what right claim ye, then, to judge fairly between men? Are your rules and principles such as to justify your persecution of Him Who, at your bidding, hath presented Himself before you, your rejection of Him, and your infliction on Him every day of grievous injury? Hath He ever, though it be for one short moment, disobeyed you? All the inhabitants of 'Iráq, and beyond them every discerning observer, will bear witness to the truth of My words.

Be fair in your judgment, O ye Ministers of State! What is it that We have committed that could justify Our banishment? What is the offense that hath warranted Our expulsion? It is We Who have sought you, and yet, behold how ye refused to receive Us! By God! This is a sore injustice that ye have perpetrated—an injustice with which no earthly injustice can measure. To this the Almighty is Himself a witness. . . .

Know ye that the world and its vanities and its embellishments shall pass away. Nothing will endure except God's Kingdom which pertaineth to none but Him, the Sovereign Lord of all, the Help in Peril, the All-Glorious, the Almighty. The days of your life shall roll away, and all the things with which ye are occupied and of which ye boast yourselves shall perish, and ye shall, most certainly, be summoned by a company of His angels to appear at the spot where the limbs of the entire creation shall be made to tremble, and the flesh of every oppressor to creep. Ye shall be asked of the things your hands have wrought in this, your vain life, and shall be repaid for your doings. This is the day that shall inevitably come upon you, the hour that none can put back. To this the Tongue of Him that speaketh the truth and is the Knower of all things hath testified.

LXVI. Fear God, ye inhabitants of the City (Constantinople), and sow not the seeds of dissension amongst men. Walk not in the paths of the Evil One. Walk ye, during the few remaining days of your life, in the ways of the one true God. Your days shall pass away as have the days of them who were before you. To dust shall ye return, even as your fathers of old did return.

Know ye that I am afraid of none except God. In none but Him have I placed My trust; to none will I cleave but Him, and wish for naught except the thing He hath wished for Me. This, indeed, is My heart's desire, did ye but know it. I have offered up My soul and My body as a sacrifice for God, the Lord of all worlds. Whoso hath known God shall know none but Him, and he that feareth God shall be afraid of no one except Him, though the powers of the whole earth rise up and be arrayed against him. I speak naught except at His bidding, and follow not, through the power of God and His might, except His truth. He, verily, shall recompense the truthful.

Narrate, O Servant, the things Thou didst behold at the time of Thine arrival in the City, that Thy testimony may endure amongst men, and serve as a warning unto them that believe. We found, upon Our arrival in the City, its governors and elders as children gathered about and disporting themselves with clay. We perceived no one sufficiently mature to acquire from Us the truths which God hath taught Us, nor ripe for Our wondrous words of wisdom. Our inner eye wept sore over them, and over their transgressions and their total disregard of the thing for which they were created. This is what We observed in that City, and which We have chosen to note down in Our Book, that it may serve as a warning unto them, and unto the rest of mankind.

Say: If ye be seekers after this life and the vanities thereof, ye should have sought them while ye were still enclosed in your mothers' wombs, for at that time ye were continually approaching them, could ye but perceive it. Ye have, on the other hand, ever since ye were born and attained maturity, been all the while receding from the world and drawing closer to dust. Why, then, exhibit such greed in amassing the treasures of the earth, when your days are numbered and your chance is well-nigh lost? Will ye not, then, O heedless ones, shake off your slumber?

Incline your ears to the counsels which this Servant giveth you for the sake of God. He, verily, asketh no recompense from you and is resigned to what God hath ordained for Him, and is entirely submissive to God's Will.

The days of your life are far spent, O people, and your end is fast approaching. Put away, therefore, the things ye have devised and to which ye cleave, and take firm hold on the precepts of God, that haply ye may attain that which He hath purposed for you, and be of them that pursue a right course. Delight not yourselves in the things of the world and its vain ornaments, neither set your hopes on them. Let your reliance be on the remembrance of God, the Most Exalted, the Most Great. He will, erelong, bring to naught all the things ye possess. Let Him be your fear, and forget not His covenant with you, and be not of them that are shut out as by a veil from Him.

Beware that ye swell not with pride before God, and disdainfully reject His loved ones. Defer ye humbly to the faithful, they that have believed in God and in His signs, whose hearts witness to His unity, whose tongues proclaim His oneness, and who speak not except by His leave. Thus do We exhort you with justice, and warn you with truth, that perchance ye may be awakened.

Lay not on any soul a load which ye would not wish to be laid upon you, and desire not for any one the things ye would not desire for yourselves. This is My best counsel unto you, did ye but observe it.

Respect ye the divines and learned amongst you, they whose conduct accords with their professions, who transgress not the bounds which God hath fixed, whose judgments are in conformity with His behests as revealed in His Book. Know ye that they are the lamps of guidance unto them that are in the heavens and on the earth. They who disregard and neglect the divines and learned that live amongst them— these have truly changed the favor with which God hath favored them.

Say: Await ye till God will have changed His favor unto you. Nothing whatsoever escapeth Him.

[128]

He knoweth the secrets both of the heavens and of the earth. His knowledge embraceth all things. Rejoice not in what ye have done, or will do in the future, nor delight in the tribulation with which ye have afflicted Us, for ye are unable by such means as these to exalt your stations, were ye to examine your works with acute discernment. Neither will ye be capable of detracting from the loftiness of Our state. Nay, God will add unto the recompense with which He shall reward Us, for having sustained with persevering patience the tribulations We have suffered. He, verily, shall increase the reward of them that endure with patience.

Know ye that trials and tribulations have, from time immemorial, been the lot of the chosen Ones of God and His beloved, and such of His servants as are detached from all else but Him, they whom neither merchandise nor traffic beguile from the remembrance of the Almighty, they that speak not till He hath spoken, and act according to His commandment. Such is God's method carried into effect of old, and such will it remain in the future. Blessed are the steadfastly enduring, they that are patient under ills and hardships, who lament not over anything that befalleth them, and who tread the path of resignation. . . .

The day is approaching when God will have raised up a people who will call to remembrance Our days,

[129]

who will tell the tale of Our trials, who will demand the restitution of Our rights from them that, without a tittle of evidence, have treated Us with manifest injustice. God, assuredly, dominateth the lives of them that wronged Us, and is well aware of their doings. He will, most certainly, lay hold on them for their sins. He, verily, is the fiercest of avengers.

Thus have We recounted unto you the tales of the one true God, and sent down unto you the things He had preordained, that haply ye may ask forgiveness of Him, may return unto Him, may truly repent, may realize your misdeeds, may shake off your slumber, may be roused from your heedlessness, may atone for the things that have escaped you, and be of them that do good. Let him who will, acknowledge the truth of My words; and as to him that willeth not, let him turn aside. My sole duty is to remind you of your failure in duty towards the Cause of God, if perchance ye may be of them that heed My warning. Wherefore, hearken ye unto My speech, and return ye to God and repent, that He, through His grace, may have mercy upon you, may wash away your sins, and forgive your trespasses. The greatness of His mercy surpasseth the fury of His wrath, and His grace encompasseth all who have been called into being and been clothed with the robe of life, be they of the past or of the future.

LXVII. There hath appeared in this Revelation what hath never appeared before. As to the infidels that have witnessed what hath been manifested, they murmur and say: "Verily, this is a sorcerer who hath devised a lie against God." They are indeed an outcast people.

Tell out to the nations, O Pen of the Ancient of Days, the things that have happened in 'Iráq. Tell them of the messenger whom the congregation of the divines of that land had delegated to meet Us, who, when attaining Our presence, questioned Us concerning certain sciences, and whom We answered by virtue of the knowledge We inherently possess. Thy Lord is, verily, the Knower of things unseen. "We testify," said he, "that the knowledge Thou dost possess is such as none can rival. Such a knowledge, however, is insufficient to vindicate the exalted station which the people ascribe to Thee. Produce, if Thou speakest the truth, what the combined forces of the peoples of the earth are powerless to produce." Thus was it irrevocably decreed in the court of the presence of thy Lord, the All-Glorious, the Loving.

"Witness! What is it thou seest?" He was dumbfounded. And when he came to himself, he said: "I truly believe in God, the All-Glorious, the All-Praised." "Go thou to the people, and tell them: 'Ask whatsoever ye please. Powerful is He to do what He willeth. Nothing whatsoever, be it of the past or of the future, can frustrate His Will.' Say: 'O ye

[131]

congregation of the divines! Choose any matter ye desire, and ask your Lord, the God of Mercy, to reveal it unto you. If He fulfil your wish, by virtue of His sovereignty, believe ye then in Him, and be not of those that reject His truth.' " "The dawn of understanding hath now broken," said he, "and the testimony of the All-Merciful is fulfilled." He arose and returned unto them that sent him, at the bidding of God, the All-Glorious, the Well-Beloved.

Days passed and he failed to come back to Us. Eventually, there came another messenger who informed Us that the people had given up what they originally had purposed. They are indeed a contemptible people. This is what happened in 'Iráq, and to what I reveal I Myself am witness. This happening was noised abroad, yet none was found to comprehend its meaning. Thus did We ordain it. Would that ye knew this!

By My Self! Whoso hath in bygone ages asked Us to produce the signs of God, hath, no sooner We revealed them to him, repudiated God's truth. The people, however, have, for the most part, remained heedless. They whose eyes are illumined with the light of understanding will perceive the sweet savors of the All-Merciful, and will embrace His truth. These are they who are truly sincere.

LXVIII. O thou who art the fruit of My Tree and the leaf thereof! On thee be My glory and My mercy.

Let not thine heart grieve over what hath befallen thee. Wert thou to scan the pages of the Book of Life, thou wouldst, most certainly, discover that which would dissipate thy sorrows and dissolve thine anguish.

Know thou, O fruit of My Tree, that the decrees of the Sovereign Ordainer, as related to fate and predestination, are of two kinds. Both are to be obeyed and accepted. The one is irrevocable, the other is, as termed by men, impending. To the former all must unreservedly submit, inasmuch as it is fixed and settled. God, however, is able to alter or repeal it. As the harm that must result from such a change will be greater than if the decree had remained unaltered, all, therefore, should willingly acquiesce in what God hath willed and confidently abide by the same.

The decree that is impending, however, is such that prayer and entreaty can succeed in averting it.

God grant that thou who art the fruit of My Tree, and they that are associated with thee, may be shielded from its evil consequences.

Say: O God, my God! Thou hast committed into mine hands a trust from Thee, and hast now according to the good-pleasure of Thy Will called it back to Thyself. It is not for me, who am a handmaid of Thine, to say, whence is this to me or wherefore hath it happened, inasmuch as Thou art glorified in all Thine acts, and art to be obeyed in Thy decree.

[133]

Thine handmaid, O my Lord, hath set her hopes on Thy grace and bounty. Grant that she may obtain that which will draw her nigh unto Thee, and will profit her in every world of Thine. Thou art the Forgiving, the All-Bountiful. There is none other God but Thee, the Ordainer, the Ancient of Days.

Vouchsafe Thy blessings, O Lord, my God, unto them that have quaffed the wine of Thy love before the face of men, and, in spite of Thine enemies, have acknowledged Thy unity, testified to Thy oneness, and confessed their belief in that which hath made the limbs of the oppressors among Thy creatures to quake, and the flesh of the proud ones of the earth to tremble. I bear witness that Thy Sovereignty can never perish, nor Thy Will be altered. Ordain for them that have set their faces towards Thee, and for Thine handmaids that have held fast by Thy Cord, that which beseemeth the Ocean of Thy bounty and the Heaven of Thy grace.

Thou art He, O God, Who hath proclaimed Himself as the Lord of Wealth, and characterized all that serve Him as poor and needy. Even as Thou hast written: "O ye that believe! Ye are but paupers in need of God; but God is the All-Possessing, the All-Praised." Having acknowledged my poverty, and recognized Thy wealth, suffer me not to be deprived of the glory of Thy riches. Thou art, verily, the Supreme Protector, the All-Knowing, the All-Wise.

LXIX.   Call thou to mind the behavior of Ashraf's mother, whose son laid down his life in the Land of Zá (Zanján). He, most certainly, is in the seat of truth, in the presence of One Who is the Most Powerful, the Almighty.

When the infidels, so unjustly, decided to put him to death, they sent and fetched his mother, that perchance she might admonish him, and induce him to recant his faith, and follow in the footsteps of them that have repudiated the truth of God, the Lord of all worlds.

No sooner did she behold the face of her son, than she spoke to him such words as caused the hearts of the lovers of God, and beyond them those of the Concourse on high, to cry out and be sore pained with grief. Truly, thy Lord knoweth what My tongue speaketh. He Himself beareth witness to My words.

And when addressing him she said: "My son, mine own son! Fail not to offer up thyself in the path of thy Lord. Beware that thou betray not thy faith in Him before Whose face have bowed down in adoration all who are in the heavens and all who are on the earth. Go thou straight on, O my son, and persevere in the path of the Lord, thy God. Haste thee to attain the presence of Him Who is the Well-Beloved of all worlds."

On her be My blessings, and My mercy, and My praise, and My glory. I Myself shall atone for the loss of her son—a son who now dwelleth within the tabernacle of My majesty and glory, and whose face beameth with a light that envelopeth with its radiance the Maids of Heaven in their celestial chambers, and beyond them the inmates of My Paradise, and the denizens of the Cities of Holiness. Were any eye to gaze on his face, he would exclaim: "Lo, this is no other than a noble angel!"

LXX. The world's equilibrium hath been upset through the vibrating influence of this most great, this new World Order. Mankind's ordered life hath been revolutionized through the agency of this unique, this wondrous System—the like of which mortal eyes have never witnessed.

Immerse yourselves in the ocean of My words, that ye may unravel its secrets, and discover all the pearls of wisdom that lie hid in its depths. Take heed that ye do not vacillate in your determination to embrace the truth of this Cause—a Cause through which the potentialities of the might of God have been revealed, and His sovereignty established. With faces beaming with joy, hasten ye unto Him. This is the changeless Faith of God, eternal in the past, eternal in the future. Let him that seeketh, attain it; and as to him that hath refused to seek it—verily, God is Self-Sufficient, above any need of His creatures.

Say: This is the infallible Balance which the Hand of God is holding, in which all who are in the heavens and all who are on the earth are weighed, and their fate determined, if ye be of them that believe and recognize this truth. Say: Through it the poor have been enriched, the learned enlightened, and the seekers enabled to ascend unto the presence of God. Beware, lest ye make it a cause of dissension amongst you. Be ye as firmly settled as the immovable mountain in the Cause of your Lord, the Mighty, the Loving.

LXXI. Be not dismayed, O peoples of the world, when the day star of My beauty is set, and the heaven of My tabernacle is concealed from your eyes. Arise to further My Cause, and to exalt My Word amongst men. We are with you at all times, and shall strengthen you through the power of truth. We are truly almighty. Whoso hath recognized Me will arise and serve Me with such determination that the powers of earth and heaven shall be unable to defeat his purpose.

The peoples of the world are fast asleep. Were they to wake from their slumber, they would hasten with eagerness unto God, the All-Knowing, the All-Wise. They would cast away everything they possess, be it all the treasures of the earth, that their Lord may remember them to the extent of addressing to them but one word. Such is the instruction given you by Him Who holdeth the knowledge of things hidden, in a Tablet which the eye of creation hath not seen, and which is revealed to none except His own Self, the omnipotent Protector of all worlds. So bewildered are they in the drunkenness of their evil desires, that they are powerless to recognize the Lord of all being, Whose voice calleth aloud from every direction: "There is none other God but Me, the Mighty, the All-Wise."

Say: Rejoice not in the things ye possess; tonight they are yours, tomorrow others will possess them. Thus warneth you He Who is the All-Knowing, the All-Informed. Say: Can ye claim that what ye own is lasting or secure? Nay! By Myself, the All-Merciful . . . The days of your life flee away as a breath of wind, and all your pomp and glory shall be folded up as were the pomp and glory of those gone before you. Reflect, O people! What hath become of your bygone days, your lost centuries? Happy the days that have been consecrated to the remembrance of God, and blessed the hours which have been spent in praise of Him Who is the All-Wise. By My life! Neither the pomp of the mighty, nor the wealth of the rich, nor even the ascendancy of the ungodly will endure. All will perish, at a word from Him. He, verily, is the All-Powerful, the All-Compelling, the Almighty. What advantage is there in the earthly things which men possess? That which shall profit them, they have utterly neglected. Erelong, they will awake from their slumber, and find themselves unable to obtain that which hath escaped them in the days of their

Lord, the Almighty, the All-Praised. Did they but know it, they would renounce their all, that their names may be mentioned before His throne. They, verily, are accounted among the dead.

LXXII. Let not your hearts be perturbed, O people, when the glory of My Presence is withdrawn, and the ocean of My utterance is stilled. In My presence amongst you there is a wisdom, and in My absence there is yet another, inscrutable to all but God, the Incomparable, the All-Knowing. Verily, We behold you from Our realm of glory, and shall aid whosoever will arise for the triumph of Our Cause with the hosts of the Concourse on high and a company of Our favored angels.

O peoples of the earth! God, the Eternal Truth, is My witness that streams of fresh and soft-flowing waters have gushed from the rocks, through the sweetness of the words uttered by your Lord, the Unconstrained; and still ye slumber. Cast away that which ye possess, and, on the wings of detachment, soar beyond all created things. Thus biddeth you the Lord of creation, the movement of Whose Pen hath revolutionized the soul of mankind.

Know ye from what heights your Lord, the All-Glorious is calling? Think ye that ye have recognized the Pen wherewith your Lord, the Lord of all names, commandeth you? Nay, by My life! Did ye but know it, ye would renounce the world, and would hasten with your whole hearts to the presence of the Well-Beloved. Your spirits would be so transported by His Word as to throw into commotion the Greater World—how much more this small and petty one! Thus have the showers of My bounty been poured down from the heaven of My loving-kindness, as a token of My grace, that ye may be of the thankful. . . .

Beware lest the desires of the flesh and of a corrupt inclination provoke divisions among you. Be ye as the fingers of one hand, the members of one body. Thus counselleth you the Pen of Revelation, if ye be of them that believe.

Consider the mercy of God and His gifts. He enjoineth upon you that which shall profit you, though He Himself can well dispense with all creatures. Your evil doings can never harm Us, neither can your good works profit Us. We summon you wholly for the sake of God. To this every man of understanding and insight will testify.

LXXIII.   It is clear and evident that when the veils that conceal the realities of the manifestations of the Names and Attributes of God, nay of all created things visible or invisible, have been rent asunder, nothing except the Sign of God will remain—a sign which He, Himself, hath placed within these realities. This sign will endure as long as is the wish of the Lord thy God, the Lord of the heavens and of the earth. If such be the blessings conferred on all created things, how superior must be the destiny of the true believer, whose existence and life are to be regarded as the originating purpose of all creation. Just as the conception of faith hath existed from the beginning that hath no beginning, and will endure till the end that hath no end, in like manner will the true believer eternally live and endure. His spirit will everlastingly circle round the Will of God. He will last as long as God, Himself, will last. He is revealed through the Revelation of God, and is hidden at His bidding. It is evident that the loftiest mansions in the Realm of Immortality have been ordained as the habitation of them that have truly believed in God and in His signs. Death can never invade that holy seat. Thus have We entrusted thee with the signs of thy Lord, that thou mayest persevere in thy love for Him, and be of them that comprehend this truth.

LXXIV. Every word that proceedeth out of the mouth of God is endowed with such potency as can instill new life into every human frame, if ye be of them that comprehend this truth. All the wondrous works ye behold in this world have been manifested through the operation of His supreme and most exalted Will, His wondrous and inflexible Purpose. Through the mere revelation of the word "Fashioner," issuing forth from His lips and proclaiming His attribute to mankind, such power is released as can generate, through successive ages, all the manifold arts which the hands of man can produce. This, verily, is a certain truth. No sooner is this resplendent word uttered, than its animating energies, stirring within all created things, give birth to the means and instruments whereby such arts can be produced and perfected. All the wondrous achievements ye now witness are the direct consequences of the Revelation of this Name. In the days to come, ye will, verily, behold things of which ye have never heard before. Thus hath it been decreed in the Tablets of God, and none can comprehend it except them whose sight is sharp. In like manner, the moment the word expressing My attribute "The Omniscient" issueth forth from My mouth, every created thing will, according to its capacity and limitations, be invested with the power to unfold the knowledge of the most marvelous sciences, and will be empowered to manifest them in the course of time at the bidding of Him Who is the Almighty, the All-Knowing. Know thou of a certainty that the Revelation of every other Name is accompanied by a similar manifestation of Divine power. Every single letter proceeding out of the mouth of God is indeed a mother letter, and every word uttered by Him Who is the Well Spring of Divine Revelation is a mother word, and His Tablet a Mother Tablet. Well is it with them that apprehend this truth.

LXXV. Tear asunder, in My Name, the veils that have grievously blinded your vision, and, through the power born of your belief in the unity of God, scatter the idols of vain imitation. Enter, then, the holy paradise of the good-pleasure of the All-Merciful. Sanctify your souls from whatsoever is not of God, and taste ye the sweetness of rest within the pale of His vast and mighty Revelation, and beneath the shadow of His supreme and infallible authority. Suffer not yourselves to be wrapt in the dense veils of your selfish desires, inasmuch as I have perfected in every one of you My creation, so that the excellence of My handiwork may be fully revealed unto men. It follows, therefore, that every man hath been, and will continue to be, able of himself to appreciate the Beauty of God, the Glorified. Had he not been endowed with such a capacity, how could he be called to account for his failure? If, in the Day when all the peoples of the earth will be gathered together, any man should, whilst standing in the presence of God, be asked: "Wherefore hast thou disbelieved in My Beauty and turned away from My Self," and if such a man should reply and say: "Inasmuch as all men have erred, and none hath been found willing to turn his face to the Truth, I, too, following their example, have grievously failed to recognize the Beauty of the Eternal," such a plea will, assuredly, be rejected. For the faith of no man can be conditioned by any one except himself.

This is one of the verities that lie enshrined in My Revelation—a verity which I have revealed in all the heavenly Books, which I have caused the Tongue of Grandeur to utter, and the Pen of Power to inscribe. Ponder a while thereon, that with both your inner and outer eye, ye may perceive the subtleties of Divine wisdom and discover the gems of heavenly knowledge which, in clear and weighty language, I have revealed in this exalted and incorruptible Tablet, and that ye may not stray far from the All-Highest Throne, from the Tree beyond which there is no passing, from the Habitation of everlasting might and glory.

The signs of God shine as manifest and resplendent as the sun amidst the works of His creatures. Whatsoever proceedeth from Him is apart, and will always remain distinguished, from the inventions of men. From the Source of His knowledge countless Luminaries of learning and wisdom have risen, and out of the Paradise of His Pen the breath of the All-Merciful hath continually been wafted to the hearts and souls of men. Happy are they that have recognized this truth.

LXXVI. Give ear, O My servant, unto that which is being sent down unto thee from the Throne of thy Lord, the Inaccessible, the Most Great. There is none other God but Him. He hath called into being His creatures, that they may know Him, Who is the

Compassionate, the All-Merciful. Unto the cities of all nations He hath sent His Messengers, Whom He hath commissioned to announce unto men tidings of the Paradise of His good pleasure, and to draw them nigh unto the Haven of abiding security, the Seat of eternal holiness and transcendent glory.

Some were guided by the Light of God, gained admittance into the court of His presence, and quaffed, from the hand of resignation, the waters of everlasting life, and were accounted of them that have truly recognized and believed in Him. Others rebelled against Him, and rejected the signs of God, the Most Powerful, the Almighty, the All-Wise.

Ages rolled away, until they attained their consummation in this, the Lord of days, the Day whereon the Day Star of the Bayán manifested itself above the horizon of mercy, the Day in which the Beauty of the All-Glorious shone forth in the exalted person of 'Alí-Muḥammad, the Báb. No sooner did He reveal Himself, than all the people rose up against Him. By some He was denounced as one that hath uttered slanders against God, the Almighty, the Ancient of Days. Others regarded Him as a man smitten with madness, an allegation which I, Myself, have heard from the lips of one of the divines. Still others disputed His claim to be the Mouthpiece of God, and stigmatized Him as one who had stolen and used as his the words of the Almighty, who had perverted their meaning, and mingled them with his

[145]

own. The Eye of Grandeur weepeth sore for the things which their mouths have uttered, while they continue to rejoice upon their seats.

"God," said He, "is My witness, O people! I am come to you with a Revelation from the Lord, your God, the Lord of your fathers of old. Look not, O people, at the things ye possess. Look rather at the things God hath sent down unto you. This, surely, will be better for you than the whole of creation, could ye but perceive it. Repeat the gaze, O people, and consider the testimony of God and His proof which are in your possession, and compare them unto the Revelation sent down unto you in this Day, that the truth, the infallible truth, may be indubitably manifested unto you. Follow not, O people, the steps of the Evil One; follow ye the Faith of the All-Merciful, and be ye of them that truly believe. What would it profit man, if he were to fail to recognize the Revelation of God? Nothing whatever. To this Mine own Self, the Omnipotent, the Omniscient, the All-Wise, will testify."

The more He exhorted them, the fiercer grew their enmity, till, at the last, they put Him to death with shameful cruelty. The curse of God be upon the oppressors!

A few believed in Him; few of Our servants are the thankful. These He admonished, in all His Tablets—nay, in every passage of His wondrous writings—not to give themselves up in the Day of the promised Revelation to anything whatever, be it in the heaven or in the earth. "O people!" said He, "I have revealed Myself for His Manifestation, and have caused My Book, the Bayán, to descend upon you for no other purpose except to establish the truth of His Cause. Fear ye God, and contend not with Him as the people of the Qur'án have contended with Me. At whatever time ye hear of Him, hasten ye towards Him, and cleave ye to whatsoever He may reveal unto you. Naught else besides Him can ever profit you, no, not though ye produce from first to last the testimonies of all those who were before you."

And when after the lapse of a few years the heaven of Divine decree was cleft asunder, and the Beauty of the Báb appeared in the clouds of the names of God, arrayed in a new raiment, these same people maliciously rose up against Him, Whose light embraceth all created things. They broke His Covenant, rejected His truth, contended with Him, caviled at His signs, treated His testimony as falsehood, and joined the company of the infidels. Eventually, they determined to take away His life. Such is the state of them who are in a far-gone error!

And when they realized their powerlessness to achieve their purpose, they arose to plot against Him. Witness how every moment they devise a fresh device to harm Him, that they may injure and dishonor the cause of God. Say: Woe be to you! By God! Your schemings cover you with shame. Your Lord, the God of mercy, can well dispense with all creatures. Nothing whatever can either increase or diminish the things He doth possess. If ye believe, to your own behoof will ye believe; and if ye believe not, ye yourselves will suffer. At no time can the hand of the infidel profane the hem of His Robe.

O My servant that believest in God! By the righteousness of the Almighty! Were I to recount to thee the tale of the things that have befallen Me, the souls and minds of men would be incapable of sustaining its weight. God Himself beareth Me witness. Watch over thyself, and follow not the footsteps of these people. Meditate diligently upon the Cause of thy Lord. Strive to know Him through His own Self and not through others. For no one else besides Him can ever profit thee. To this all created things will testify, couldst thou but perceive it.

Emerge from behind the veil, by the leave of thy Lord, the All-Glorious, the Most Powerful, and seize, before the eyes of those who are in the heavens and those who are on the earth, the Chalice of Immortality, in the name of thy Lord, the Inaccessible, the Most High, and quaff thy fill, and be not of them that tarry. I swear by God! The moment thou touchest the Cup with thy lips, the Concourse on high will acclaim thee saying, "Drink with healthy relish, O man that hast truly believed in God!" and the inhabitants of the Cities of Immortality will cry out, "Joy be to thee, O thou that hast drained the Cup of His love!" and the Tongue of Grandeur will hail thee, "Great is the blessedness that awaiteth thee, O My servant, for thou hast attained unto that which none hath attained, except such as have detached themselves from all that is in the heavens and all that is on the earth, and who are the emblems of true detachment."

LXXVII. And now, concerning thy question regarding the creation of man. Know thou that all men have been created in the nature made by God, the Guardian, the Self-Subsisting. Unto each one hath been prescribed a pre-ordained measure, as decreed in God's mighty and guarded Tablets. All that which ye potentially possess can, however, be manifested only as a result of your own volition. Your own acts testify to this truth. Consider, for instance, that which hath been forbidden, in the Bayán, unto men. God hath in that Book, and by His behest, decreed as lawful whatsoever He hath pleased to decree, and hath, through the power of His sovereign might, forbidden whatsoever He elected to forbid. To this testifieth the text of that Book. Will ye not bear witness? Men, however, have wittingly broken His law. Is such a behavior to be attributed to God, or to their proper selves? Be fair in your judgment. Every good thing is of God, and every evil thing is from yourselves. Will ye not comprehend? This same truth hath been revealed in all the Scriptures, if ye be of them that understand. Every act ye meditate is as clear to Him as is that act when already accomplished. There is none other God besides Him. His is all creation and its empire. All stands revealed before Him; all is recorded in His holy and hidden Tablets. This fore-knowledge of God, however, should not be regarded as having caused the actions of men, just as your own previous knowledge that a certain event is to occur, or your desire that it should happen, is not and can never be the reason for its occurrence.

LXXVIII.   As to thy question concerning the origin of creation. Know assuredly that God's creation hath existed from eternity, and will continue to exist forever. Its beginning hath had no beginning, and its end knoweth no end. His name, the Creator, presupposeth a creation, even as His title, the Lord of Men, must involve the existence of a servant.

As to those sayings, attributed to the Prophets of old, such as, "In the beginning was God; there was no creature to know Him," and "The Lord was alone; with no one to adore Him," the meaning of these and similar sayings is clear and evident, and should at no time be misapprehended. To this same truth bear witness these words which He hath revealed: "God was alone; there was none else besides Him. He will always remain what He hath ever been." Every discerning eye will readily perceive that

[150]

the Lord is now manifest, yet there is none to recognize His glory. By this is meant that the habitation wherein the Divine Being dwelleth is far above the reach and ken of any one besides Him. Whatsoever in the contingent world can either be expressed or apprehended, can never transgress the limits which, by its inherent nature, have been imposed upon it. God, alone, transcendeth such limitations. He, verily, is from everlasting. No peer or partner has been, or can ever be, joined with Him. No name can be compared with His Name. No pen can portray His nature, neither can any tongue depict His glory. He will, for ever, remain immeasurably exalted above any one except Himself.

Consider the hour at which the supreme Manifestation of God revealeth Himself unto men. Ere that hour cometh, the Ancient Being, Who is still unknown of men and hath not as yet given utterance to the Word of God, is Himself the All-Knower in a world devoid of any man that hath known Him. He is indeed the Creator without a creation. For at the very moment preceding His Revelation, each and every created thing shall be made to yield up its soul to God. This is indeed the Day of which it hath been written: "Whose shall be the Kingdom this Day?" And none can be found ready to answer!

LXXIX. As to thy question concerning the worlds of God. Know thou of a truth that the worlds of God are countless in their number, and infinite in their range. None can reckon or comprehend them except God, the All-Knowing, the All-Wise. Consider thy state when asleep. Verily, I say, this phenomenon is the most mysterious of the signs of God amongst men, were they to ponder it in their hearts. Behold how the thing which thou hast seen in thy dream is, after a considerable lapse of time, fully realized. Had the world in which thou didst find thyself in thy dream been identical with the world in which thou livest, it would have been necessary for the event occurring in that dream to have transpired in this world at the very moment of its occurrence. Were it so, you yourself would have borne witness unto it. This being not the case, however, it must necessarily follow that the world in which thou livest is different and apart from that which thou hast experienced in thy dream. This latter world hath neither beginning nor end. It would be true if thou wert to contend that this same world is, as decreed by the All-Glorious and Almighty God, within thy proper self and is wrapped up within thee. It would equally be true to maintain that thy spirit, having transcended the limitations of sleep and having stripped itself of all earthly attachment, hath, by the act of God, been made to traverse a realm which lieth hidden in the innermost reality of this world. Verily I say, the creation of God embraceth worlds besides this world, and creatures apart from these creatures. In each of these worlds He hath ordained things which none can search except Himself, the All-Searching, the All-Wise. Do thou meditate on that which We have revealed unto thee, that thou mayest discover the purpose of God, thy Lord, and the Lord of all worlds. In these words the mysteries of Divine Wisdom have been treasured. We have refrained from dwelling upon this theme owing to the sorrow that hath encompassed Us from the actions of them that have been created through Our words, if ye be of them that will hearken unto Our Voice.

LXXX. Thou hast asked Me whether man, as apart from the Prophets of God and His chosen ones, will retain, after his physical death, the self-same individuality, personality, consciousness, and understanding that characterize his life in this world. If this should be the case, how is it, thou hast observed, that whereas such slight injuries to his mental faculties as fainting and severe illness deprive him of his understanding and consciousness, his death, which must involve the decomposition of his body and the dissolution of its elements, is powerless to destroy that understanding and extinguish that consciousness? How can any one imagine that man's consciousness and personality will be maintained, when the very instruments necessary to their existence and function will have completely disintegrated?

Know thou that the soul of man is exalted above,

and is independent of all infirmities of body or mind. That a sick person showeth signs of weakness is due to the hindrances that interpose themselves between his soul and his body, for the soul itself remaineth unaffected by any bodily ailments. Consider the light of the lamp. Though an external object may interfere with its radiance, the light itself continueth to shine with undiminished power. In like manner, every malady afflicting the body of man is an impediment that preventeth the soul from manifesting its inherent might and power. When it leaveth the body, however, it will evince such ascendancy, and reveal such influence as no force on earth can equal. Every pure, every refined and sanctified soul will be endowed with tremendous power, and shall rejoice with exceeding gladness.

Consider the lamp which is hidden under a bushel. Though its light be shining, yet its radiance is concealed from men. Likewise, consider the sun which hath been obscured by the clouds. Observe how its splendor appeareth to have diminished, when in reality the source of that light hath remained unchanged. The soul of man should be likened unto this sun, and all things on earth should be regarded as his body. So long as no external impediment interveneth between them, the body will, in its entirety, continue to reflect the light of the soul, and to be sustained by its power. As soon as, however, a veil interposeth itself between them, the brightness of that light seemeth to lessen.

Consider again the sun when it is completely hidden behind the clouds. Though the earth is still illumined with its light, yet the measure of light which it receiveth is considerably reduced. Not until the clouds have dispersed, can the sun shine again in the plenitude of its glory. Neither the presence of the cloud nor its absence can, in any way, affect the inherent splendor of the sun. The soul of man is the sun by which his body is illumined, and from which it draweth its sustenance, and should be so regarded.

Consider, moreover, how the fruit, ere it is formed, lieth potentially within the tree. Were the tree to be cut into pieces, no sign nor any part of the fruit, however small, could be detected. When it appeareth, however, it manifesteth itself, as thou hast observed, in its wondrous beauty and glorious perfection. Certain fruits, indeed, attain their fullest development only after being severed from the tree.

LXXXI.   And now concerning thy question regarding the soul of man and its survival after death. Know thou of a truth that the soul, after its separation from the body, will continue to progress until it attaineth the presence of God, in a state and condition which neither the revolution of ages and centuries, nor the changes and chances of this world, can alter. It will endure as long as the Kingdom of

God, His sovereignty, His dominion and power will endure. It will manifest the signs of God and His attributes, and will reveal His loving-kindness and bounty. The movement of My Pen is stilled when it attempteth to befittingly describe the loftiness and glory of so exalted a station. The honor with which the Hand of Mercy will invest the soul is such as no tongue can adequately reveal, nor any other earthly agency describe. Blessed is the soul which, at the hour of its separation from the body, is sanctified from the vain imaginings of the peoples of the world. Such a soul liveth and moveth in accordance with the Will of its Creator, and entereth the all-highest Paradise. The Maids of Heaven, inmates of the loftiest mansions, will circle around it, and the Prophets of God and His chosen ones will seek its companionship. With them that soul will freely converse, and will recount unto them that which it hath been made to endure in the path of God, the Lord of all worlds. If any man be told that which hath been ordained for such a soul in the worlds of God, the Lord of the throne on high and of earth below, his whole being will instantly blaze out in his great longing to attain that most exalted, that sanctified and resplendent station. . . . The nature of the soul after death can never be described, nor is it meet and permissible to reveal its whole character to the eyes of men. The Prophets and Messengers of God have been sent down for the sole purpose of guiding mankind to the straight Path of Truth. The purpose underlying Their revelation hath been to educate all men, that they may, at the hour of death, ascend, in the utmost purity and sanctity and with absolute detachment, to the throne of the Most High. The light which these souls radiate is responsible for the progress of the world and the advancement of its peoples. They are like unto leaven which leaveneth the world of being, and constitute the animating force through which the arts and wonders of the world are made manifest. Through them the clouds rain their bounty upon men, and the earth bringeth forth its fruits. All things must needs have a cause, a motive power, an animating principle. These souls and symbols of detachment have provided, and will continue to provide, the supreme moving impulse in the world of being. The world beyond is as different from this world as this world is different from that of the child while still in the womb of its mother. When the soul attaineth the Presence of God, it will assume the form that best befitteth its immortality and is worthy of its celestial habitation. Such an existence is a contingent and not an absolute existence, inasmuch as the former is preceded by a cause, whilst the latter is independent thereof. Absolute existence is strictly confined to God, exalted be His glory. Well is it with them that apprehend this truth. Wert thou to ponder in thine heart the behavior of the Prophets of God thou wouldst assuredly and readily testify

[157]

that there must needs be other worlds besides this world. The majority of the truly wise and learned have, throughout the ages, as it hath been recorded by the Pen of Glory in the Tablet of Wisdom, borne witness to the truth of that which the holy Writ of God hath revealed. Even the materialists have testified in their writings to the wisdom of these divinely-appointed Messengers, and have regarded the references made by the Prophets to Paradise, to hell fire, to future reward and punishment, to have been actuated by a desire to educate and uplift the souls of men. Consider, therefore, how the generality of mankind, whatever their beliefs or theories, have recognized the excellence, and admitted the superiority, of these Prophets of God. These Gems of Detachment are acclaimed by some as the embodiments of wisdom, while others believe them to be the mouthpiece of God Himself. How could such Souls have consented to surrender themselves unto their enemies if they believed all the worlds of God to have been reduced to this earthly life? Would they have willingly suffered such afflictions and torments as no man hath ever experienced or witnessed?

LXXXII. Thou hast asked Me concerning the nature of the soul. Know, verily, that the soul is a sign of God, a heavenly gem whose reality the most learned of men hath failed to grasp, and whose mystery no mind, however acute, can ever hope to unravel. It is the first among all created things to declare the excellence of its Creator, the first to recognize His glory, to cleave to His truth, and to bow down in adoration before Him. If it be faithful to God, it will reflect His light, and will, eventually, return unto Him. If it fail, however, in its allegiance to its Creator, it will become a victim to self and passion, and will, in the end, sink in their depths.

Whoso hath, in this Day, refused to allow the doubts and fancies of men to turn him away from Him Who is the Eternal Truth, and hath not suffered the tumult provoked by the ecclesiastical and secular authorities to deter him from recognizing His Message, such a man will be regarded by God, the Lord of all men, as one of His mighty signs, and will be numbered among them whose names have been inscribed by the Pen of the Most High in His Book. Blessed is he that hath recognized the true stature of such a soul, that hath acknowledged its station, and discovered its virtues.

Much hath been written in the books of old concerning the various stages in the development of the soul, such as concupiscence, irascibility, inspiration, benevolence, contentment, Divine good-pleasure, and the like; the Pen of the Most High, however, is disinclined to dwell upon them. Every soul that walketh humbly with its God, in this Day, and cleaveth unto Him, shall find itself invested with the honor and glory of all goodly names and stations.

[159]

When man is asleep, his soul can, in no wise, be said to have been inherently affected by any external object. It is not susceptible of any change in its original state or character. Any variation in its functions is to be ascribed to external causes. It is to these external influences that any variations in its environment, its understanding, and perception should be attributed.

Consider the human eye. Though it hath the faculty of perceiving all created things, yet the slightest impediment may so obstruct its vision as to deprive it of the power of discerning any object whatsoever. Magnified be the name of Him Who hath created, and is the Cause of, these causes, Who hath ordained that every change and variation in the world of being be made dependent upon them. Every created thing in the whole universe is but a door leading into His knowledge, a sign of His sovereignty, a revelation of His names, a symbol of His majesty, a token of His power, a means of admittance into His straight Path. . . .

Verily I say, the human soul is, in its essence, one of the signs of God, a mystery among His mysteries. It is one of the mighty signs of the Almighty, the harbinger that proclaimeth the reality of all the worlds of God. Within it lieth concealed that which the world is now utterly incapable of apprehending. Ponder in thine heart the revelation of the Soul of God that pervadeth all His Laws, and contrast it with that base and appetitive nature that hath rebelled against Him, that forbiddeth men to turn unto the Lord of Names, and impelleth them to walk after their lusts and wickedness. Such a soul hath, in truth, wandered far in the path of error. . . .

Thou hast, moreover, asked Me concerning the state of the soul after its separation from the body. Know thou, of a truth, that if the soul of man hath walked in the ways of God, it will, assuredly, return and be gathered to the glory of the Beloved. By the righteousness of God! It shall attain a station such as no pen can depict, or tongue describe. The soul that hath remained faithful to the Cause of God, and stood unwaveringly firm in His Path shall, after his ascension, be possessed of such power that all the worlds which the Almighty hath created can benefit through him. Such a soul provideth, at the bidding of the Ideal King and Divine Educator, the pure leaven that leaveneth the world of being, and furnisheth the power through which the arts and wonders of the world are made manifest. Consider how meal needeth leaven to be leavened with. Those souls that are the symbols of detachment are the leaven of the world. Meditate on this, and be of the thankful.

In several of Our Tablets We have referred to this theme, and have set forth the various stages in the development of the soul. Verily I say, the human soul is exalted above all egress and regress. It is still, and yet it soareth; it moveth, and yet it is still. It is, in itself, a testimony that beareth witness to the existence of a world that is contingent, as well as to the reality of a world that hath neither beginning nor end. Behold how the dream thou hast dreamed is, after the lapse of many years, re-enacted before thine eyes. Consider how strange is the mystery of the world that appeareth to thee in thy dream. Ponder in thine heart upon the unsearchable wisdom of God, and meditate on its manifold revelations. . . .

Witness the wondrous evidences of God's handiwork, and reflect upon its range and character. He Who is the Seal of the Prophets hath said: "Increase my wonder and amazement at Thee, O God!"

As to thy question whether the physical world is subject to any limitations, know thou that the comprehension of this matter dependeth upon the observer himself. In one sense, it is limited; in another, it is exalted beyond all limitations. The one true God hath everlastingly existed, and will everlastingly continue to exist. His creation, likewise, hath had no beginning, and will have no end. All that is created, however, is preceded by a cause. This fact, in itself, establisheth, beyond the shadow of a doubt, the unity of the Creator.

Thou hast, moreover, asked Me concerning the nature of the celestial spheres. To comprehend their nature, it would be necessary to inquire into the meaning of the allusions that have been made in the Books of old to the celestial spheres and the heavens, and to discover the character of their relationship to this physical world, and the influence which they exert upon it. Every heart is filled with wonder at so bewildering a theme, and every mind is perplexed by its mystery. God, alone, can fathom its import. The learned men, that have fixed at several thousand years the life of this earth, have failed, throughout the long period of their observation, to consider either the number or the age of the other planets. Consider, moreover, the manifold divergencies that have resulted from the theories propounded by these men. Know thou that every fixed star hath its own planets, and every planet its own creatures, whose number no man can compute.

O thou that hast fixed thine eyes upon My countenance! The Day Spring of Glory hath, in this Day, manifested its radiance, and the Voice of the Most High is calling. We have formerly uttered these words: "This is not the day for any man to question his Lord. It behoveth whosoever hath hearkened to the Call of God, as voiced by Him Who is the Day Spring of Glory, to arise and cry out: 'Here am I, here am I, O Lord of all Names; here am I, here am I, O Maker of the heavens! I testify that, through Thy Revelation, the things hidden in the Books of God have been revealed, and that whatsoever hath been recorded by Thy Messengers in the sacred Scriptures hath been fulfilled.'"

LXXXIII. Consider the rational faculty with which God hath endowed the essence of man. Examine thine own self, and behold how thy motion and stillness, thy will and purpose, thy sight and hearing, thy sense of smell and power of speech, and whatever else is related to, or transcendeth, thy physical senses or spiritual perceptions, all proceed from, and owe their existence to, this same faculty. So closely are they related unto it, that if in less than the twinkling of an eye its relationship to the human body be severed, each and every one of these senses will cease immediately to exercise its function, and will be deprived of the power to manifest the evidences of its activity. It is indubitably clear and evident that each of these afore-mentioned instruments has depended, and will ever continue to depend, for its proper functioning on this rational faculty, which should be regarded as a sign of the revelation of Him Who is the sovereign Lord of all. Through its manifestation all these names and attributes have been revealed, and by the suspension of its action they are all destroyed and perish.

It would be wholly untrue to maintain that this faculty is the same as the power of vision, inasmuch as the power of vision is derived from it and acteth in dependence upon it. It would, likewise, be idle to contend that this faculty can be identified with the sense of hearing, as the sense of hearing receiveth

[164]

from the rational faculty the requisite energy for performing its functions.

This same relationship bindeth this faculty with whatsoever hath been the recipient of these names and attributes within the human temple. These diverse names and revealed attributes have been generated through the agency of this sign of God. Immeasurably exalted is this sign, in its essence and reality, above all such names and attributes. Nay, all else besides it will, when compared with its glory, fade into utter nothingness and become a thing forgotten.

Wert thou to ponder in thine heart, from now until the end that hath no end, and with all the concentrated intelligence and understanding which the greatest minds have attained in the past or will attain in the future, this divinely ordained and subtle Reality, this sign of the revelation of the All-Abiding, All-Glorious God, thou wilt fail to comprehend its mystery or to appraise its virtue. Having recognized thy powerlessness to attain to an adequate understanding of that Reality which abideth within thee, thou wilt readily admit the futility of such efforts as may be attempted by thee, or by any of the created things, to fathom the mystery of the Living God, the Day Star of unfading glory, the Ancient of everlasting days. This confession of helplessness which mature contemplation must eventually impel every mind to make is in itself the acme of human understanding, and marketh the culmination of man's development.

LXXXIV. Regard thou the one true God as One Who is apart from, and immeasurably exalted above, all created things. The whole universe reflecteth His glory, while He is Himself independent of, and transcendeth His creatures. This is the true meaning of Divine unity. He Who is the Eternal Truth is the one Power Who exerciseth undisputed sovereignty over the world of being, Whose image is reflected in the mirror of the entire creation. All existence is dependent upon Him, and from Him is derived the source of the sustenance of all things. This is what is meant by Divine unity; this is its fundamental principle.

Some, deluded by their idle fancies, have conceived all created things as associates and partners of God, and imagined themselves to be the exponents of His unity. By Him Who is the one true God! Such men have been, and will continue to remain, the victims of blind imitation, and are to be numbered with them that have restricted and limited the conception of God.

He is a true believer in Divine unity who, far from confusing duality with oneness, refuseth to allow any notion of multiplicity to becloud his conception of the singleness of God, who will regard the Divine

Being as One Who, by His very nature, transcendeth the limitations of numbers.

The essence of belief in Divine unity consisteth in regarding Him Who is the Manifestation of God and Him Who is the invisible, the inaccessible, the unknowable Essence as one and the same. By this is meant that whatever pertaineth to the former, all His acts and doings, whatever He ordaineth or forbiddeth, should be considered, in all their aspects, and under all circumstances, and without any reservation, as identical with the Will of God Himself. This is the loftiest station to which a true believer in the unity of God can ever hope to attain. Blessed is the man that reacheth this station, and is of them that are steadfast in their belief.

LXXXV. O My servants! It behoveth you to refresh and revive your souls through the gracious favors which, in this Divine, this soul-stirring Springtime, are being showered upon you. The Day Star of His great glory hath shed its radiance upon you, and the clouds of His limitless grace have overshadowed you. How high the reward of him that hath not deprived himself of so great a bounty, nor failed to recognize the beauty of his Best-Beloved in this, His new attire.

Say: O people! The Lamp of God is burning; take heed, lest the fierce winds of your disobedience extinguish its light. Now is the time to arise and magnify the Lord, your God. Strive not after bodily comforts, and keep your heart pure and stainless. The Evil One is lying in wait, ready to entrap you. Gird yourselves against his wicked devices, and, led by the light of the name of the one true God, deliver yourselves from the darkness that surroundeth you. Center your thoughts in the Well-Beloved, rather than in your own selves.

Say: O ye that have strayed and lost your way! The Divine Messenger, Who speaketh naught but the truth, hath announced unto you the coming of the Best-Beloved. Behold, He is now come. Wherefore are ye downcast and dejected? Why remain despondent when the Pure and Hidden One hath appeared unveiled amongst you? He Who is both the Beginning and the End, He Who is both Stillness and Motion, is now manifest before your eyes. Behold how, in this Day, the Beginning is reflected in the End, how out of Stillness Motion hath been engendered. This motion hath been generated by the potent energies which the words of the Almighty have released throughout the entire creation. Whoso hath been quickened by its vitalizing power, will find himself impelled to attain the court of the Beloved; and whoso hath deprived himself therefrom, will sink into irretrievable despondency. He is truly wise whom the world and all that is therein have not deterred from recognizing the light of this Day, who will not allow men's idle talk to cause him to swerve from the

[168]

way of righteousness. He is indeed as one dead who, at the wondrous dawn of this Revelation, hath failed to be quickened by its soul-stirring breeze. He is indeed a captive who hath not recognized the Supreme Redeemer, but hath suffered his soul to be bound, distressed and helpless, in the fetters of his desires.

O My servants! Whoso hath tasted of this Fountain hath attained unto everlasting Life, and whoso hath refused to drink therefrom is even as the dead. Say: O ye workers of iniquity! Covetousness hath hindered you from giving a hearing ear unto the sweet voice of Him Who is the All-Sufficing. Wash it away from your hearts, that His Divine secret may be made known unto you. Behold Him manifest and resplendent as the sun in all its glory.

Say: O ye that are bereft of understanding! A severe trial pursueth you, and will suddenly overtake you. Bestir yourselves, that haply it may pass and inflict no harm upon you. Acknowledge the exalted character of the name of the Lord, your God, Who hath come unto you in the greatness of His glory. He, verily, is the All-Knowing, the All-Possessing, the Supreme Protector.

LXXXVI. And now concerning thy question whether human souls continue to be conscious one of another after their separation from the body. Know thou that the souls of the people of Bahá, who have entered and been established within the Crimson Ark, shall associate and commune intimately one with another, and shall be so closely associated in their lives, their aspirations, their aims and strivings as to be even as one soul. They are indeed the ones who are well-informed, who are keen-sighted, and who are endued with understanding. Thus hath it been decreed by Him Who is the All-Knowing, the All-Wise.

The people of Bahá, who are the inmates of the Ark of God, are, one and all, well aware of one another's state and condition, and are united in the bonds of intimacy and fellowship. Such a state, however, must depend upon their faith and their conduct. They that are of the same grade and station are fully aware of one another's capacity, character, accomplishments and merits. They that are of a lower grade, however, are incapable of comprehending adequately the station, or of estimating the merits, of those that rank above them. Each shall receive his share from thy Lord. Blessed is the man that hath turned his face towards God, and walked steadfastly in His love, until his soul hath winged its flight unto God, the Sovereign Lord of all, the Most Powerful, the Ever-Forgiving, the All-Merciful.

The souls of the infidels, however, shall—and to this I bear witness—when breathing their last be made aware of the good things that have escaped them, and shall bemoan their plight, and shall humble themselves before God. They shall continue doing so after the separation of their souls from their bodies.

It is clear and evident that all men shall, after their physical death, estimate the worth of their deeds, and realize all that their hands have wrought. I swear by the Day Star that shineth above the horizon of Divine power! They that are the followers of the one true God shall, the moment they depart out of this life, experience such joy and gladness as would be impossible to describe, while they that live in error shall be seized with such fear and trembling, and shall be filled with such consternation, as nothing can exceed. Well is it with him that hath quaffed the choice and incorruptible wine of faith through the gracious favor and the manifold bounties of Him Who is the Lord of all Faiths. . . .

This is the Day when the loved ones of God should keep their eyes directed towards His Manifestation, and fasten them upon whatsoever that Manifestation may be pleased to reveal. Certain traditions of bygone ages rest on no foundations whatever, while the notions entertained by past generations, and which they have recorded in their books, have, for the most part, been influenced by the desires of a corrupt inclination. Thou dost witness how most of the commentaries and interpretations of the words of God, now current amongst men, are devoid of truth. Their falsity hath, in some cases, been exposed when the intervening veils were rent asunder. They themselves have acknowledged their failure in apprehending the meaning of any of the words of God.

Our purpose is to show that should the loved ones of God sanctify their hearts and their ears from the vain sayings that were uttered aforetime, and turn with their inmost souls to Him Who is the Day Spring of His Revelation, and to whatsoever things He hath manifested, such behavior would be regarded as highly meritorious in the sight of God. . . .

Magnify His Name, and be thou of the thankful. Convey My greetings to My loved ones, whom God hath singled out for His love, and caused them to achieve their objects. All glory be to God, the Lord of all worlds.

LXXXVII.   And now regarding thy question, "How is it that no records are to be found concerning the Prophets that have preceded Adam, the Father of Mankind, or of the kings that lived in the days of those Prophets?" Know thou that the absence of any reference to them is no proof that they did not actually exist. That no records concerning them are now available should be attributed to their extreme remoteness, as well as to the vast changes which the earth hath undergone since their time.

Moreover such forms and modes of writing as are now current amongst men were unknown to the generations that were before Adam. There was even a time when men were wholly ignorant of the art of writing, and had adopted a system entirely different from the one which they now use. For a proper exposition of this an elaborate explanation would be required.

Consider the differences that have arisen since the days of Adam. The divers and widely-known languages now spoken by the peoples of the earth were originally unknown, as were the varied rules and customs now prevailing amongst them. The people of those times spoke a language different from those now known. Diversities of language arose in a later age, in a land known as Babel. It was given the name Babel, because the term signifieth "the place where the confusion of tongues arose."

Subsequently Syriac became prominent among the existing languages. The Sacred Scriptures of former times were revealed in that tongue. Later, Abraham, the Friend of God, appeared and shed upon the world the light of Divine Revelation. The language He spoke while He crossed the Jordan became known as Hebrew ('Ibrání), which meaneth "the language of the crossing." The Books of God and the Sacred Scriptures were then revealed in that tongue, and not until after a considerable lapse of time did Arabic become the language of Revelation. . . .

Witness, therefore, how numerous and far-reaching have been the changes in language, speech, and writing since the days of Adam. How much greater must have been the changes before Him!

Our purpose in revealing these words is to show that the one true God hath, in His all-highest and transcendent station, ever been, and will everlastingly continue to be, exalted above the praise and conception of all else but Him. His creation hath ever existed, and the Manifestations of His Divine glory and the Day Springs of eternal holiness have been sent down from time immemorial, and been commissioned to summon mankind to the one true God. That the names of some of them are forgotten and the records of their lives lost is to be attributed to the disturbances and changes that have overtaken the world.

Mention hath been made in certain books of a deluge which caused all that existed on earth, historical records as well as other things, to be destroyed. Moreover, many cataclysms have occurred which have effaced the traces of many events. Furthermore, among existing historical records differences are to be found, and each of the various peoples of the world hath its own account of the age of the earth and of its history. Some trace their history as far back as eight thousand years, others as far as twelve thousand years. To any one that hath read the book of Júk it is clear and evident how much the accounts given by the various books have differed.

Please God thou wilt turn thine eyes towards the

Most Great Revelation, and entirely disregard these conflicting tales and traditions.

LXXXVIII. Know verily that the essence of justice and the source thereof are both embodied in the ordinances prescribed by Him Who is the Manifestation of the Self of God amongst men, if ye be of them that recognize this truth. He doth verily incarnate the highest, the infallible standard of justice unto all creation. Were His law to be such as to strike terror into the hearts of all that are in heaven and on earth, that law is naught but manifest justice. The fears and agitation which the revelation of this law provokes in men's hearts should indeed be likened to the cries of the suckling babe weaned from his mother's milk, if ye be of them that perceive. Were men to discover the motivating purpose of God's Revelation, they would assuredly cast away their fears, and, with hearts filled with gratitude, rejoice with exceeding gladness.

LXXXIX. Know assuredly that just as thou firmly believest that the Word of God, exalted be His glory, endureth for ever, thou must, likewise, believe with undoubting faith that its meaning can never be exhausted. They who are its appointed interpreters, they whose hearts are the repositories of its secrets, are, however, the only ones who can comprehend its manifold wisdom. Whoso, while reading the Sacred

Scriptures, is tempted to choose therefrom whatever may suit him with which to challenge the authority of the Representative of God among men, is, indeed, as one dead, though to outward seeming he may walk and converse with his neighbors, and share with them their food and their drink.

Oh, would that the world could believe Me! Were all the things that lie enshrined within the heart of Bahá, and which the Lord, His God, the Lord of all names, hath taught Him, to be unveiled to mankind, every man on earth would be dumbfounded.

How great the multitude of truths which the garment of words can never contain! How vast the number of such verities as no expression can adequately describe, whose significance can never be unfolded, and to which not even the remotest allusions can be made! How manifold are the truths which must remain unuttered until the appointed time is come! Even as it hath been said: "Not everything that a man knoweth can be disclosed, nor can everything that he can disclose be regarded as timely, nor can every timely utterance be considered as suited to the capacity of those who hear it."

Of these truths some can be disclosed only to the extent of the capacity of the repositories of the light of Our knowledge, and the recipients of Our hidden grace. We beseech God to strengthen thee with His power, and enable thee to recognize Him Who is the Source of all knowledge, that thou mayest detach thyself from all human learning, for, "what would it profit any man to strive after learning when he hath already found and recognized Him Who is the Object of all knowledge?" Cleave to the Root of Knowledge, and to Him Who is the Fountain thereof, that thou mayest find thyself independent of all who claim to be well versed in human learning, and whose claim no clear proof, nor the testimony of any enlightening book, can support.

xc. Whatever is in the heavens and whatever is on the earth is a direct evidence of the revelation within it of the attributes and names of God, inasmuch as within every atom are enshrined the signs that bear eloquent testimony to the revelation of that Most Great Light. Methinks, but for the potency of that revelation, no being could ever exist. How resplendent the luminaries of knowledge that shine in an atom, and how vast the oceans of wisdom that surge within a drop! To a supreme degree is this true of man, who, among all created things, hath been invested with the robe of such gifts, and hath been singled out for the glory of such distinction. For in him are potentially revealed all the attributes and names of God to a degree that no other created being hath excelled or surpassed. All these names and attributes are applicable to him. Even as He hath said: "Man is My mystery, and I am his mystery." Manifold are the verses that have been repeatedly revealed

[177]

in all the Heavenly Books and the Holy Scriptures, expressive of this most subtle and lofty theme. Even as He hath revealed: "We will surely show them Our signs in the world and within themselves." Again He saith: "And also in your own selves: will ye not, then, behold the signs of God?" And yet again He revealeth: "And be ye not like those who forget God, and whom He hath therefore caused to forget their own selves." In this connection, He Who is the eternal King—may the souls of all that dwell within the mystic Tabernacle be a sacrifice unto Him—hath spoken: "He hath known God who hath known himself."

. . . From that which hath been said it becometh evident that all things, in their inmost reality, testify to the revelation of the names and attributes of God within them. Each according to its capacity, indicateth, and is expressive of, the knowledge of God. So potent and universal is this revelation, that it hath encompassed all things visible and invisible. Thus hath He revealed: "Hath aught else save Thee a power of revelation which is not possessed by Thee, that it could have manifested Thee? Blind is the eye which doth not perceive Thee." Likewise hath the eternal King spoken: "No thing have I perceived, except that I perceived God within it, God before it, or God after it." Also in the tradition of Kumayl it is written: "Behold, a light hath shone forth out of the morn of eternity, and lo, its waves have penetrated the inmost reality of all men." Man, the noblest and most perfect of all created things, excelleth them all in the intensity of this revelation, and is a fuller expression of its glory. And of all men, the most accomplished, the most distinguished, and the most excellent are the Manifestations of the Sun of Truth. Nay, all else besides these Manifestations, live by the operation of Their Will, and move and have their being through the outpourings of Their grace.

XCI. Amongst the proofs demonstrating the truth of this Revelation is this, that in every age and Dispensation, whenever the invisible Essence was revealed in the person of His Manifestation, certain souls, obscure and detached from all worldly entanglements, would seek illumination from the Sun of Prophethood and Moon of Divine guidance, and would attain unto the Divine Presence. For this reason, the divines of the age and those possessed of wealth, would scorn and scoff at these people. Even as He hath revealed concerning them that erred: "Then said the chiefs of His people who believed not, 'We see in Thee but a man like ourselves; and we see not any who have followed Thee except our meanest ones of hasty judgment, nor see we any excellence in you above ourselves: nay, we deem you liars.'" They caviled at those holy Manifestations, and protested saying: "None hath followed you except the abject amongst us, those who are worthy of no attention." Their aim was to show that no one amongst the learned, the wealthy, and the renowned believed in them. By this and similar proofs they sought to demonstrate the falsity of Him that speaketh naught but the truth.

In this most resplendent Dispensation, however, this most mighty Sovereignty, a number of illumined divines, of men of consummate learning, of doctors of mature wisdom, have attained unto His Court, drunk the cup of His divine Presence, and been invested with the honor of His most excellent favor. They have renounced, for the sake of the Beloved, the world and all that is therein. . . .

All these were guided by the light of the Sun of Divine Revelation, confessed and acknowledged His truth. Such was their faith, that most of them renounced their substance and kindred, and cleaved to the good pleasure of the All-Glorious. They laid down their lives for their Well-Beloved, and surrendered their all in His path. Their breasts were made targets for the darts of the enemy, and their heads adorned the spears of the infidel. No land remained which did not drink the blood of these embodiments of detachment, and no sword that did not bruise their necks. Their deeds, alone, testify to the truth of their words. Doth not the testimony of these holy souls, who have so gloriously risen to offer up their lives for their Beloved that the whole world marveled at the manner of their sacrifice, suffice the people of this day? Is it not sufficient witness against the faith-lessness of those who for a trifle betrayed their faith, who bartered away immortality for that which per-isheth, who gave up the Kawthar of the Divine Presence for salty springs, and whose one aim in life is to usurp the property of others? Even as thou dost witness how all of them have busied themselves with the vanities of the world, and have strayed far from Him Who is the Lord, the Most High.

Be fair: Is the testimony of those acceptable and worthy of attention whose deeds agree with their words, whose outward behavior conforms with their inner life? The mind is bewildered at their deeds, and the soul marveleth at their fortitude and bodily endurance. Or is the testimony of these faithless souls who breathe naught but the breath of selfish desire, and who lie imprisoned in the cage of their idle fan-cies, acceptable? Like the bats of darkness, they lift not their heads from their couch except to pursue the transient things of the world, and find no rest by night except as they labor to advance the aims of their sordid life. Immersed in their selfish schemes, they are oblivious of the Divine decree. In the day-time they strive with all their soul after worldly benefits, and in the night season their sole occupa-tion is to gratify their carnal desires. By what law or standard could men be justified in cleaving to the denials of such petty-minded souls and in ignoring the faith of them that have renounced, for the sake of the good pleasure of God, their life and substance, their fame and renown, their reputation and honor? . . .

With what love, what devotion, what exultation and holy rapture, they sacrificed their lives in the path of the All-Glorious! To the truth of this all witness. And yet, how can they belittle this Revelation? Hath any age witnessed such momentous happenings? If these companions be not the true strivers after God, who else could be called by this name? Have these companions been seekers after power or glory? Have they ever yearned for riches? Have they cherished any desire except the good pleasure of God? If these companions, with all their marvelous testimonies and wondrous works, be false, who then is worthy to claim for himself the truth? I swear by God! Their very deeds are a sufficient testimony, and an irrefutable proof unto all the peoples of the earth, were men to ponder in their hearts the mysteries of Divine Revelation. "And they who act unjustly shall soon know what lot awaiteth them!" . . .

Consider these martyrs of unquestionable sincerity, to whose truthfulness testifieth the explicit text of the Book, and all of whom, as thou hast witnessed, have sacrificed their life, their substance, their wives, their children, their all, and ascended unto the loftiest chambers of Paradise. Is it fair to reject the testimony of these detached and exalted beings to the truth of this pre-eminent and Glorious Revelation, and to regard as acceptable the denunciations which have been uttered against this resplendent Light by this faithless people, who for gold have forsaken their faith, and who for the sake of leadership have repudiated Him Who is the First Leader of all mankind? This, although their character is now revealed unto all people who have recognized them as those who will in no wise relinquish one jot or one tittle of their temporal authority for the sake of God's holy Faith, how much less their life, their substance, and the like.

XCII. The Book of God is wide open, and His Word is summoning mankind unto Him. No more than a mere handful, however, hath been found willing to cleave to His Cause, or to become the instruments for its promotion. These few have been endued with the Divine Elixir that can, alone, transmute into purest gold the dross of the world, and have been empowered to administer the infallible remedy for all the ills that afflict the children of men. No man can obtain everlasting life, unless he embraceth the truth of this inestimable, this wondrous, and sublime Revelation.

Incline your ears, O friends of God, to the voice of Him Whom the world hath wronged, and hold fast unto whatsoever will exalt His Cause. He, verily, guideth whomsoever He pleaseth unto His straight

Path. This is a Revelation that infuseth strength into the feeble, and crowneth with wealth the destitute.

With the utmost friendliness and in a spirit of perfect fellowship take ye counsel together, and dedicate the precious days of your lives to the betterment of the world and the promotion of the Cause of Him Who is the Ancient and Sovereign Lord of all. He, verily, enjoineth upon all men what is right, and forbiddeth whatsoever degradeth their station.

XCIII. Know thou that every created thing is a sign of the revelation of God. Each, according to its capacity, is, and will ever remain, a token of the Almighty. Inasmuch as He, the sovereign Lord of all, hath willed to reveal His sovereignty in the kingdom of names and attributes, each and every created thing hath, through the act of the Divine Will, been made a sign of His glory. So pervasive and general is this revelation that nothing whatsoever in the whole universe can be discovered that doth not reflect His splendor. Under such conditions every consideration of proximity and remoteness is obliterated. . . . Were the Hand of Divine power to divest of this high endowment all created things, the entire universe would become desolate and void.

Behold, how immeasurably exalted is the Lord your God above all created things! Witness the majesty of His sovereignty, His ascendancy, and supreme power. If the things which have been created by

Him—magnified be His glory—and ordained to be the manifestations of His names and attributes, stand, by virtue of the grace with which they have been endowed, exalted beyond all proximity and remoteness, how much loftier must be that Divine Essence that hath called them into being? . . .

Meditate on what the poet hath written: "Wonder not, if my Best-Beloved be closer to me than mine own self; wonder at this, that I, despite such nearness, should still be so far from Him." . . . Considering what God hath revealed, that "We are closer to man than his life-vein," the poet hath, in allusion to this verse, stated that, though the revelation of my Best-Beloved hath so permeated my being that He is closer to me than my life-vein, yet, notwithstanding my certitude of its reality and my recognition of my station, I am still so far removed from Him. By this he meaneth that his heart, which is the seat of the All-Merciful and the throne wherein abideth the splendor of His revelation, is forgetful of its Creator, hath strayed from His path, hath shut out itself from His glory, and is stained with the defilement of earthly desires.

It should be remembered in this connection that the one true God is in Himself exalted beyond and above proximity and remoteness. His reality transcendeth such limitations. His relationship to His creatures knoweth no degrees. That some are near and others are far is to be ascribed to the manifestations themselves.

That the heart is the throne, in which the Revelation of God the All-Merciful is centered, is attested by the holy utterances which We have formerly revealed. Among them is this saying: "Earth and heaven cannot contain Me; what can alone contain Me is the heart of him that believeth in Me, and is faithful to My Cause." How often hath the human heart, which is the recipient of the light of God and the seat of the revelation of the All-Merciful, erred from Him Who is the Source of that light and the Well Spring of that revelation. It is the waywardness of the heart that removeth it far from God, and condemneth it to remoteness from Him. Those hearts, however, that are aware of His Presence, are close to Him, and are to be regarded as having drawn nigh unto His throne.

Consider, moreover, how frequently doth man become forgetful of his own self, whilst God remaineth, through His all-encompassing knowledge, aware of His creature, and continueth to shed upon him the manifest radiance of His glory. It is evident, therefore, that, in such circumstances, He is closer to him than his own self. He will, indeed, so remain for ever, for, whereas the one true God knoweth all things, perceiveth all things, and comprehendeth all things, mortal man is prone to err, and is ignorant of the mysteries that lie enfolded within him. . . .

Let no one imagine that by Our assertion that all created things are the signs of the revelation of God is meant that—God forbid—all men, be they good or evil, pious or infidel, are equal in the sight of God. Nor doth it imply that the Divine Being—magnified be His name and exalted be His glory—is, under any circumstances, comparable unto men, or can, in any way, be associated with His creatures. Such an error hath been committed by certain foolish ones who, after having ascended into the heavens of their idle fancies, have interpreted Divine Unity to mean that all created things are the signs of God, and that, consequently, there is no distinction whatsoever between them. Some have even outstripped them by maintaining that these signs are peers and partners of God Himself. Gracious God! He, verily, is one and indivisible; one in His essence, one in His attributes. Everything besides Him is as nothing when brought face to face with the resplendent revelation of but one of His names, with no more than the faintest intimation of His glory—how much less when confronted with His own Self!

By the righteousness of My name, the All-Merciful! The Pen of the Most High trembleth with a great trembling and is sore shaken at the revelation of these words. How puny and insignificant is the evanescent drop when compared with the waves and billows of God's limitless and everlasting Ocean, and how utterly contemptible must every contingent and perishable thing appear when brought face to face with the uncreated, the unspeakable glory of the Eternal! We implore pardon of God, the All-Powerful, for them that entertain such beliefs, and give utterance to such words. Say: O people! How can a fleeting fancy compare with the Self-Subsisting, and how can the Creator be likened unto His creatures, who are but as the script of His Pen? Nay, His script excelleth all things, and is sanctified from, and immeasurably exalted above, all creatures.

Furthermore, consider the signs of the revelation of God in their relation one to another. Can the sun, which is but one of these signs, be regarded as equal in rank to darkness? The one true God beareth Me witness! No man can believe it, unless he be of those whose hearts are straitened, and whose eyes have become deluded. Say: Consider your own selves. Your nails and eyes are both parts of your bodies. Do ye regard them of equal rank and value? If ye say, yea; say, then: ye have indeed charged with imposture, the Lord, my God, the All-Glorious, inasmuch as ye pare the one, and cherish the other as dearly as your own life.

To transgress the limits of one's own rank and station is, in no wise, permissible. The integrity of every rank and station must needs be preserved. By this is meant that every created thing should be viewed in the light of the station it hath been ordained to occupy.

It should be borne in mind, however, that when the light of My Name, the All-Pervading, hath shed its radiance upon the universe, each and every created thing hath, according to a fixed decree, been endowed with the capacity to exercise a particular influence, and been made to possess a distinct virtue. Consider the effect of poison. Deadly though it is, it possesseth the power of exerting, under certain conditions, a beneficial influence. The potency infused into all created things is the direct consequence of the revelation of this most blessed Name. Glorified be He, Who is the Creator of all names and attributes! Cast into the fire the tree that hath rot and dried up, and abide under the shadow of the green and goodly Tree, and partake of the fruit thereof.

The people living in the days of the Manifestations of God have, for the most part, uttered such unseemly sayings. These have been set down circumstantially in the revealed Books and Holy Scriptures.

He is really a believer in the Unity of God who recognizeth in each and every created thing the sign of the revelation of Him Who is the Eternal Truth, and not he who maintaineth that the creature is indistinguishable from the Creator.

Consider, for instance, the revelation of the light of the Name of God, the Educator. Behold, how in all things the evidences of such a revelation are manifest, how the betterment of all beings dependeth upon it. This education is of two kinds.

The one is universal. Its influence pervadeth all things and sustaineth them. It is for this reason that God hath assumed the title, "Lord of all worlds." The other is confined to them that have come under the shadow of this Name, and sought the shelter of this most mighty Revelation. They, however, that have failed to seek this shelter, have deprived themselves of this privilege, and are powerless to benefit from the spiritual sustenance that hath been sent down through the heavenly grace of this Most Great Name. How great the gulf fixed between the one and the other! If the veil were lifted, and the full glory of the station of those that have turned wholly towards God, and have, in their love for Him, renounced the world, were made manifest, the entire creation would be dumbfounded. The true believer in the Unity of God will, as it hath already been explained, recognize, in the believer and the unbeliever, the evidences of the revelation of both of these Names. Were this revelation to be withdrawn, all would perish.

Consider, in like manner, the revelation of the light of the Name of God, the Incomparable. Behold, how this light hath enveloped the entire creation, how each and every thing manifesteth the sign of His Unity, testifieth to the reality of Him Who is the Eternal Truth, proclaimeth His sovereignty, His oneness, and His power. This revelation is a token of His mercy that hath encompassed all created things.

[190]

They that have joined partners with Him, however, are unaware of such a revelation, and are deprived of the Faith through which they can draw near unto, and be united with, Him. Witness how the divers peoples and kindreds of the earth bear witness to His unity, and recognize His oneness. But for the sign of the Unity of God within them, they would have never acknowledged the truth of the words, "There is none other God but God." And yet, consider how grievously they have erred, and strayed from His path. Inasmuch as they have failed to recognize the Sovereign Revealer, they have ceased to be reckoned among those who may be regarded as true believers in the Unity of God.

This sign of the revelation of the Divine Being in them that have joined partners with Him may, in a sense, be regarded as a reflection of the glory with which the faithful are illumined. None, however, can comprehend this truth save men endued with understanding. They that have truly recognized the Unity of God should be regarded as the primary manifestations of this Name. It is they who have quaffed the wine of Divine Unity from the cup which the hand of God hath proffered unto them, and who have turned their faces towards Him. How vast the distance that separateth these sanctified beings from those men that are so far away from God! . . .

God grant that, with a penetrating vision, thou mayest perceive, in all things, the sign of the revela-

[191]

tion of Him Who is the Ancient King, and recognize how exalted and sanctified from the whole creation is that most holy and sacred Being. This, in truth, is the very root and essence of belief in the unity and singleness of God. "God was alone; there was none else besides Him." He, now, is what He hath ever been. There is none other God but Him, the One, the Incomparable, the Almighty, the Most Exalted, the Most Great.

XCIV. And now concerning thy reference to the existence of two Gods. Beware, beware, lest thou be led to join partners with the Lord, thy God. He is, and hath from everlasting been, one and alone, without peer or equal, eternal in the past, eternal in the future, detached from all things, ever-abiding, unchangeable, and self-subsisting. He hath assigned no associate unto Himself in His Kingdom, no counsellor to counsel Him, none to compare unto Him, none to rival His glory. To this every atom of the universe beareth witness, and beyond it the inmates of the realms on high, they that occupy the most exalted seats, and whose names are remembered before the Throne of Glory.

Bear thou witness in thine inmost heart unto this testimony which God hath Himself and for Himself pronounced, that there is none other God but Him, that all else besides Him have been created by His behest, have been fashioned by His leave, are subject to His law, are as a thing forgotten when compared to the glorious evidences of His oneness, and are as nothing when brought face to face with the mighty revelations of His unity.

He, in truth, hath, throughout eternity, been one in His Essence, one in His attributes, one in His works. Any and every comparison is applicable only to His creatures, and all conceptions of association are conceptions that belong solely to those that serve Him. Immeasurably exalted is His Essence above the descriptions of His creatures. He, alone, occupieth the Seat of transcendent majesty, of supreme and inaccessible glory. The birds of men's hearts, however high they soar, can never hope to attain the heights of His unknowable Essence. It is He Who hath called into being the whole of creation, Who hath caused every created thing to spring forth at His behest. Shall, then, the thing that was born by virtue of the word which His Pen hath revealed, and which the finger of His Will hath directed, be regarded as partner with Him, or an embodiment of His Self? Far be it from His glory that human pen or tongue should hint at His mystery, or that human heart conceive His Essence. All else besides Him stand poor and desolate at His door, all are powerless before the greatness of His might, all are but slaves in His Kingdom. He is rich enough to dispense with all creatures.

The tie of servitude established between the worshiper and the adored One, between the creature and the Creator, should in itself be regarded as a token of His gracious favor unto men, and not as an indication of any merit they may possess. To this testifieth every true and discerning believer.

xcv. Know thou that, according to what thy Lord, the Lord of all men, hath decreed in His Book, the favors vouchsafed by Him unto mankind have been, and will ever remain, limitless in their range. First and foremost among these favors, which the Almighty hath conferred upon man, is the gift of understanding. His purpose in conferring such a gift is none other except to enable His creature to know and recognize the one true God—exalted be His glory. This gift giveth man the power to discern the truth in all things, leadeth him to that which is right, and helpeth him to discover the secrets of creation. Next in rank, is the power of vision, the chief instrument whereby his understanding can function. The senses of hearing, of the heart, and the like, are similarly to be reckoned among the gifts with which the human body is endowed. Immeasurably exalted is the Almighty Who hath created these powers, and revealed them in the body of man.

Every one of these gifts is an undoubted evidence of the majesty, the power, the ascendancy, the all-embracing knowledge of the one true God—exalted be His glory. Consider the sense of touch. Witness how its power hath spread itself over the entire human body. Whereas the faculties of sight and of hearing are each localized in a particular center, the sense of touch embraceth the whole human frame. Glorified be His power, magnified be His sovereignty!

These gifts are inherent in man himself. That which is preeminent above all other gifts, is incorruptible in nature, and pertaineth to God Himself, is the gift of Divine Revelation. Every bounty conferred by the Creator upon man, be it material or spiritual, is subservient unto this. It is, in its essence, and will ever so remain, the Bread which cometh down from Heaven. It is God's supreme testimony, the clearest evidence of His truth, the sign of His consummate bounty, the token of His all-encompassing mercy, the proof of His most loving providence, the symbol of His most perfect grace. He hath, indeed, partaken of this highest gift of God who hath recognized His Manifestation in this Day.

Render thanks unto thy Lord for having vouchsafed unto thee so great a bounty. Lift up thy voice and say: All praise be to Thee, O Thou, the Desire of every understanding heart!

XCVI. The Pen of the Most High is unceasingly calling; and yet, how few are those that have inclined their ear to its voice! The dwellers of the kingdom of names have busied themselves with the gay livery of the world, forgetful that every man that hath eyes to perceive and ears to hear cannot but readily recognize how evanescent are its colors.

A new life is, in this age, stirring within all the peoples of the earth; and yet none hath discovered its cause or perceived its motive. Consider the peoples of the West. Witness how, in their pursuit of that which is vain and trivial, they have sacrificed, and are still sacrificing, countless lives for the sake of its establishment and promotion. The peoples of Persia, on the other hand, though the repository of a perspicuous and luminous Revelation, the glory of whose loftiness and renown hath encompassed the whole earth, are dispirited and sunk in deep lethargy.

O friends! Be not careless of the virtues with which ye have been endowed, neither be neglectful of your high destiny. Suffer not your labors to be wasted through the vain imaginations which certain hearts have devised. Ye are the stars of the heaven of understanding, the breeze that stirreth at the break of day, the soft-flowing waters upon which must depend the very life of all men, the letters inscribed upon His sacred scroll. With the utmost unity, and in a spirit of perfect fellowship, exert yourselves, that ye may be enabled to achieve that which beseemeth this Day of God. Verily I say, strife and dissension, and whatsoever the mind of man abhorreth are entirely unworthy of his station. Center your energies in the propagation of the Faith of God. Whoso is worthy of so high a calling, let him arise and promote it. Whoso is unable, it is his duty to appoint him who will, in his stead, proclaim this Revelation, whose power hath caused the foundations of the mightiest structures to quake, every mountain to be crushed into dust, and every soul to be dumb-founded. Should the greatness of this Day be revealed in its fullness, every man would forsake a myriad lives in his longing to partake, though it be for one moment, of its great glory—how much more this world and its corruptible treasures!

Be ye guided by wisdom in all your doings, and cleave ye tenaciously unto it. Please God ye may all be strengthened to carry out that which is the Will of God, and may be graciously assisted to appreciate the rank conferred upon such of His loved ones as have arisen to serve Him and magnify His name. Upon them be the glory of God, the glory of all that is in the heavens and all that is on the earth, and the glory of the inmates of the most exalted Paradise, the heaven of heavens.

XCVII. Consider the doubts which they who have joined partners with God have instilled into the hearts of the people of this land. "Is it ever possible," they ask, "for copper to be transmuted into gold?" Say, Yes, by my Lord, it is possible. Its secret, however, lieth hidden in Our Knowledge. We will reveal it unto whom We will. Whoso doubteth Our power, let him ask the Lord his God, that He may disclose unto him the secret, and assure him of its truth. That copper can be turned into gold is in itself sufficient proof that gold can, in like manner, be transmuted into copper, if they be of them that can apprehend this truth. Every mineral can be made to acquire the density, form, and substance of each and every other mineral. The knowledge thereof is with Us in the Hidden Book.

XCVIII.   Say: O leaders of religion! Weigh not the Book of God with such standards and sciences as are current amongst you, for the Book itself is the unerring balance established amongst men. In this most perfect balance whatsoever the peoples and kindreds of the earth possess must be weighed, while the measure of its weight should be tested according to its own standard, did ye but know it.

The eye of My loving-kindness weepeth sore over you, inasmuch as ye have failed to recognize the One upon Whom ye have been calling in the daytime and in the night season, at even and at morn. Advance, O people, with snow-white faces and radiant hearts, unto the blest and crimson Spot, wherein the Sadratu'l-Muntahá is calling: "Verily, there is none other God beside Me, the Omnipotent Protector, the Self-Subsisting!"

O ye leaders of religion! Who is the man amongst you that can rival Me in vision or insight? Where is he to be found that dareth to claim to be My equal in utterance or wisdom? No, by My Lord, the All-Merciful! All on the earth shall pass away; and this is the face of your Lord, the Almighty, the Well-Beloved.

We have decreed, O people, that the highest and last end of all learning be the recognition of Him Who is the Object of all knowledge; and yet, behold how ye have allowed your learning to shut you out, as by a veil, from Him Who is the Dayspring of this Light, through Whom every hidden thing hath been revealed. Could ye but discover the source whence the splendor of this utterance is diffused, ye would cast away the peoples of the world and all that they possess, and would draw nigh unto this most blessed Seat of glory.

Say: This, verily, is the heaven in which the Mother Book is treasured, could ye but comprehend it. He it is Who hath caused the Rock to shout, and the Burning Bush to lift up its voice, upon the Mount rising above the Holy Land, and proclaim: "The Kingdom is God's, the sovereign Lord of all, the All-Powerful, the Loving!"

We have not entered any school, nor read any of your dissertations. Incline your ears to the words of this unlettered One, wherewith He summoneth you unto God, the Ever-Abiding. Better is this for you than all the treasures of the earth, could ye but comprehend it.

[199]

XCIX. The vitality of men's belief in God is dying out in every land; nothing short of His wholesome medicine can ever restore it. The corrosion of ungodliness is eating into the vitals of human society; what else but the Elixir of His potent Revelation can cleanse and revive it? Is it within human power, O Ḥakím, to effect in the constituent elements of any of the minute and indivisible particles of matter so complete a transformation as to transmute it into purest gold? Perplexing and difficult as this may appear, the still greater task of converting satanic strength into heavenly power is one that We have been empowered to accomplish. The Force capable of such a transformation transcendeth the potency of the Elixir itself. The Word of God, alone, can claim the distinction of being endowed with the capacity required for so great and far-reaching a change.

C. The voice of the Divine Herald, proceeding out of the throne of God, declareth: O ye My loved ones! Suffer not the hem of My sacred vesture to be smirched and mired with the things of this world, and follow not the promptings of your evil and corrupt desires. The Day Star of Divine Revelation, that shineth in the plenitude of its glory in the heaven of this Prison, beareth Me witness. They whose hearts are turned towards Him Who is the Object of the adoration of the entire creation must needs, in this

Day, pass beyond and be sanctified from all created things, visible and invisible. If they arise to teach My Cause, they must let the breath of Him Who is the Unconstrained stir them, and must spread it abroad on the earth with high resolve, with minds that are wholly centered in Him, and with hearts that are completely detached from and independent of all things, and with souls that are sanctified from the world and its vanities. It behoveth them to choose as the best provision for their journey reliance upon God, and to clothe themselves with the love of their Lord, the Most Exalted, the All-Glorious. If they do so, their words shall influence their hearers.

How great, how very great, the gulf that separateth Us from them who, in this Day, are occupied with their evil passions, and have set their hopes on the things of the earth and its fleeting glory! Many a time hath the court of the All-Merciful been to outward seeming so denuded of the riches of this world that they who lived in close association with Him suffered from dire want. Despite their sufferings, the Pen of the Most High hath, at no time, been willing to refer, nor even to make the slightest allusion, to the things that pertain to this world and its treasures. And if, at any time, any gift were presented to Him, that gift was accepted as a token of His grace unto him that offered it. Should it ever please Us to appropriate to Our own use all the treasures of the earth, to none is given the right to question

Our authority, or to challenge Our right. It would be impossible to conceive any act more contemptible than soliciting, in the name of the one true God, the riches which men possess.

It is incumbent upon thee, and upon the followers of Him Who is the Eternal Truth, to summon all men to whatsoever shall sanctify them from all attachment to the things of the earth and purge them from its defilements, that the sweet smell of the raiment of the All-Glorious may be smelled from all them that love Him.

They who are possessed of riches, however, must have the utmost regard for the poor, for great is the honor destined by God for those poor who are steadfast in patience. By My life! There is no honor, except what God may please to bestow, that can compare to this honor. Great is the blessedness awaiting the poor that endure patiently and conceal their sufferings, and well is it with the rich who bestow their riches on the needy and prefer them before themselves.

Please God, the poor may exert themselves and strive to earn the means of livelihood. This is a duty which, in this most great Revelation, hath been prescribed unto every one, and is accounted in the sight of God as a goodly deed. Whoso observeth this duty, the help of the invisible One shall most certainly aid him. He can enrich, through His grace, whomsoever

He pleaseth. He, verily, hath power over all things. . . .

Tell, O 'Alí, the loved ones of God that equity is the most fundamental among human virtues. The evaluation of all things must needs depend upon it. Ponder a while on the woes and afflictions which this Prisoner hath sustained. I have, all the days of My life, been at the mercy of Mine enemies, and have suffered each day, in the path of the love of God, a fresh tribulation. I have patiently endured until the fame of the Cause of God was spread abroad on the earth. If any one should now arise and, prompted by the vain imaginations his heart hath devised, endeavor, openly or in secret, to sow the seeds of dissension amongst men—can such a man be said to have acted with equity? No, by Him Whose might extendeth over all things! By My life! Mine heart groaneth and mine eyes weep sore for the Cause of God and for them that understand not what they say and imagine what they cannot comprehend.

It beseemeth all men, in this Day, to take firm hold on the Most Great Name, and to establish the unity of all mankind. There is no place to flee to, no refuge that any one can seek, except Him. Should any man be led to utter such words as will turn away the people from the shores of God's limitless ocean, and cause them to fix their hearts on anything except this glorious and manifest Being, that hath assumed a form subject to human limitations—such a man, however

[203]

lofty the station he may occupy, shall be denounced by the entire creation as one that hath deprived himself of the sweet savors of the All-Merciful.

Say: Observe equity in your judgment, ye men of understanding heart! He that is unjust in his judgment is destitute of the characteristics that distinguish man's station. He Who is the Eternal Truth knoweth well what the breasts of men conceal. His long forbearance hath emboldened His creatures, for not until the appointed time is come will He rend any veil asunder. His surpassing mercy hath restrained the fury of His wrath, and caused most people to imagine that the one true God is unaware of the things they have privily committed. By Him Who is the All-Knowing, the All-Informed! The mirror of His knowledge reflecteth, with complete distinctness, precision and fidelity, the doings of all men. Say: Praise be to Thee, O Concealer of the sins of the weak and helpless! Magnified be Thy name, O Thou that forgivest the heedless ones that trespass against Thee!

We have forbidden men to walk after the imaginations of their hearts, that they may be enabled to recognize Him Who is the sovereign Source and Object of all knowledge, and may acknowledge whatsoever He may be pleased to reveal. Witness how they have entangled themselves with their idle fancies and vain imaginations. By My life! They are themselves the victims of what their own hearts have devised, and yet they perceive it not. Vain and profitless is the talk of their lips, and yet they understand not.

We beseech God that He may graciously vouchsafe His grace unto all men, and enable them to attain the knowledge of Him and of themselves. By My life! Whoso hath known Him shall soar in the immensity of His love, and shall be detached from the world and all that is therein. Nothing on earth shall deflect him from his course, how much less they who, prompted by their vain imaginations, speak those things which God hath forbidden.

Say: This is the Day when every ear must needs be attentive to His voice. Hearken ye to the Call of this wronged One, and magnify ye the name of the one true God, and adorn yourselves with the ornament of His remembrance, and illumine your hearts with the light of His love. This is the key that unlocketh the hearts of men, the burnish that shall cleanse the souls of all beings. He that is careless of what hath poured out from the finger of the Will of God liveth in manifest error. Amity and rectitude of conduct, rather than dissension and mischief, are the marks of true faith.

Proclaim unto men what He, Who speaketh the truth and is the Bearer of the Trust of God, hath bidden thee observe. My glory be with thee, O thou that callest upon My name, whose eyes are directed towards My court, and whose tongue uttereth the praise of thy Lord, the Beneficent.

CI. The purpose underlying the revelation of every heavenly Book, nay, of every divinely-revealed verse, is to endue all men with righteousness and understanding, so that peace and tranquillity may be firmly established amongst them. Whatsoever instilleth assurance into the hearts of men, whatsoever exalteth their station or promoteth their contentment, is acceptable in the sight of God. How lofty is the station which man, if he but choose to fulfill his high destiny, can attain! To what depths of degradation he can sink, depths which the meanest of creatures have never reached! Seize, O friends, the chance which this Day offereth you, and deprive not yourselves of the liberal effusions of His grace. I beseech God that He may graciously enable every one of you to adorn himself, in this blessed Day, with the ornament of pure and holy deeds. He, verily, doeth whatsoever He willeth.

CII. Give a hearing ear, O people, to that which I, in truth, say unto you. The one true God, exalted be His glory, hath ever regarded, and will continue to regard, the hearts of men as His own, His exclusive possession. All else, whether pertaining to land or sea, whether riches or glory, He hath bequeathed unto the Kings and rulers of the earth. From the beginning that hath no beginning the ensign proclaiming the words "He doeth whatsoever He willeth" hath been unfurled in all its splendor before His

Manifestation. What mankind needeth in this day is obedience unto them that are in authority, and a faithful adherence to the cord of wisdom. The instruments which are essential to the immediate protection, the security and assurance of the human race have been entrusted to the hands, and lie in the grasp, of the governors of human society. This is the wish of God and His decree. . . . We cherish the hope that one of the kings of the earth will, for the sake of God, arise for the triumph of this wronged, this oppressed people. Such a king will be eternally extolled and glorified. God hath prescribed unto this people the duty of aiding whosoever will aid them, of serving his best interests, and of demonstrating to him their abiding loyalty. They who follow Me must strive, under all circumstances, to promote the welfare of whosoever will arise for the triumph of My Cause, and must at all times prove their devotion and fidelity unto him. Happy is the man that hearkeneth and observeth My counsel. Woe unto him that faileth to fulfil My wish.

CIII.   God hath, through His tongue that uttereth the truth, testified in all His Tablets to these words: "I am He that liveth in the Abhá Realm of Glory."

By the righteousness of God! He, from the heights of this sublime, this holy, this mighty, and transcendent station, seeth all things, heareth all things, and is, at this hour, proclaiming: Blessed art thou, O

Javád, inasmuch as thou hast attained unto that which no man before thee hath attained. I swear by Him Who is the Eternal Truth! Through thee the eyes of the inmates of the Exalted Paradise have been gladdened. The people, however, are utterly heedless. Were We to reveal thy station, the hearts of men would be sorely agitated, their footsteps would slip, the embodiments of vain-glory would be dumb-founded, would fall down upon the ground, and would thrust the fingers of heedlessness into their ears, for fear of hearing.

Grieve thou not over those that have busied themselves with the things of this world, and have forgotten the remembrance of God, the Most Great. By Him Who is the Eternal Truth! The day is approaching when the wrathful anger of the Almighty will have taken hold of them. He, verily, is the Omnipotent, the All-Subduing, the Most Powerful. He shall cleanse the earth from the defilement of their corruption, and shall give it for an heritage unto such of His servants as are nigh unto Him.

Say: O people! Dust fill your mouths, and ashes blind your eyes, for having bartered away the Divine Joseph for the most paltry of prices. Oh, the misery that resteth upon you, ye that are far astray! Have ye imagined in your hearts that ye possess the power to outstrip Him and His Cause? Far from it! To this He, Himself, the All-Powerful, the Most Exalted, the Most Great, doth testify.

[208]

Soon shall the blasts of His chastisement beat upon you, and the dust of hell enshroud you. Those men who, having amassed the vanities and ornaments of the earth, have turned away disdainfully from God —these have lost both this world and the world to come. Ere long, will God, with the Hand of Power, strip them of their possessions, and divest them of the robe of His bounty. To this they themselves shall soon witness. Thou, too, shalt testify.

Say: O people! Let not this life and its deceits deceive you, for the world and all that is therein is held firmly in the grasp of His Will. He bestoweth His favor on whom He willeth, and from whom He willeth He taketh it away. He doth whatsoever He chooseth. Had the world been of any worth in His sight, He surely would never have allowed His enemies to possess it, even to the extent of a grain of mustard seed. He hath, however, caused you to be entangled with its affairs, in return for what your hands have wrought in His Cause. This, indeed, is a chastisement which ye, of your own will, have inflicted upon yourselves, could ye but perceive it. Are ye rejoicing in the things which, according to the estimate of God, are contemptible and worthless, things wherewith He proveth the hearts of the doubtful?

CIV. O ye peoples of the world! Know, verily, that an unforeseen calamity is following you, and that grievous retribution awaiteth you. Think not the deeds ye have committed have been blotted from My sight. By My beauty! All your doings hath My Pen graven with open characters upon tablets of chrysolite.

cv. O kings of the earth! He Who is the sovereign Lord of all is come. The Kingdom is God's, the omnipotent Protector, the Self-Subsisting. Worship none but God, and, with radiant hearts, lift up your faces unto your Lord, the Lord of all names. This is a Revelation to which whatever ye possess can never be compared, could ye but know it.

We see you rejoicing in that which ye have amassed for others and shutting out yourselves from the worlds which naught except My guarded Tablet can reckon. The treasures ye have laid up have drawn you far away from your ultimate objective. This ill beseemeth you, could ye but understand it. Wash your hearts from all earthly defilements, and hasten to enter the Kingdom of your Lord, the Creator of earth and heaven, Who caused the world to tremble and all its peoples to wail, except them that have renounced all things and clung to that which the Hidden Tablet hath ordained.

This is the Day in which He Who held converse with God hath attained the light of the Ancient of Days, and quaffed the pure waters of reunion from

[210]

this Cup that hath caused the seas to swell. Say: By the one true God! Sinai is circling round the Dayspring of Revelation, while from the heights of the Kingdom the Voice of the Spirit of God is heard proclaiming: "Bestir yourselves, ye proud ones of the earth, and hasten ye unto Him." Carmel hath, in this Day, hastened in longing adoration to attain His court, whilst from the heart of Zion there cometh the cry: "The promise is fulfilled. That which had been announced in the holy Writ of God, the Most Exalted, the Almighty, the Best-Beloved, is made manifest."

O kings of the earth! The Most Great Law hath been revealed in this Spot, this scene of transcendent splendor. Every hidden thing hath been brought to light, by virtue of the Will of the Supreme Ordainer, He Who hath ushered in the Last Hour, through Whom the Moon hath been cleft, and every irrevocable decree expounded.

Ye are but vassals, O kings of the earth! He Who is the King of Kings hath appeared, arrayed in His most wondrous glory, and is summoning you unto Himself, the Help in Peril, the Self-Subsisting. Take heed lest pride deter you from recognizing the Source of Revelation, lest the things of this world shut you out as by a veil from Him Who is the Creator of heaven. Arise, and serve Him Who is the Desire of all nations, Who hath created you through a word

[211]

from Him, and ordained you to be, for all time, the emblems of His sovereignty.

By the righteousness of God! It is not Our wish to lay hands on your kingdoms. Our mission is to seize and possess the hearts of men. Upon them the eyes of Bahá are fastened. To this testifieth the Kingdom of Names, could ye but comprehend it. Whoso followeth his Lord will renounce the world and all that is therein; how much greater, then, must be the detachment of Him Who holdeth so august a station! Forsake your palaces, and haste ye to gain admittance into His Kingdom. This, indeed, will profit you both in this world and in the next. To this testifieth the Lord of the realm on high, did ye but know it.

How great the blessedness that awaiteth the king who will arise to aid My Cause in My Kingdom, who will detach himself from all else but Me! Such a king is numbered with the companions of the Crimson Ark—the Ark which God hath prepared for the people of Bahá. All must glorify his name, must reverence his station, and aid him to unlock the cities with the keys of My Name, the omnipotent Protector of all that inhabit the visible and invisible kingdoms. Such a king is the very eye of mankind, the luminous ornament on the brow of creation, the fountainhead of blessings unto the whole world. Offer up, O people of Bahá, your substance, nay your very lives, for his assistance.

CVI. The All-Knowing Physician hath His finger on the pulse of mankind. He perceiveth the disease, and prescribeth, in His unerring wisdom, the remedy. Every age hath its own problem, and every soul its particular aspiration. The remedy the world needeth in its present-day afflictions can never be the same as that which a subsequent age may require. Be anxiously concerned with the needs of the age ye live in, and center your deliberations on its exigencies and requirements.

We can well perceive how the whole human race is encompassed with great, with incalculable afflictions. We see it languishing on its bed of sickness, sore-tried and disillusioned. They that are intoxicated by self-conceit have interposed themselves between it and the Divine and infallible Physician. Witness how they have entangled all men, themselves included, in the mesh of their devices. They can neither discover the cause of the disease, nor have they any knowledge of the remedy. They have conceived the straight to be crooked, and have imagined their friend an enemy.

Incline your ears to the sweet melody of this Prisoner. Arise, and lift up your voices, that haply they that are fast asleep may be awakened. Say: O ye who are as dead! The Hand of Divine bounty proffereth unto you the Water of Life. Hasten and drink your fill. Whoso hath been re-born in this Day, shall never die; whoso remaineth dead, shall never live.

CVII. He Who is your Lord, the All-Merciful, cherisheth in His heart the desire of beholding the entire human race as one soul and one body. Haste ye to win your share of God's good grace and mercy in this Day that eclipseth all other created Days. How great the felicity that awaiteth the man that forsaketh all he hath in a desire to obtain the things of God! Such a man, We testify, is among God's blessed ones.

CVIII. We have a fixed time for you, O peoples. If ye fail, at the appointed hour, to turn towards God, He, verily, will lay violent hold on you, and will cause grievous afflictions to assail you from every direction. How severe, indeed, is the chastisement with which your Lord will then chastise you!

CIX. O Kamál! The heights which, through the most gracious favor of God, mortal man can attain, in this Day, are as yet unrevealed to his sight. The world of being hath never had, nor doth it yet possess the capacity for such a revelation. The day, however, is approaching when the potentialities of so great a favor will, by virtue of His behest, be manifested unto men. Though the forces of the nations be arrayed against Him, though the kings of the earth be leagued to undermine His Cause, the power of His might shall stand unshaken. He, verily, speaketh the truth, and summoneth all mankind to the way of Him Who is the Incomparable, the All-Knowing.

All men have been created to carry forward an ever-advancing civilization. The Almighty beareth Me witness: To act like the beasts of the field is unworthy of man. Those virtues that befit his dignity are forbearance, mercy, compassion and loving-kindness towards all the peoples and kindreds of the earth. Say: O friends! Drink your fill from this crystal stream that floweth through the heavenly grace of Him Who is the Lord of Names. Let others partake of its waters in My name, that the leaders of men in every land may fully recognize the purpose for which the Eternal Truth hath been revealed, and the reason for which they themselves have been created.

CX. The Great Being saith: O ye children of men! The fundamental purpose animating the Faith of God and His Religion is to safeguard the interests and promote the unity of the human race, and to foster the spirit of love and fellowship amongst men. Suffer it not to become a source of dissension and discord, of hate and enmity. This is the straight Path, the fixed and immovable foundation. Whatsoever is raised on this foundation, the changes and chances of the world can never impair its strength, nor will the revolution of countless centuries undermine its structure. Our hope is that the world's religious leaders and the rulers thereof will unitedly arise for the reformation of this age and the rehabilitation of its fortunes. Let them, after meditating on its needs, take counsel together and, through anxious and full deliberation, administer to a diseased and sorely-afflicted world the remedy it requireth. . . . It is incumbent upon them who are in authority to exercise moderation in all things. Whatsoever passeth beyond the limits of moderation will cease to exert a beneficial influence. Consider for instance such things as liberty, civilization and the like. However much men of understanding may favorably regard them, they will, if carried to excess, exercise a pernicious influence upon men. . . . Please God, the peoples of the world may be led, as the result of the high endeavors exerted by their rulers and the wise and learned amongst men, to recognize their best interests. How long will humanity persist in its waywardness? How long will injustice continue? How long is chaos and confusion to reign amongst men? How long will discord agitate the face of society? . . . The winds of despair are, alas, blowing from every direction, and the strife that divideth and afflicteth the human race is daily increasing. The signs of impending convulsions and chaos can now be discerned, inasmuch as the prevailing order appeareth to be lamentably defective. I beseech God, exalted be His glory, that He may graciously awaken the peoples of the earth, may grant that the end of their conduct may be profitable unto them, and aid them to accomplish that which beseemeth their station.

CXI. O contending peoples and kindreds of the earth! Set your faces towards unity, and let the radiance of its light shine upon you. Gather ye together, and for the sake of God resolve to root out whatever is the source of contention amongst you. Then will the effulgence of the world's great Luminary envelop the whole earth, and its inhabitants become the citizens of one city, and the occupants of one and the same throne. This wronged One hath, ever since the early days of His life, cherished none other desire but this, and will continue to entertain no wish except this wish. There can be no doubt whatever that the peoples of the world, of whatever race or religion, derive their inspiration from one heavenly Source, and are the subjects of one God. The difference between the ordinances under which they abide should be attributed to the varying requirements and exigencies of the age in which they were revealed. All of them, except a few which are the outcome of human perversity, were ordained of God, and are a reflection of His Will and Purpose. Arise and, armed with the power of faith, shatter to pieces the gods of your vain imaginings, the sowers of dissension amongst you. Cleave unto that which draweth you together and uniteth you. This, verily, is the most exalted Word which the Mother Book hath sent down and revealed unto you. To this beareth witness the Tongue of Grandeur from His habitation of glory.

CXII. Behold the disturbances which, for many a long year, have afflicted the earth, and the perturbation that hath seized its peoples. It hath either been ravaged by war, or tormented by sudden and unforeseen calamities. Though the world is encompassed with misery and distress, yet no man hath paused to reflect what the cause or source of that may be. Whenever the True Counsellor uttered a word in admonishment, lo, they all denounced Him as a mover of mischief and rejected His claim. How bewildering, how confusing is such behavior! No two men can be found who may be said to be outwardly and inwardly united. The evidences of discord and malice are apparent everywhere, though all were made for harmony and union. The Great Being saith: O wellbeloved ones! The tabernacle of unity hath been raised; regard ye not one another as strangers. Ye are the fruits of one tree, and the leaves of one branch. We cherish the hope that the light of justice may shine upon the world and sanctify it from tyranny. If the rulers and kings of the earth, the symbols of the power of God, exalted be His glory, arise and resolve to dedicate themselves to whatever will promote the highest interests of the whole of humanity, the reign of justice will assuredly be established

amongst the children of men, and the effulgence of
its light will envelop the whole earth. The Great
Being saith: The structure of world stability and
order hath been reared upon, and will continue to be
sustained by, the twin pillars of reward and punishment. . . . In another passage He hath written: Take
heed, O concourse of the rulers of the world! There
is no force on earth that can equal in its conquering
power the force of justice and wisdom. . . . Blessed is
the king who marcheth with the ensign of wisdom
unfurled before him, and the battalions of justice
massed in his rear. He verily is the ornament that
adorneth the brow of peace and the countenance of
security. There can be no doubt whatever that if
the day star of justice, which the clouds of tyranny
have obscured, were to shed its light upon men, the
face of the earth would be completely transformed.

CXIII. Dost thou imagine, O Minister of the <u>Sh</u>áh
in the City (Constantinople), that I hold within My
grasp the ultimate destiny of the Cause of God?
Thinkest thou that My imprisonment, or the shame
I have been made to suffer, or even My death and
utter annihilation, can deflect its course? Wretched
is what thou hast imagined in thine heart! Thou art
indeed of them that walk after the vain imaginings
which their hearts devise. No God is there but Him.
Powerful is He to manifest His Cause, and to exalt
His testimony, and to establish whatsoever is His

Will, and to elevate it to so eminent a position that neither thine own hands, nor the hands of them that have turned away from Him, can ever touch or harm it.

Dost thou believe thou hast the power to frustrate His Will, to hinder Him from executing His judgment, or to deter Him from exercising His sovereignty? Pretendest thou that aught in the heavens or in the earth can resist His Faith? No, by Him Who is the Eternal Truth! Nothing whatsoever in the whole of creation can thwart His Purpose. Cast away, therefore, the mere conceit thou dost follow, for mere conceit can never take the place of truth. Be thou of them that have truly repented and returned to God, the God Who hath created thee, Who hath nourished thee, and made thee a minister among them that profess thy faith.

Know thou, moreover, that He it is Who hath, by His own behest, created all that is in the heavens and all that is on the earth. How can, then, the thing that hath been created at His bidding prevail against Him? High is God exalted above what ye imagine about Him, ye people of malice! If this Cause be of God, no man can prevail against it; and if it be not of God, the divines amongst you, and they that follow their corrupt desires and such as have rebelled against Him will surely suffice to overpower it.

Hast thou not heard what a man of the family of Pharaoh, a believer, hath said of old, and which God recounted unto His Apostle, Whom He hath chosen above all human beings, and entrusted with His Message, and made the source of His mercy unto all them that dwell on earth? He said, and He, verily, speaketh the truth: "Will ye slay a man because he saith my Lord is God, when he hath already come to you with proofs of his mission? And if he be a liar, on him will be his lie, but if he be a man of truth, part at least of what he threateneth will fall upon you." This is what God hath revealed unto His Well-Beloved One, in His unerring Book.

And yet, ye have failed to incline your ears unto His bidding, have disregarded His law, have rejected His counsel as recorded in His Book, and have been of them that have strayed far from Him. How many those who, every year, and every month, have because of you been put to death! How manifold the injustices ye have perpetrated—injustices the like of which the eye of creation hath not seen, which no chronicler hath ever recorded! How numerous the babes and sucklings who were made orphans, and the fathers who lost their sons, because of your cruelty, O ye unjust doers! How oft hath a sister pined away and mourned over her brother, and how oft hath a wife lamented after her husband and sole sustainer!

Your iniquity waxed greater and greater until ye slew Him Who had never taken His eyes away from the face of God, the Most Exalted, the Most Great. Would that ye had put Him to death after the man-

[221]

ner men are wont to put one another to death! Ye
slew Him, however, in such circumstances as no man
hath ever witnessed. The heavens wept sore over Him,
and the souls of them who are nigh unto God cried
out for His affliction. Was He not a Scion of your
Prophet's ancient House? Had not His fame as a
direct descendant of the Apostle been spread abroad
amongst you? Why, then, did ye inflict upon Him
what no man, however far ye may look back, hath
inflicted upon another? By God! The eye of creation
hath never beheld your like. Ye slay Him Who is a
Scion of your Prophet's House, and rejoice and make
merry while seated on your seats of honor! Ye utter
your imprecations against them who were before you,
and who have perpetrated what ye have perpetrated,
and remain yourselves all the time unaware of your
enormities!

Be fair in your judgment. Did they whom you
curse, upon whom ye invoke evil, act differently
from yourselves? Have they not slain the descendant
of their Prophet as ye have slain the descendant of
your own? Is not your conduct similar to their conduct? Wherefore, then, claim ye to be different from
them, O ye sowers of dissension amongst men?

And when ye took away His life, one of His followers arose to avenge His death. He was unknown
of men, and the design he had conceived was un-
noticed by any one. Eventually he committed what
had been preordained. It behoveth you, therefore, to

attach blame to no one except to yourselves, for the things ye have committed, if ye but judge fairly. Who is there on the whole earth who hath done what ye have done? None, by Him Who is the Lord of all worlds!

All the rulers and kings of the earth honor and revere the descendants of their Prophets and holy men, could ye but perceive it. Ye, on the other hand, are responsible for such acts as no man hath, at any time, performed. Your misdeeds have caused every understanding heart to be consumed with grief. And yet, ye have remained sunk in your heedlessness, and failed to realize the wickedness of your actions.

Ye have persisted in your waywardness until ye rose up against Us, though We had committed nothing to justify your enmity. Fear ye not God Who hath created you, and fashioned you, and caused you to attain your strength, and joined you with them that have resigned themselves to Him (Muslims)? How long will ye persist in your waywardness? How long will ye refuse to reflect? How long ere ye shake off your slumber and are roused from your heedlessness? How long will ye remain unaware of the truth?

Ponder in thine heart. Did ye, notwithstanding your behavior and the things your hands have wrought, succeed in quenching the fire of God or in putting out the light of His Revelation—a light that hath enveloped with its brightness them that are

[223]

immersed in the billowing oceans of immortality, and hath attracted the souls of such as truly believe in and uphold His unity? Know ye not that the Hand of God is over your hands, that His irrevocable Decree transcendeth all your devices, that He is supreme over His servants, that He is equal to His Purpose, that He doth what He wisheth, that He shall not be asked of whatever He willeth, that He ordaineth what He pleaseth, that He is the Most Powerful, the Almighty? If ye believe this to be the truth, wherefore, then, will ye not cease from troubling and be at peace with yourselves?

Ye perpetrate every day a fresh injustice, and treat Me as ye treated Me in times past, though I never attempted to meddle with your affairs. At no time have I opposed you, neither have I rebelled against your laws. Behold how ye have, at the last, made Me a prisoner in this far-off land! Know for a certainty, however, that whatever your hands or the hands of the infidels have wrought will never, as they never did of old, change the Cause of God or alter His ways.

Give heed to My warning, ye people of Persia! If I be slain at your hands, God will assuredly raise up one who will fill the seat made vacant through My death, for such is God's method carried into effect of old, and no change can ye find in God's method of dealing. Seek ye to put out God's light that shineth upon His earth? Averse is God from what ye desire.

[224]

He shall perfect His light, albeit ye abhor it in the secret of your hearts.

Pause for but a little while and reflect, O Minister, and be fair in thy judgment. What is it that We have committed that could justify thee in having slandered Us unto the King's Ministers, in following thy desires, in perverting the truth, and in uttering thy calumnies against Us? We have never met each other except when We met thee in thy father's house, in the days when the martyrdom of Imám Ḥusayn was being commemorated. On those occasions no one could have the chance of making known to others his views and beliefs in conversation or in discourse. Thou wilt bear witness to the truth of My words, if thou be of the truthful. I have frequented no other gatherings in which thou couldst have learned My mind or in which any other could have done so. How, then, didst thou pronounce thy verdict against Me, when thou hadst not heard My testimony from Mine own lips? Hast thou not heard what God, exalted be His glory, hath said: "Say not to every one who meeteth you with a greeting, 'Thou art not a believer'." "Thrust not away those who cry to their Lord at morn and even, craving to behold His face." Thou hast indeed forsaken what the Book of God hath prescribed, and yet thou deemest thyself to be a believer!

Despite what thou hast done I entertain—and to this God is My witness—no ill-will against thee,

nor against any one, though from thee and others
We receive such hurt as no believer in the unity of
God can sustain. My cause is in the hand of none
except God, and My trust is in no one else but Him.
Erelong shall your days pass away, as shall pass away
the days of those who now, with flagrant pride,
vaunt themselves over their neighbor. Soon shall ye be
gathered together in the presence of God, and shall be
asked of your doings, and shall be repaid for what
your hands have wrought, and wretched the abode
of the wicked doers!

By God! Wert thou to realize what thou hast done,
thou wouldst surely weep sore over thyself, and
wouldst flee for refuge to God, and wouldst pine
away and mourn all the days of thy life, till God will
have forgiven thee, for He, verily, is the Most Generous, the All-Bountiful. Thou wilt, however, persist,
till the hour of thy death, in thy heedlessness, inasmuch as thou hast, with all thine heart, thy soul and
inmost being, busied thyself with the vanities of the
world. Thou shalt, after thy departure, discover what
We have revealed unto thee, and shalt find all thy
doings recorded in the Book wherein the works of all
them that dwell on earth, be they greater or less than
the weight of an atom, are noted down. Heed, therefore, My counsel, and hearken thou, with the hearing of thine heart, unto My speech, and be not careless of My words, nor be of them that reject My
truth. Glory not in the things that have been given

thee. Set before thine eyes what hath been revealed in the Book of God, the Help in Peril, the All-Glorious: "And when they had forgotten their warnings, We set open to them the gates of all things," even as We did set open to thee and to thy like the gates of this earth and the ornaments thereof. Wait thou, therefore, for what hath been promised in the latter part of this holy verse, for this is a promise from Him Who is the Almighty, the All-Wise— a promise that will not prove untrue.

I know not the path ye have chosen and which ye tread, O congregation of My ill-wishers! We summon you to God, We remind you of His Day, We announce unto you tidings of your reunion with Him, We draw you nigh unto His court, and send down upon you tokens of His wondrous wisdom, and yet lo, behold how ye reject Us, how ye condemn Us, through the things which your lying mouths have uttered, as an infidel, how ye devise your devices against Us! And when We manifest unto you what God hath, through His bountiful favor, bestowed upon Us, ye say, "It is but plain magic." The same words were spoken by the generations that were before you and were what you are, did ye but perceive it. Ye have thereby deprived yourselves of the bounty of God and of His grace, and shall never obtain them till the day when God will have judged between Us and you, and He, verily, is the best of Judges.

Certain ones among you have said: "He it is Who hath laid claim to be God." By God! This is a gross calumny. I am but a servant of God Who hath believed in Him and in His signs, and in His Prophets and in His angels. My tongue, and My heart, and My inner and My outer being testify that there is no God but Him, that all others have been created by His behest, and been fashioned through the operation of His Will. There is none other God but Him, the Creator, the Raiser from the dead, the Quickener, the Slayer. I am He that telleth abroad the favors with which God hath, through His bounty, favored Me. If this be My transgression, then I am truly the first of the transgressors. I and My kindred are at your mercy. Do ye as ye please, and be not of them that hesitate, that I might return to God My Lord, and reach the place where I can no longer behold your faces. This, indeed, is My dearest wish, My most ardent desire. Of My state God is, verily, sufficiently informed, observant.

Imagine thyself to be under the eye of God, O Minister! If thou seest Him not, He, in truth, clearly seeth thee. Observe, and judge fairly Our Cause. What is it that We have committed that could have induced thee to rise up against Us, and to slander Us to the people, if thou be of them who are just? We departed out of Ṭihrán, at the bidding of the King, and, by his leave, transferred Our residence to 'Iráq. If I had transgressed against him, why, then, did he release Me? And if I were innocent of guilt, wherefore did ye afflict Us with such tribulation as none among them that profess your faith hath suffered? Hath any of Mine acts, after Mine arrival in 'Iráq, been such as to subvert the authority of the government? Who is it that can be said to have detected any thing reprehensible in Our behavior? Enquire for thyself of its people, that thou mayest be of them who have discerned the truth.

For eleven years We dwelt in that land, until the Minister representing thy government arrived, whose name Our pen is loth to mention, who was given to wine, who followed his lusts, and committed wickedness, and was corrupt and corrupted 'Iráq. To this will bear witness most of the inhabitants of Baghdád, wert thou to inquire of them, and be of such as seek the truth. He it was who wrongfully seized the substance of his fellow-men, who forsook all the commandments of God, and perpetrated whatever God had forbidden. Eventually, he, following his desires, rose up against Us, and walked in the ways of the unjust. He accused Us, in his letter to thee, and thou didst believe him and followed in his way, without seeking any proof or trustworthy evidence from him. Thou didst ask for no explanation, nor didst thou attempt either to investigate or ascertain the matter, that the truth might be distinguished from falsehood in thy sight, and that thou mightest be clear in thy discernment. Find out for thyself the sort of man he

[229]

was by asking those Ministers who were, at that time, in 'Iráq, as well as the Governor of the City (Baghdád) and its high Counsellor, that the truth may be revealed to thee, and that thou mayest be of the well-informed.

God is Our witness! We have, under no circumstances, opposed either him, or others. We observed, under all conditions, the precepts of God, and were never one of those that wrought disorders. To this he himself doth testify. His intention was to lay hold on Us, and send Us back to Persia, that he might thereby exalt his fame and reputation. Thou hast committed the same crime, and for the self-same purpose. Ye both are of equal grade in the sight of God, the sovereign Lord of all, the All-Knowing.

It is not Our purpose in addressing to thee these words to lighten the burden of Our woe, or to induce thee to intercede for Us with any one. No, by Him Who is the Lord of all worlds! We have set forth the whole matter before thee, that perchance thou might realize what thou hast done, might desist from inflicting on others the hurt thou hast inflicted on Us, and might be of them that have truly repented to God, Who created thee and created all things, and might act with discernment in the future. Better is this for thee than all thou dost possess, than thy ministry whose days are numbered.

Beware lest thou be led to connive at injustice. Set thy heart firmly upon justice, and alter not the

Cause of God, and be of them whose eyes are directed towards the things that have been revealed in His Book. Follow not, under any condition, the promptings of thine evil desires. Keep thou the law of God, thy Lord, the Beneficent, the Ancient of Days. Thou shalt most certainly return to dust, and shalt perish like all the things in which thou takest delight. This is what the Tongue of truth and glory hath spoken.

Rememberest thou not God's warning uttered in times past, that thou mayest be of them that heed His warning? He said, and He, verily, speaketh the truth: "From it (earth) have We created you, and unto it will We return you, and out of it will We bring you forth a second time." This is what God ordained unto all them that dwell on earth, be they high or low. It behoveth not, therefore, him who was created from dust, who will return unto it, and will again be brought forth out of it, to swell with pride before God, and before His loved ones, to proudly scorn them, and be filled with disdainful arrogance. Nay, rather it behoveth thee and those like thee to submit yourselves to them Who are the Manifestations of the unity of God, and to defer humbly to the faithful, who have forsaken their all for the sake of God, and have detached themselves from the things which engross men's attention, and lead them astray from the path of God, the All-Glorious, the All-Praised. Thus do We send down upon you that which

GLEANINGS FROM THE WRITINGS OF BAHÁ'U'LLÁH

shall profit you and profit them that have placed their whole trust and confidence in their Lord.

CXIV. Hearken, O King (Sultán 'Abdu'l-'Azíz), to the speech of Him that speaketh the truth, Him that doth not ask thee to recompense Him with the things God hath chosen to bestow upon thee, Him Who unerringly treadeth the straight Path. He it is Who summoneth thee unto God, thy Lord, Who showeth thee the right course, the way that leadeth to true felicity, that haply thou mayest be of them with whom it shall be well.

Beware, O King, that thou gather not around thee such ministers as follow the desires of a corrupt inclination, as have cast behind their backs that which hath been committed into their hands and manifestly betrayed their trust. Be bounteous to others as God hath been bounteous to thee, and abandon not the interests of thy people to the mercy of such ministers as these. Lay not aside the fear of God, and be thou of them that act uprightly. Gather around thee those ministers from whom thou canst perceive the fragrance of faith and of justice, and take thou counsel with them, and choose whatever is best in thy sight, and be of them that act generously.

Know thou for a certainty that whoso disbelieveth in God is neither trustworthy nor truthful. This, indeed, is the truth, the undoubted truth. He that acteth treacherously towards God will, also, act

[232]

treacherously towards his king. Nothing whatever can deter such a man from evil, nothing can hinder him from betraying his neighbor, nothing can induce him to walk uprightly.

Take heed that thou resign not the reins of the affairs of thy state into the hands of others, and repose not thy confidence in ministers unworthy of thy trust, and be not of them that live in heedlessness. Shun them whose hearts are turned away from thee, and place not thy confidence in them, and entrust them not with thine affairs and the affairs of such as profess thy faith. Beware that thou allow not the wolf to become the shepherd of God's flock, and surrender not the fate of His loved ones to the mercy of the malicious. Expect not that they who violate the ordinances of God will be trustworthy or sincere in the faith they profess. Avoid them, and preserve strict guard over thyself, lest their devices and mischief hurt thee. Turn away from them, and fix thy gaze upon God, thy Lord, the All-Glorious, the Most Bountiful. He that giveth up himself wholly to God, God shall, assuredly, be with him; and he that placeth his complete trust in God, God shall, verily, protect him from whatsoever may harm him, and shield him from the wickedness of every evil plotter.

Wert thou to incline thine ear unto My speech and observe My counsel, God would exalt thee to so eminent a position that the designs of no man on the whole earth can ever touch or hurt thee. Observe, O

King, with thine inmost heart and with thy whole being, the precepts of God, and walk not in the paths of the oppressor. Seize thou, and hold firmly within the grasp of thy might, the reins of the affairs of thy people, and examine in person whatever pertaineth unto them. Let nothing escape thee, for therein lieth the highest good.

Render thanks unto God for having chosen thee out of the whole world, and made thee king over them that profess thy faith. It well beseemeth thee to appreciate the wondrous favors with which God hath favored thee, and to magnify continually His name. Thou canst best praise Him if thou lovest His loved ones, and dost safeguard and protect His servants from the mischief of the treacherous, that none may any longer oppress them. Thou shouldst, moreover, arise to enforce the law of God amongst them, that thou mayest be of those who are firmly established in His law.

Shouldst thou cause rivers of justice to spread their waters amongst thy subjects, God would surely aid thee with the hosts of the unseen and of the seen, and would strengthen thee in thine affairs. No God is there but Him. All creation and its empire are His. Unto Him return the works of the faithful.

Place not thy reliance on thy treasures. Put thy whole confidence in the grace of God, thy Lord. Let Him be thy trust in whatever thou doest, and be of them that have submitted themselves to His Will.

Let Him be thy helper and enrich thyself with His treasures, for with Him are the treasuries of the heavens and of the earth. He bestoweth them upon whom He will, and from whom He will He withholdeth them. There is none other God but Him, the All-Possessing, the All-Praised. All are but paupers at the door of His mercy; all are helpless before the revelation of His sovereignty, and beseech His favors.

Overstep not the bounds of moderation, and deal justly with them that serve thee. Bestow upon them according to their needs, and not to the extent that will enable them to lay up riches for themselves, to deck their persons, to embellish their homes, to acquire the things that are of no benefit unto them, and to be numbered with the extravagant. Deal with them with undeviating justice, so that none among them may either suffer want, or be pampered with luxuries. This is but manifest justice.

Allow not the abject to rule over and dominate them who are noble and worthy of honor, and suffer not the high-minded to be at the mercy of the contemptible and worthless, for this is what We observed upon Our arrival in the City (Constantinople), and to it We bear witness. We found among its inhabitants some who were possessed of an affluent fortune and lived in the midst of excessive riches, while others were in dire want and abject poverty. This ill beseemeth thy sovereignty, and is unworthy of thy rank.

Let My counsel be acceptable to thee, and strive thou to rule with equity among men, that God may exalt thy name and spread abroad the fame of thy justice in all the world. Beware lest thou aggrandize thy ministers at the expense of thy subjects. Fear the sighs of the poor and of the upright in heart who, at every break of day, bewail their plight, and be unto them a benignant sovereign. They, verily, are thy treasures on earth. It behoveth thee, therefore, to safeguard thy treasures from the assaults of them who wish to rob thee. Inquire into their affairs, and ascertain, every year, nay every month, their condition, and be not of them that are careless of their duty.

Set before thine eyes God's unerring Balance and, as one standing in His Presence, weigh in that Balance thine actions every day, every moment of thy life. Bring thyself to account ere thou art summoned to a reckoning, on the Day when no man shall have strength to stand for fear of God, the Day when the hearts of the heedless ones shall be made to tremble.

It behoveth every king to be as bountiful as the sun, which fostereth the growth of all beings, and giveth to each its due, whose benefits are not inherent in itself, but are ordained by Him Who is the Most Powerful, the Almighty. The King should be as generous, as liberal in his mercy as the clouds, the outpourings of whose bounty are showered upon every

[236]

land, by the behest of Him Who is the Supreme Ordainer, the All-Knowing.

Have a care not to entrust thine affairs of state entirely into another's hands. None can discharge thy functions better than thine own self. Thus do We make clear unto thee Our words of wisdom, and send down upon thee that which can enable thee to pass over from the left hand of oppression to the right hand of justice, and approach the resplendent ocean of His favors. Such is the path which the kings that were before thee have trodden, they that acted equitably towards their subjects, and walked in the ways of undeviating justice.

Thou art God's shadow on earth. Strive, therefore, to act in such a manner as befitteth so eminent, so august a station. If thou dost depart from following the things We have caused to descend upon thee and taught thee, thou wilt, assuredly, be derogating from that great and priceless honor. Return, then, and cleave wholly unto God, and cleanse thine heart from the world and all its vanities, and suffer not the love of any stranger to enter and dwell therein. Not until thou dost purify thine heart from every trace of such love can the brightness of the light of God shed its radiance upon it, for to none hath God given more than one heart. This, verily, hath been decreed and written down in His ancient Book. And as the human heart, as fashioned by God, is one and undivided, it behoveth thee to take heed that its affections be, also,

[237]

one and undivided. Cleave thou, therefore, with the whole affection of thine heart, unto His love, and withdraw it from the love of any one besides Him, that He may aid thee to immerse thyself in the ocean of His unity, and enable thee to become a true upholder of His oneness. God is My witness. My sole purpose in revealing to thee these words is to sanctify thee from the transitory things of the earth, and aid thee to enter the realm of everlasting glory, that thou mayest, by the leave of God, be of them that abide and rule therein. . . .

I swear by God, O King! It is not My wish to make My plaint to thee against them that persecute Me. I only plead My grief and My sorrow to God, Who hath created Me and them, Who well knoweth our state and Who watcheth over all things. My wish is to warn them of the consequences of their actions, if perchance they might desist from treating others as they have treated Me, and be of them that heed My warning.

The tribulations that have touched Us, the destitution from which We suffer, the various troubles with which We are encompassed, shall all pass away, as shall pass away the pleasures in which they delight and the affluence they enjoy. This is the truth which no man on earth can reject. The days in which We have been compelled to dwell in the dust will soon be ended, as will the days in which they occupied the seats of honor. God shall, assuredly, judge with truth between Us and them, and He, verily, is the best of judges.

We render thanks unto God for whatsoever hath befallen Us, and We patiently endure the things He hath ordained in the past or will ordain in the future. In Him have I placed My trust; and into His hands have I committed My Cause. He will, certainly, repay all them that endure with patience and put their confidence in Him. His is the creation and its empire. He exalteth whom He will, and whom He will He doth abase. He shall not be asked of His doings. He, verily, is the All-Glorious, the Almighty.

Let thine ear be attentive, O King, to the words We have addressed to thee. Let the oppressor desist from his tyranny, and cut off the perpetrators of injustice from among them that profess thy faith. By the righteousness of God! The tribulations We have sustained are such that any pen that recounteth them cannot but be overwhelmed with anguish. No one of them that truly believe and uphold the unity of God can bear the burden of their recital. So great have been Our sufferings that even the eyes of Our enemies have wept over Us, and beyond them those of every discerning person. And to all these trials have We been subjected, in spite of Our action in approaching thee, and in bidding the people to enter beneath thy shadow, that thou mightest be a stronghold unto them that believe in and uphold the unity of God.

Have I, O King, ever disobeyed thee? Have I, at any time, transgressed any of thy laws? Can any of thy ministers that represented thee in 'Iráq produce any proof that can establish my disloyalty to thee? No, by Him Who is the Lord of all worlds! Not for one short moment did We rebel against thee, or against any of thy ministers. Never, God willing, shall We revolt against thee, though We be exposed to trials more severe than any We suffered in the past.

In the day time and in the night season, at even and at morn, We pray to God on thy behalf, that He may graciously aid thee to be obedient unto Him and to observe His commandment, that He may shield thee from the hosts of the evil ones. Do, therefore, as it pleaseth thee, and treat Us as befitteth thy station and beseemeth thy sovereignty. Be not forgetful of the law of God in whatever thou desirest to achieve, now or in the days to come. Say: Praise be to God, the Lord of all worlds!

cxv. The Pen of Revelation, O Dhabíḥ, hath, in most of the divinely-revealed Tablets, recorded these words: We have admonished all the loved ones of God to take heed lest the hem of Our sacred vesture be smirched with the mire of unlawful deeds, or be stained with the dust of reprehensible conduct. We have, moreover, exhorted them to fix their gaze upon whatsoever hath been revealed in Our Tablets. Had their inner ears been attentive to the Divine counsels which have shone forth from the Day Spring of the Pen of the All-Merciful, and hearkened unto His Voice, most of the peoples of the earth would have by now been adorned with the ornament of His guidance. What had been pre-ordained, however, hath come to pass.

Once again doth the Tongue of the Ancient of Days reveal, while in this Most Great Prison, these words which are recorded in this snow-white Scroll: O ye the beloved of the one true God! Pass beyond the narrow retreats of your evil and corrupt desires, and advance into the vast immensity of the realm of God, and abide ye in the meads of sanctity and of detachment, that the fragrance of your deeds may lead the whole of mankind to the ocean of God's unfading glory. Forbear ye from concerning yourselves with the affairs of this world and all that pertaineth unto it, or from meddling with the activities of those who are its outward leaders.

The one true God, exalted be His glory, hath bestowed the government of the earth upon the kings. To none is given the right to act in any manner that would run counter to the considered views of them who are in authority. That which He hath reserved for Himself are the cities of men's hearts; and of these the loved ones of Him Who is the Sovereign Truth are, in this Day, as the keys. Please God they may, one and all, be enabled to unlock, through the power of the Most Great Name, the gates of these cities. This is what is meant by aiding the one true God—a theme to which the Pen of Him Who causeth the dawn to break hath referred in all His Books and Tablets.

It behoveth, likewise, the loved ones of God to be forbearing towards their fellow-men, and to be so sanctified and detached from all things, and to evince such sincerity and fairness, that all the peoples of the earth may recognize them as the trustees of God amongst men. Consider to what lofty heights the injunctions of the Almighty have soared, and how abject is the habitation wherein these feeble souls are now abiding. Blessed are they who, on the wings of certitude, have flown in the heavens which the Pen of thy Lord, the All-Merciful, hath spread.

Behold, O Dhabíh, the works which God, the Sovereign Truth, hath wrought. Say thou: How great, how very great, is the power of His might that encompasseth all worlds! Exalted, immeasurably exalted, is His detachment above the reach and ken of the entire creation! Glorified, glorified be His meekness—a meekness that hath melted the hearts of them that have been brought nigh unto God!

Though afflicted with countless tribulations, which We have suffered at the hands of Our enemies, We have proclaimed unto all the rulers of the earth what God hath willed to proclaim, that all nations may know that no manner of affliction can deter the Pen

[242]

of the Ancient of Days from achieving its purpose. His Pen moveth by the leave of God, Who fashioneth the crumbling and rotten bones.

Considering this most mighty enterprise, it beseemeth them that love Him to gird up the loins of their endeavor, and to fix their thoughts on whatever will ensure the victory of the cause of God, rather than commit vile and contemptible deeds. Wert thou to consider, for but a little while, the outward works and doings of Him Who is the Eternal Truth, thou wouldst fall down upon the ground, and exclaim: O Thou Who art the Lord of Lords! I testify that Thou art the Lord of all creation, and the Educator of all beings, visible and invisible. I bear witness that Thy power hath encompassed the entire universe, and that the hosts of the earth can never dismay Thee, nor can the dominion of all peoples and nations deter Thee from executing Thy purpose. I confess that Thou hast no desire except the regeneration of the whole world, and the establishment of the unity of its peoples, and the salvation of all them that dwell therein.

Reflect a while, and consider how they who are the loved ones of God must conduct themselves, and to what heights they must soar. Beseech thou, at all times, thy Lord, the God of Mercy, to aid them to do what He willeth. He, verily, is the Most Powerful, the All-Glorious, the All-Knowing.

The imprisonment inflicted on this wronged One,

O Ḏhabíḥ, did to Him no harm nor can it ever do so; nor can the loss of all His earthly goods, His exile, or even His martyrdom and outward humiliation, do Him any hurt. That which can hurt Him are the evil deeds which the beloved of God commit, and which they impute to Him Who is the Sovereign Truth. This is the affliction from which I suffer, and to this He, Himself, Who is potent over all things, beareth Me witness. That which hath sorely hurt Me are the claims which the people of the Bayán are advancing every day. Some have proclaimed their allegiance to one of My Branches (Sons), while others have asserted independently their claims, and acted after their own desires.

O Ḏhabíḥ! The Tongue of Grandeur saith: By Myself that speaketh the truth! In this most mighty Revelation all the Dispensations of the past have attained their highest and final consummation. Whoso layeth claim to a Revelation after Him, such a man is assuredly a lying impostor. We pray God that He may graciously assist him to retract and repudiate such claim. Should he repent, God will no doubt forgive him. If, however, he persisteth in his error, God will assuredly send down one who will deal mercilessly with him. He, verily, is the Almighty, the Most Powerful.

Behold how the people of the Bayán have utterly failed to recognize that the sole object of whatsoever My Previous Manifestation and Harbinger of My

Beauty hath revealed hath been My Revelation and the proclamation of My Cause. Never—and to this He Who is the Sovereign Truth beareth Me witness —would He have, but for Me, pronounced what He did pronounce. Witness how this foolish people have treated the Cause of Him Who is the All-Possessing, the Inaccessible, as a play and pastime! Their hearts devise each day a new device, and their fancy leadeth them to seek a fresh retreat. If what they say be true, how then can the stability of the Cause of thy Lord be ensured? Ponder this in thine heart, and be thou of them who are sharp-sighted, who scan heedfully, who are steadfast in their purpose and confident in their belief. Such should be thy certitude that if all mankind were to advance such claims as no man hath ever advanced, or any mind conceived, thou wouldst completely ignore them, wouldst cast them from thee, and would set thy face towards Him Who is the Object of the adoration of all worlds.

By the righteousness of Mine own Self! Great, immeasurably great is this Cause! Mighty, inconceivably mighty is this Day! Blessed indeed is the man that hath forsaken all things, and fastened his eyes upon Him Whose face hath shed illumination upon all who are in the heavens and all who are on the earth.

Sharp must be thy sight, O Ḏhabíḥ, and adamant thy soul, and brass-like thy feet, if thou wishest to be unshaken by the assaults of the selfish desires that whisper in men's breasts. This is the firm injunction which the Pen of the Most Great Name hath, by virtue of the Will of the Ancient King, been moved to reveal. Keep it as the apple of thine eye, and be thou of the thankful. Strive thou day and night to serve the Cause of Him Who is the Eternal Truth, and be thou detached from all else but Him. By Myself! Whatever thou seest in this Day shall perish. Supremely lofty will be thy station, if thou remainest steadfast in the Cause of thy Lord. Towards Him are thy busy movements directed, and in Him is thy final resting-place.

cxvi. O kings of Christendom! Heard ye not the saying of Jesus, the Spirit of God, "I go away, and come again unto you"? Wherefore, then, did ye fail, when He did come again unto you in the clouds of heaven, to draw nigh unto Him, that ye might behold His face, and be of them that attained His Presence? In another passage He saith: "When He, the Spirit of Truth, is come, He will guide you into all truth." And yet, behold how, when He did bring the truth, ye refused to turn your faces towards Him, and persisted in disporting yourselves with your pastimes and fancies. Ye welcomed Him not, neither did ye seek His Presence, that ye might hear the verses of God from His own mouth, and partake of the manifold wisdom of the Almighty, the All-Glorious, the All-Wise. Ye have, by reason of your failure, hindered the breath of God from being wafted over you, and have withheld from your souls the sweetness of its fragrance. Ye continue roving with delight in the valley of your corrupt desires. Ye, and all ye possess, shall pass away. Ye shall, most certainly, return to God, and shall be called to account for your doings in the presence of Him Who shall gather together the entire creation . . .

Twenty years have passed, O kings, during which We have, each day, tasted the agony of a fresh tribulation. No one of them that were before Us hath endured the things We have endured. Would that ye could perceive it! They that rose up against Us have put us to death, have shed our blood, have plundered our property, and violated our honor. Though aware of most of our afflictions, ye, nevertheless, have failed to stay the hand of the aggressor. For is it not your clear duty to restrain the tyranny of the oppressor, and to deal equitably with your subjects, that your high sense of justice may be fully demonstrated to all mankind?

God hath committed into your hands the reins of the government of the people, that ye may rule with justice over them, safeguard the rights of the downtrodden, and punish the wrong-doers. If ye neglect the duty prescribed unto you by God in His Book, your names shall be numbered with those of the unjust in His sight. Grievous, indeed, will be your error. Cleave ye to that which your imaginations have devised, and cast behind your backs the commandments of God, the Most Exalted, the Inaccessible, the All-Compelling, the Almighty? Cast away the things ye possess, and cling to that which God hath bidden you observe. Seek ye His grace, for he that seeketh it treadeth His straight Path.

Consider the state in which We are, and behold ye the ills and troubles that have tried Us. Neglect Us not, though it be for a moment, and judge ye between Us and Our enemies with equity. This will, surely, be a manifest advantage unto you. Thus do We relate to you Our tale, and recount the things that have befallen Us, that ye might take off Our ills and ease Our burden. Let him who will, relieve Us from Our trouble; and as to him that willeth not, My Lord is assuredly the best of helpers.

Warn and acquaint the people, O Servant, with the things We have sent down unto Thee, and let the fear of no one dismay Thee, and be Thou not of them that waver. The day is approaching when God will have exalted His Cause and magnified His testimony in the eyes of all who are in the heavens and all who are on the earth. Place, in all circumstances, Thy whole trust in Thy Lord, and fix Thy gaze upon Him, and turn away from all them that repudiate His truth. Let God, Thy Lord, be Thy sufficing succorer and helper. We have pledged Ourselves to secure Thy triumph upon earth and to exalt Our Cause above all men, though no king be found who would turn his face towards Thee.

CXVII. The Great Being, wishing to reveal the prerequisites of the peace and tranquillity of the world and the advancement of its peoples, hath written: The time must come when the imperative necessity for the holding of a vast, an all-embracing assemblage of men will be universally realized. The rulers and kings of the earth must needs attend it, and, participating in its deliberations, must consider such ways and means as will lay the foundations of the world's Great Peace amongst men. Such a peace demandeth that the Great Powers should resolve, for the sake of the tranquillity of the peoples of the earth, to be fully reconciled among themselves. Should any king take up arms against another, all should unitedly arise and prevent him. If this be done, the nations of the world will no longer require any armaments, except for the purpose of preserving the security of their realms and of maintaining internal order within their territories. This will ensure the peace and composure of every people, government and nation. We fain would hope that the kings and rulers of the earth, the mirrors of the gracious and almighty name of God, may attain unto this station, and shield mankind from the onslaught of tyranny. . . . The day is approaching when all the peoples of the world will have adopted one universal language and one common script. When this is achieved, to whatsoever city a man may journey, it shall be as if he were entering his own home. These things are obligatory and absolutely essential. It is incumbent upon every man of insight and understanding to strive to translate that which hath been written into reality and action. . . . That one indeed is a man who, today, dedicateth himself to the service of the entire human race. The Great Being saith: Blessed and happy is he that ariseth to promote the best interests of the peoples and kindreds of the earth. In another passage He hath proclaimed: It is not for him to pride himself who loveth his own country, but rather for him who loveth the whole world. The earth is but one country, and mankind its citizens.

CXVIII.   Lay not aside the fear of God, O kings of the earth, and beware that ye transgress not the bounds which the Almighty hath fixed. Observe the injunctions laid upon you in His Book, and take good heed not to overstep their limits. Be vigilant, that ye may not do injustice to anyone, be it to the extent of a grain of mustard seed. Tread ye the path of justice, for this, verily, is the straight path.

Compose your differences, and reduce your armaments, that the burden of your expenditures may be lightened, and that your minds and hearts may be tranquillized. Heal the dissensions that divide you, and ye will no longer be in need of any armaments except what the protection of your cities and territories demandeth. Fear ye God, and take heed not to outstrip the bounds of moderation, and be numbered among the extravagant.

We have learned that you are increasing your outlay every year, and are laying the burden thereof on your subjects. This, verily, is more than they can bear, and is a grievous injustice. Decide justly between men, and be ye the emblems of justice amongst them. This, if ye judge fairly, is the thing that behoveth you, and beseemeth your station.

Beware not to deal unjustly with any one that appealeth to you, and entereth beneath your shadow. Walk ye in the fear of God, and be ye of them that lead a godly life. Rest not on your power, your armies, and treasures. Put your whole trust and confidence in God, Who hath created you, and seek ye His help in all your affairs. Succor cometh from Him alone. He succoreth whom He will with the hosts of the heavens and of the earth.

Know ye that the poor are the trust of God in your midst. Watch that ye betray not His trust, that ye deal not unjustly with them and that ye walk not in the ways of the treacherous. Ye will most certainly be called upon to answer for His trust on the day when the Balance of Justice shall be set, the day when unto every one shall be rendered his due, when the doings of all men, be they rich or poor, shall be weighed.

If ye pay no heed unto the counsels which, in peerless and unequivocal language, We have revealed in this Tablet, Divine chastisement shall assail you from every direction, and the sentence of His justice shall be pronounced against you. On that day ye shall have no power to resist Him, and shall recognize your own impotence. Have mercy on yourselves and on those beneath you. Judge ye between them according to the precepts prescribed by God in His most holy and exalted Tablet, a Tablet wherein He hath assigned to each and every thing its settled measure, in which He hath given, with distinctness, an explanation of all things, and which is in itself a monition unto them that believe in Him.

Examine Our Cause, inquire into the things that have befallen Us, and decide justly between Us and Our enemies, and be ye of them that act equitably towards their neighbor. If ye stay not the hand of the oppressor, if ye fail to safeguard the rights of the down-trodden, what right have ye then to vaunt yourselves among men? What is it of which ye can rightly boast? Is it on your food and your drink that ye pride yourselves, on the riches ye lay up in your treasuries, on the diversity and the cost of the ornaments with which ye deck yourselves? If true glory were to consist in the possession of such perishable things, then the earth on which ye walk must needs vaunt itself over you, because it supplieth you, and bestoweth upon you, these very things, by the decree of the Almighty. In its bowels are contained, according to what God hath ordained, all that ye possess. From it, as a sign of His mercy, ye derive your riches. Behold then your state, the thing in which ye glory! Would that ye could perceive it!

Nay! By Him Who holdeth in His grasp the kingdom of the entire creation! Nowhere doth your true and abiding glory reside except in your firm adherence unto the precepts of God, your wholehearted observance of His laws, your resolution to see that they do not remain unenforced, and to pursue steadfastly the right course.

CXIX. O ye rulers of the earth! Wherefore have ye clouded the radiance of the Sun, and caused it to cease from shining? Hearken unto the counsel given you by the Pen of the Most High, that haply both ye and the poor may attain unto tranquillity and peace. We beseech God to assist the kings of the earth to establish peace on earth. He, verily, doth what He willeth.

O kings of the earth! We see you increasing every year your expenditures, and laying the burden thereof on your subjects. This, verily, is wholly and grossly unjust. Fear the sighs and tears of this wronged One, and lay not excessive burdens on your peoples. Do not rob them to rear palaces for yourselves; nay rather choose for them that which ye choose for yourselves. Thus We unfold to your eyes that which profiteth you, if ye but perceive. Your people are your treasures. Beware lest your rule violate the commandments of God, and ye deliver your wards to the hands of the robber. By them ye rule, by their means ye subsist, by their aid ye conquer. Yet, how disdainfully ye look upon them! How strange, how very strange!

Now that ye have refused the Most Great Peace, hold ye fast unto this, the Lesser Peace, that haply ye may in some degree better your own condition and that of your dependents.

O rulers of the earth! Be reconciled among yourselves, that ye may need no more armaments save in a measure to safeguard your territories and dominions. Beware lest ye disregard the counsel of the All-Knowing, the Faithful.

Be united, O kings of the earth, for thereby will the tempest of discord be stilled amongst you, and your peoples find rest, if ye be of them that comprehend. Should any one among you take up arms against another, rise ye all against him, for this is naught but manifest justice.

cxx.   O ye the elected representatives of the people in every land! Take ye counsel together, and let your concern be only for that which profiteth mankind, and bettereth the condition thereof, if ye be of them that scan heedfully. Regard the world as the human body which, though at its creation whole and perfect, hath been afflicted, through various causes, with grave disorders and maladies. Not for one day did it gain ease, nay its sickness waxed more severe, as it fell under the treatment of ignorant physicians, who gave full rein to their personal desires, and have erred grievously. And if, at one time, through the care of an able physician, a member of that body was healed, the rest remained afflicted as before. Thus informeth you the All-Knowing, the All-Wise.

We behold it, in this day, at the mercy of rulers so drunk with pride that they cannot discern clearly their own best advantage, much less recognize a Revelation so bewildering and challenging as this. And whenever any one of them hath striven to improve its condition, his motive hath been his own gain, whether confessedly so or not; and the unworthiness of this motive hath limited his power to heal or cure.

That which the Lord hath ordained as the sovereign remedy and mightiest instrument for the healing of all the world is the union of all its peoples in one universal Cause, one common Faith. This can in no wise be achieved except through the power of a skilled, an all-powerful and inspired Physician. This, verily, is the truth, and all else naught but error.

CXXI. Say: O ye that envy Me and seek My hurt! The fury of your wrath against Me confound you! Lo, the Day Star of Glory hath risen above the horizon of My Revelation, and enveloped with its radiance the whole of mankind. And yet, behold how ye have shut out yourselves from its splendor and are sunk in utter heedlessness. Have mercy upon yourselves, and repudiate not the claim of Him Whose truth ye have already recognized, and be not of them that transgress.

By the righteousness of the one true God! If ye reject this Revelation, all the nations of the earth will laugh you to scorn and mock you, for it is you that have produced, before their eyes, and for the purpose of vindicating the truth of your Cause, the testimonies of God, the Sovereign Protector, the Most Powerful, the All-Glorious, the All-Knowing. And yet, no sooner was His subsequent Revelation, clothed with the glory of an all-compelling sovereignty, sent down unto you, than ye cast it behind your backs, O ye that are numbered with the heedless ones!

What! Believe ye in your hearts that ye possess the power to extinguish the radiance of the Sun, or to eclipse its splendor? Nay, by My life! Ye will never and can never achieve your purpose, though ye summon to your aid all that is in the heavens and all that is on the earth. Walk ye in the fear of God, and render not your works vain. Incline your ears to His words, and be not of them that are shut out as by a veil from Him. Say: God is My witness! I have wished nothing whatever for Myself. What I have wished is the victory of God and the triumph of His

[256]

Cause. He is Himself a sufficient witness between you and Me. Were ye to cleanse your eyes, ye would readily perceive how My deeds testify to the truth of My words, how My words are a guide to My deeds.

Blinded are your eyes! Perceived ye not the greatness of the power of God and of His sovereignty? Beheld ye not His majesty and glory? Woe unto you, ye congregation of the malicious and envious! Hearken unto My speech, and tarry not though it be for less than a moment. Thus biddeth you He Who is the Beauty of the All-Merciful, that haply ye may detach yourselves from the things ye possess, and ascend to the heights from which ye can discover the whole creation sheltered beneath the shadow of His Revelation.

Say: There is no place of refuge for you, no asylum to which ye can flee, no one to defend or to protect you in this Day from the fury of the wrath of God and from His vehement power, unless and until ye seek the shadow of His Revelation. This, indeed, is His Revelation which hath been manifested unto you in the person of this Youth. Glorified, then, be God for so effulgent, so precious, so wondrous a vision.

Detach yourselves from all else but Me, and turn your faces towards My face, for better is this for you than the things ye possess. The Tongue of God testifieth to the truth of My words, through Mine own Word that speaketh the truth, and embraceth and comprehendeth all things.

[257]

Say: Think ye that your allegiance to His Cause can ever profit Him, or your repudiation of its truth cause Him any loss? No, by My Self, the All-Subduing, the Inaccessible, the Most High! Tear ye asunder the veils of names and cleave ye their kingdom. By My Beauty! He Who is the Monarch of all names is come, He at Whose bidding every single name hath, from the beginning that hath no beginning, been created, He Who shall continue to create them as He pleaseth. He, verily, is the All-Powerful, the All-Wise.

Beware that ye divest not yourselves of the raiment of Divine guidance. Drink ye your fill from the Cup which the Youths of Heaven have raised above your heads. Thus biddeth you He Who hath more mercy upon you than your own selves, He Who asketh not any recompense or thanks from you. His reward is from Him Who hath, through the power of truth, sent Him down unto you, and singled Him out and proclaimed Him as His own Testimony unto the whole of creation. He it is Who hath empowered Him to manifest all His signs. Repeat the gaze, that ye may perceive the things whereunto the Tongue of the Ancient of Days hath summoned you, that haply ye may be of them that have apprehended the truth. Heard it ye ever reported by your fathers of old, or by the generations that preceded them, even unto the first Adam, that any one coming in the clouds of revelation, being invested with manifest and transcendent sovereignty, having on his right hand the Kingdom of God and on his left all the power and glory of His everlasting dominion, any one preceded by the hosts of God, the Almighty, the All-Compelling, the Most Powerful, and uttering continually verses whose import the minds of the most learned and wisest of men are powerless to fathom, should yet be the bearer of a message that is not of God? Be discerning, then, and speak ye the truth, the very truth, if ye claim to be honest and high-minded.

Say: The verses We have revealed are as numerous as those which, in the preceding Revelation, were sent down upon the Báb. Let him that doubteth the words which the Spirit of God hath spoken seek the court of Our presence and hear Our divinely-revealed verses, and be an eye-witness of the clear proof of Our claim.

Say: By the righteousness of the Almighty! The measure of the favors of God hath been filled up, His Word hath been perfected, the light of His countenance hath been revealed, His sovereignty hath encompassed the whole of creation, the glory of His Revelation hath been made manifest, and His bounties have rained upon all mankind.

CXXII. Man is the supreme Talisman. Lack of a proper education hath, however, deprived him of that which he doth inherently possess. Through a word proceeding out of the mouth of God he was called into being; by one word more he was guided to recognize the Source of his education; by yet another word his station and destiny were safeguarded. The Great Being saith: Regard man as a mine rich in gems of inestimable value. Education can, alone, cause it to reveal its treasures, and enable mankind to benefit therefrom. If any man were to meditate on that which the Scriptures, sent down from the heaven of God's holy Will, have revealed, he would readily recognize that their purpose is that all men shall be regarded as one soul, so that the seal bearing the words "The Kingdom shall be God's" may be stamped on every heart, and the light of Divine bounty, of grace, and mercy may envelop all mankind. The one true God, exalted be His glory, hath wished nothing for Himself. The allegiance of mankind profiteth Him not, neither doth its perversity harm Him. The Bird of the Realm of Utterance voiceth continually this call: "All things have I willed for thee, and thee, too, for thine own sake." If the learned and worldly-wise men of this age were to allow mankind to inhale the fragrance of fellowship and love, every understanding heart would apprehend the meaning of true liberty, and discover the secret of undisturbed peace and absolute composure. Were the earth to attain this station and be illumined with its light it could then be truly said of it: "Thou shall see in it no hollows or rising hills."

CXXIII. The generations that have gone on before you—whither are they fled? And those round whom in life circled the fairest and the loveliest of the land, where now are they? Profit by their example, O people, and be not of them that are gone astray.

Others ere long will lay hands on what ye possess, and enter into your habitations. Incline your ears to My words, and be not numbered among the foolish.

For every one of you his paramount duty is to choose for himself that on which no other may infringe and none usurp from him. Such a thing—and to this the Almighty is My witness—is the love of God, could ye but perceive it.

Build ye for yourselves such houses as the rain and floods can never destroy, which shall protect you from the changes and chances of this life. This is the instruction of Him Whom the world hath wronged and forsaken.

CXXIV. How wondrous is the unity of the Living, the Ever-Abiding God—a unity which is exalted above all limitations, that transcendeth the comprehension of all created things! He hath, from everlasting, dwelt in His inaccessible habitation of holiness and glory, and will unto everlasting continue to be enthroned upon the heights of His independent sovereignty and grandeur. How lofty hath been His incorruptible Essence, how completely independent of the knowledge of all created things, and how immensely exalted will it remain above the praise of all the inhabitants of the heavens and the earth!

From the exalted source, and out of the essence of His favor and bounty He hath entrusted every created thing with a sign of His knowledge, so that none of His creatures may be deprived of its share in expressing, each according to its capacity and rank, this knowledge. This sign is the mirror of His beauty in the world of creation. The greater the effort exerted for the refinement of this sublime and noble mirror, the more faithfully will it be made to reflect the glory of the names and attributes of God, and reveal the wonders of His signs and knowledge. Every created thing will be enabled (so great is this reflecting power) to reveal the potentialities of its pre-ordained station, will recognize its capacity and limitations, and will testify to the truth that "He, verily, is God; there is none other God besides Him." . . .

There can be no doubt whatever that, in consequence of the efforts which every man may consciously exert and as a result of the exertion of his own spiritual faculties, this mirror can be so cleansed from the dross of earthly defilements and purged from satanic fancies as to be able to draw nigh unto the meads of eternal holiness and attain the courts of everlasting fellowship. In pursuance, however, of the principle that for every thing a time hath been fixed, and for every fruit a season hath been ordained, the latent energies of such a bounty can best be released, and the vernal glory of such a gift can only be manifested, in the Days of God. Invested though each day may be with its pre-ordained share of God's wondrous grace, the Days immediately associated with the Manifestation of God possess a unique distinction and occupy a station which no mind can ever comprehend. Such is the virtue infused into them that if the hearts of all that dwell in the heavens and the earth were, in those days of everlasting delight, to be brought face to face with that Day Star of unfading glory and attuned to His Will, each would find itself exalted above all earthly things, radiant with His light, and sanctified through His grace. All hail to this grace which no blessing, however great, can excel, and all honor to such a loving-kindness the like of which the eye of creation hath not seen! Exalted is He above that which they attribute unto Him or recount about Him!

It is for this reason that, in those days, no man shall ever stand in need of his neighbor. It hath already been abundantly demonstrated that in that divinely-appointed Day the majority of them that have sought and attained His holy court have revealed such knowledge and wisdom, a drop of which none else besides these holy and sanctified souls, however long he may have taught or studied, hath grasped or will ever comprehend. It is by virtue of this power that the beloved of God have, in the days of the Manifestation of the Day Star of Truth, been exalted above, and made independent of, all human learning. Nay, from their hearts and the springs of their innate powers hath gushed out unceasingly the inmost essence of human learning and wisdom.

CXXV. O My brother! When a true seeker determineth to take the step of search in the path leading unto the knowledge of the Ancient of Days, he must, before all else, cleanse his heart, which is the seat of the revelation of the inner mysteries of God, from the obscuring dust of all acquired knowledge, and the allusions of the embodiments of satanic fancy. He must purge his breast, which is the sanctuary of the abiding love of the Beloved, of every defilement, and sanctify his soul from all that pertaineth to water and clay, from all shadowy and ephemeral attachments. He must so cleanse his heart that no remnant of either love or hate may linger therein, lest that love blindly incline him to error, or that hate repel him away from the truth. Even as thou dost witness in this Day how most of the people, because of such love and hate, are bereft of the immortal Face, have strayed far from the Embodiments of the Divine mysteries, and, shepherdless, are roaming through the wilderness of oblivion and error.

That seeker must, at all times, put his trust in God, must renounce the peoples of the earth, must detach himself from the world of dust, and cleave unto Him Who is the Lord of Lords. He must never seek to exalt himself above any one, must wash away from the tablet of his heart every trace of pride and vain-glory, must cling unto patience and resignation, observe silence and refrain from idle talk. For the tongue is a smoldering fire, and excess of speech a deadly poison. Material fire consumeth the body, whereas the fire of the tongue devoureth both heart and soul. The force of the former lasteth but for a time, whilst the effects of the latter endure a century.

That seeker should, also, regard backbiting as grievous error, and keep himself aloof from its dominion, inasmuch as backbiting quencheth the light of the heart, and extinguisheth the life of the soul. He should be content with little, and be freed from all inordinate desire. He should treasure the companionship of them that have renounced the world, and regard avoidance of boastful and worldly people a precious benefit. At the dawn of every day he should commune with God, and, with all his soul, persevere in the quest of his Beloved. He should consume every wayward thought with the flame of His loving mention, and, with the swiftness of lightning, pass by all else save Him. He should succor the dispossessed, and never withhold his favor from the destitute. He should show kindness to animals, how much more unto his fellow-man, to him who is endowed with the power of utterance. He should not hesitate to offer up his life for his Beloved, nor allow the cen-

[265]

sure of the people to turn him away from the Truth. He should not wish for others that which he doth not wish for himself, nor promise that which he doth not fulfil. With all his heart he should avoid fellowship with evil-doers, and pray for the remission of their sins. He should forgive the sinful, and never despise his low estate, for none knoweth what his own end shall be. How often hath a sinner attained, at the hour of death, to the essence of faith, and, quaffing the immortal draught, hath taken his flight unto the Concourse on high! And how often hath a devout believer, at the hour of his soul's ascension, been so changed as to fall into the nethermost fire!

Our purpose in revealing these convincing and weighty utterances is to impress upon the seeker that he should regard all else beside God as transient, and count all things save Him, Who is the Object of all adoration, as utter nothingness.

These are among the attributes of the exalted, and constitute the hall-mark of the spiritually-minded. They have already been mentioned in connection with the requirements of the wayfarers that tread the path of Positive Knowledge. When the detached wayfarer and sincere seeker hath fulfilled these essential conditions, then and only then can he be called a true seeker. Whensoever he hath fulfilled the conditions implied in the verse: "Whoso maketh efforts for Us," he shall enjoy the blessings conferred by the words: "In Our Ways shall We assuredly guide him."

Only when the lamp of search, of earnest striving, of longing desire, of passionate devotion, of fervid love, of rapture, and ecstasy, is kindled within the seeker's heart, and the breeze of His loving-kindness is wafted upon his soul, will the darkness of error be dispelled, the mists of doubts and misgivings be dissipated, and the lights of knowledge and certitude envelop his being. At that hour will the Mystic Herald, bearing the joyful tidings of the Spirit, shine forth from the City of God resplendent as the morn, and, through the trumpet-blast of knowledge, will awaken the heart, the soul, and the spirit from the slumber of heedlessness. Then will the manifold favors and outpouring grace of the holy and everlasting Spirit confer such new life upon the seeker that he will find himself endowed with a new eye, a new ear, a new heart, and a new mind. He will contemplate the manifest signs of the universe, and will penetrate the hidden mysteries of the soul. Gazing with the eye of God, he will perceive within every atom a door that leadeth him to the stations of absolute certitude. He will discover in all things the mysteries of Divine Revelation, and the evidences of an everlasting Manifestation.

I swear by God! Were he that treadeth the path of guidance and seeketh to scale the heights of righteousness to attain unto this glorious and exalted station, he would inhale, at a distance of a thousand leagues, the fragrance of God, and would perceive the resplendent morn of a Divine guidance rising above the dayspring of all things. Each and every thing, however small, would be to him a revelation, leading him to his Beloved, the Object of his quest. So great shall be the discernment of this seeker that he will discriminate between truth and falsehood, even as he doth distinguish the sun from shadow. If in the uttermost corners of the East the sweet savors of God be wafted, he will assuredly recognize and inhale their fragrance, even though he be dwelling in the uttermost ends of the West. He will, likewise, clearly distinguish all the signs of God—His wondrous utterances, His great works, and mighty deeds—from the doings, the words and ways of men, even as the jeweler who knoweth the gem from the stone, or the man who distinguisheth the spring from autumn, and heat from cold. When the channel of the human soul is cleansed of all worldly and impeding attachments, it will unfailingly perceive the breath of the Beloved across immeasurable distances, and will, led by its perfume, attain and enter the City of Certitude.

Therein he will discern the wonders of His ancient Wisdom, and will perceive all the hidden teachings from the rustling leaves of the Tree that flourisheth in that City. With both his inner and outer ear, he will hear from its dust the hymns of glory and praise ascending unto the Lord of Lords, and with his inner eye will he discover the mysteries of "return" and "revival."

How unspeakably glorious are the signs, the tokens, the revelations, and splendors which He, Who is the King of Names and Attributes, hath destined for that City! The attainment unto this City quencheth thirst without water, and kindleth the love of God without fire. Within every blade of grass are enshrined the mysteries of an inscrutable Wisdom, and upon every rose-bush a myriad nightingales pour out, in blissful rapture, their melody. Its wondrous tulips unfold the mystery of the undying Fire in the Burning Bush, and its sweet savors of holiness breathe the perfume of the Messianic Spirit. It bestoweth wealth without gold, and conferreth immortality without death. In each one of its leaves ineffable delights are treasured, and within every chamber unnumbered mysteries lie hidden.

They that valiantly labor in quest of God, will, when once they have renounced all else but Him, be so attached and wedded unto that City, that a moment's separation from it would to them be unthinkable. They will hearken unto infallible proofs from the Hyacinth of that assembly, and will receive the surest testimonies from the beauty of its Rose, and the melody of its Nightingale. Once in about a thousand years shall this City be renewed and re-adorned. . . .

That City is none other than the Word of God revealed in every age and dispensation. In the days of Moses it was the Pentateuch; in the days of Jesus, the Gospel; in the days of Muḥammad, the Messenger of God, the Qur'án; in this day, the Bayán; and in the Dispensation of Him Whom God will make manifest, His own Book—the Book unto which all the Books of former Dispensations must needs be referred, the Book that standeth amongst them all transcendent and supreme.

CXXVI. To whatever place We may be banished, however great the tribulation We may suffer, they who are the people of God must, with fixed resolve and perfect confidence, keep their eyes directed towards the Day Spring of Glory, and be busied in whatever may be conducive to the betterment of the world and the education of its peoples. All that hath befallen Us in the past hath advanced the interests of Our Revelation and blazoned its fame; and all that may befall Us in the future will have a like result. Cling ye, with your inmost hearts, to the Cause of God, a Cause that hath been sent down by Him Who is the Ordainer, the All-Wise. We have, with the utmost kindliness and mercy, summoned and directed all peoples and nations to that which shall truly profit them.

The Day Star of Truth that shineth in its meridian splendor beareth Us witness! They who are the people of God have no ambition except to revive the world, to ennoble its life, and regenerate its peoples. Truthfulness and good-will have, at all times, marked their relations with all men. Their outward conduct is but a reflection of their inward life, and their inward life a mirror of their outward conduct. No veil hideth or obscureth the verities on which their Faith is established. Before the eyes of all men these verities have been laid bare, and can be unmistakably recognized. Their very acts attest the truth of these words.

Every discerning eye can, in this Day, perceive the dawning light of God's Revelation, and every attentive ear can recognize the Voice that was heard from the Burning Bush. Such is the rushing of the waters of Divine mercy, that He Who is the Day Spring of the signs of God and the Revealer of the evidences of His glory is without veil or concealment associating and conversing with the peoples of the earth and its kindreds. How numerous are those who, with hearts intent upon malice, have sought Our Presence, and departed from it loyal and loving friends! The portals of grace are wide open before the face of all men. In Our outward dealings with them We have treated alike the righteous and the sinner, that perchance the evil-doer may attain the limitless ocean of Divine forgiveness. Our name "the Concealer" hath shed such a light upon men that the froward hath imagined himself to be numbered with the pious. No man that seeketh Us will We ever disappoint, neither shall he that hath set his face towards Us be denied access unto Our court. . . .

O friends! Help ye the one true God, exalted be His glory, by your goodly deeds, by such conduct and character as shall be acceptable in His sight. He that seeketh to be a helper of God in this Day, let him close his eyes to whatever he may possess, and open them to the things of God. Let him cease to occupy himself with that which profiteth him, and concern himself with that which shall exalt the all-compelling name of the Almighty. He should cleanse his heart from all evil passions and corrupt desires, for the fear of God is the weapon that can render him victorious, the primary instrument whereby he can achieve his purpose. The fear of God is the shield that defendeth His Cause, the buckler that enableth His people to attain to victory. It is a standard that no man can abase, a force that no power can rival. By its aid, and by the leave of Him Who is the Lord of Hosts, they that have drawn nigh unto God have been able to subdue and conquer the citadels of the hearts of men.

CXXVII. If it be your wish, O people, to know God and to discover the greatness of His might, look, then, upon Me with Mine own eyes, and not with the eyes of any one besides Me. Ye will, otherwise, be never capable of recognizing Me, though ye ponder

My Cause as long as My Kingdom endureth, and meditate upon all created things throughout the eternity of God, the Sovereign Lord of all, the Omnipotent, the Ever-Abiding, the All-Wise. Thus have We manifested the truth of Our Revelation, that haply the people may be roused from their heedlessness, and be of them that understand.

Behold the low estate of these men who know full well how I have offered up Mine own Self and My kindred in the path of God and for the preservation of their faith in Him, who are well aware how Mine enemies have compassed Me about, in the days when the hearts of men feared and trembled, the days when they hid themselves from the eyes of the loved ones of God and of His enemies, and were busied in ensuring their own security and peace.

We eventually succeeded in manifesting the Cause of God, and exalted it to so eminent a position that all the people, except those who cherished ill-will in their hearts against this Youth and joined partners with the Almighty, acknowledged the sovereignty of God and His mighty dominion. And yet, notwithstanding this Revelation whose influence hath pervaded all created things, and despite the brightness of this Light, the like of which none of them hath ever beheld, witness how the people of the Bayán have denied and contended with Me. Some have turned away from the Path of God, rejected the authority of Him in Whom they had believed, and acted insolently towards God, the Most Powerful, the Supreme Protector, the Most Exalted, the Most Great. Others hesitated and halted in His Path, and regarded the Cause of the Creator, in its inmost truth, as invalid unless substantiated by the approval of him who was created through the operation of My Will. Thus have their works come to naught, and yet they failed to perceive it. Among them is he who sought to measure God with the measure of his own self, and was so misled by the names of God as to rise up against Me, who condemned Me as one that deserved to be put to death, and who imputed to Me the very offenses of which he himself was guilty.

Wherefore, do I plead My grief and My sorrow to Him Who created Me and entrusted Me with His Message. Unto Him do I render thanks and praise for the things He hath ordained, for My loneliness, and the anguish I suffer at the hands of these men who have strayed so far from Him. I have patiently sustained, and will continue to sustain, the tribulation that touched Me, and will put My whole trust and confidence in God. Him will I supplicate saying: Guide Thy servants, O My Lord, unto the court of Thy favor and bounty, and suffer them not to be deprived of the wonders of Thy grace and of Thy manifold blessings. For they know not what Thou hast ordained for them by virtue of Thy mercy that encompasseth the whole of creation. Outwardly, O Lord, they are weak and helpless; inwardly they are but orphans. Thou art the All-Bountiful, the Munificent, the Most Exalted, the Most Great. Cast not, O My God, the fury of Thy wrath upon them, and cause them to tarry until such time when the wonders of Thy mercy will have been made manifest, that haply they may return unto Thee, and ask forgiveness of Thee for the things they have committed against Thee. Verily, Thou art the Forgiving, the All-Merciful.

cxxviii. Say: Doth it beseem a man while claiming to be a follower of his Lord, the All-Merciful, he should yet in his heart do the very deeds of the Evil One? Nay, it ill beseemeth him, and to this He Who is the Beauty of the All-Glorious will bear Me witness. Would that ye could comprehend it!

Cleanse from your hearts the love of worldly things, from your tongues every remembrance except His remembrance, from your entire being whatsoever may deter you from beholding His face, or may tempt you to follow the promptings of your evil and corrupt inclinations. Let God be your fear, O people, and be ye of them that tread the path of righteousness.

Say: Should your conduct, O people, contradict your professions, how think ye, then, to be able to distinguish yourselves from them who, though professing their faith in the Lord their God, have, as soon as He came unto them in the cloud of holiness, refused to acknowledge Him, and repudiated His truth? Disencumber yourselves of all attachment to this world and the vanities thereof. Beware that ye approach them not, inasmuch as they prompt you to walk after your own lusts and covetous desires, and hinder you from entering the straight and glorious Path.

Know ye that by "the world" is meant your unawareness of Him Who is your Maker, and your absorption in aught else but Him. The "life to come," on the other hand, signifieth the things that give you a safe approach to God, the All-Glorious, the Incomparable. Whatsoever deterreth you, in this Day, from loving God is nothing but the world. Flee it, that ye may be numbered with the blest. Should a man wish to adorn himself with the ornaments of the earth, to wear its apparels, or partake of the benefits it can bestow, no harm can befall him, if he alloweth nothing whatever to intervene between him and God, for God hath ordained every good thing, whether created in the heavens or in the earth, for such of His servants as truly believe in Him. Eat ye, O people, of the good things which God hath allowed you, and deprive not yourselves from His wondrous bounties. Render thanks and praise unto Him, and be of them that are truly thankful.

O thou that hast fled thy home and sought the presence of God! Proclaim unto men the Message of thy Lord, that it may haply deter them from following the promptings of their evil and corrupt desires, and bring them to the remembrance of God, the Most Exalted, the Most Great. Say: Fear God, O people, and refrain from shedding the blood of any one. Contend not with your neighbor, and be ye of them that do good. Beware that ye commit no disorders on the earth after it hath been well ordered, and follow not the footsteps of them that are gone astray.

Whoso ariseth among you to teach the Cause of his Lord, let him, before all else, teach his own self, that his speech may attract the hearts of them that hear him. Unless he teacheth his own self, the words of his mouth will not influence the heart of the seeker. Take heed, O people, lest ye be of them that give good counsel to others but forget to follow it themselves. The words of such as these, and beyond the words the realities of all things, and beyond these realities the angels that are nigh unto God, bring against them the accusation of falsehood.

Should such a man ever succeed in influencing any one, this success should be attributed not to him, but rather to the influence of the words of God, as decreed by Him Who is the Almighty, the All-Wise. In the sight of God he is regarded as a lamp that imparteth its light, and yet is all the while being consumed within itself.

Say: Commit not, O people, that which will bring shame upon you or dishonor the Cause of God in the eyes of men, and be not of the mischief-makers. Ap-

[277]

proach not the things which your minds condemn. Eschew all manner of wickedness, for such things are forbidden unto you in the Book which none touch except such as God hath cleansed from every taint of guilt, and numbered among the purified.

Be fair to yourselves and to others, that the evidences of justice may be revealed, through your deeds, among Our faithful servants. Beware lest ye encroach upon the substance of your neighbor. Prove yourselves worthy of his trust and confidence in you, and withhold not from the poor the gifts which the grace of God hath bestowed upon you. He, verily, shall recompense the charitable, and doubly repay them for what they have bestowed. No God is there but Him. All creation and its empire are His. He bestoweth His gifts on whom He will, and from whom He will He withholdeth them. He is the Great Giver, the Most Generous, the Benevolent.

Say: Teach ye the Cause of God, O people of Bahá, for God hath prescribed unto every one the duty of proclaiming His Message, and regardeth it as the most meritorious of all deeds. Such a deed is acceptable only when he that teacheth the Cause is already a firm believer in God, the Supreme Protector, the Gracious, the Almighty. He hath, moreover, ordained that His Cause be taught through the power of men's utterance, and not through resort to violence. Thus hath His ordinance been sent down from the Kingdom of Him Who is the Most Exalted, the All-Wise.

Beware lest ye contend with any one, nay, strive to make him aware of the truth with kindly manner and most convincing exhortation. If your hearer respond, he will have responded to his own behoof, and if not, turn ye away from him, and set your faces towards God's sacred Court, the seat of resplendent holiness.

Dispute not with any one concerning the things of this world and its affairs, for God hath abandoned them to such as have set their affection upon them. Out of the whole world He hath chosen for Himself the hearts of men—hearts which the hosts of revelation and of utterance can subdue. Thus hath it been ordained by the Fingers of Bahá, upon the Tablet of God's irrevocable decree, by the behest of Him Who is the Supreme Ordainer, the All-Knowing.

CXXIX. O wayfarer in the path of God! Take thou thy portion of the ocean of His grace, and deprive not thyself of the things that lie hidden in its depths. Be thou of them that have partaken of its treasures. A dewdrop out of this ocean would, if shed upon all that are in the heavens and on the earth, suffice to enrich them with the bounty of God, the Almighty, the All-Knowing, the All-Wise. With the hands of renunciation draw forth from its life-giving waters, and sprinkle therewith all created things, that they may be cleansed from all man-made limitations and may approach the mighty seat of God, this hallowed and resplendent Spot.

Be not grieved if thou performest it thyself alone. Let God be all-sufficient for thee. Commune intimately with His Spirit, and be thou of the thankful. Proclaim the Cause of thy Lord unto all who are in the heavens and on the earth. Should any man respond to thy call, lay bare before him the pearls of the wisdom of the Lord, thy God, which His Spirit hath sent down unto thee, and be thou of them that truly believe. And should any one reject thine offer, turn thou away from him, and put thy trust and confidence in the Lord, thy God, the Lord of all worlds.

By the righteousness of God! Whoso openeth his lips in this Day and maketh mention of the name of his Lord, the hosts of Divine inspiration shall descend upon him from the heaven of My name, the All-Knowing, the All-Wise. On him shall also descend the Concourse on high, each bearing aloft a chalice of pure light. Thus hath it been foreordained in the realm of God's Revelation, by the behest of Him Who is the All-Glorious, the Most Powerful.

There lay concealed within the Holy Veil, and prepared for the service of God, a company of His chosen ones who shall be manifested unto men, who shall aid His Cause, who shall be afraid of no one, though the entire human race rise up and war against them. These are the ones who, before the gaze of the dwellers on earth and the denizens of heaven, shall arise and, shouting aloud, acclaim the name of the Almighty, and summon the children of men to the path of God, the All-Glorious, the All-Praised. Walk thou in their way, and let no one dismay thee. Be of them whom the tumult of the world, however much it may agitate them in the path of their Creator, can never sadden, whose purpose the blame of the blamer will never defeat.

Go forth with the Tablet of God and His signs, and rejoin them that have believed in Me, and announce unto them tidings of Our most holy Paradise. Warn, then, those that have joined partners with Him. Say: I am come to you, O people, from the Throne of glory, and bear you an announcement from God, the Most Powerful, the Most Exalted, the Most Great. In mine hand I carry the testimony of God, your Lord and the Lord of your sires of old. Weigh it with the just Balance that ye possess, the Balance of the testimony of the Prophets and Messengers of God. If ye find it to be established in truth, if ye believe it to be of God, beware, then, lest ye cavil at it, and render your works vain, and be numbered with the infidels. It is indeed the sign of God that hath been sent down through the power of truth, through which the validity of His Cause hath been demonstrated unto His creatures, and the ensigns of purity lifted up betwixt earth and heaven. Say: This is the sealed and mystic Scroll, the repository of God's irrevocable Decree, bearing the words which the Finger of Holiness hath traced, that lay wrapt within the veil of impenetrable mystery, and hath now been sent down as a token of the grace of Him Who is the Almighty, the Ancient of Days. In it have We decreed the destinies of all the dwellers of the earth and the denizens of heaven, and written down the knowledge of all things from first to last. Nothing whatsoever can escape or frustrate Him, whether created in the past or to be created in the future, could ye but perceive it.

Say: The Revelation sent down by God hath most surely been repeated, and the outstretched Hand of Our power hath overshadowed all that are in the heavens and all that are on the earth. We have, through the power of truth, the very truth, manifested an infinitesimal glimmer of Our impenetrable Mystery, and lo, they that have recognized the radiance of the Sinaic splendor expired, as they caught a lightening glimpse of this Crimson Light enveloping the Sinai of Our Revelation. Thus hath He Who is the Beauty of the All-Merciful come down in the clouds of His testimony, and the decree accomplished by virtue of the Will of God, the All-Glorious, the All-Wise.

Say: Step out of Thy holy chamber, O Maid of Heaven, inmate of the Exalted Paradise! Drape thyself in whatever manner pleaseth Thee in the silken Vesture of Immortality, and put on, in the name of the All-Glorious, the broidered Robe of Light. Hear, then, the sweet, the wondrous accent of the Voice that cometh from the Throne of Thy Lord, the Inaccessible, the Most High. Unveil Thy face, and manifest the beauty of the black-eyed Damsel, and suffer not the servants of God to be deprived of the light of Thy shining countenance. Grieve not if Thou hearest the sighs of the dwellers of the earth, or the voice of the lamentation of the denizens of heaven. Leave them to perish on the dust of extinction. Let them be reduced to nothingness, inasmuch as the flame of hatred hath been kindled within their breasts. Intone, then, before the face of the peoples of earth and heaven, and in a most melodious voice, the anthem of praise, for a remembrance of Him Who is the King of the names and attributes of God. Thus have We decreed Thy destiny. Well able are We to achieve Our purpose.

Beware that Thou divest not Thyself, Thou Who art the Essence of Purity, of Thy robe of effulgent glory. Nay, enrich Thyself increasingly, in the kingdom of creation, with the incorruptible vestures of Thy God, that the beauteous image of the Almighty may be reflected through Thee in all created things and the grace of Thy Lord be infused in the plenitude of its power into the entire creation.

If Thou smellest from any one the smell of the love of Thy Lord, offer up Thyself for him, for We have created Thee to this end, and have covenanted

[283]

with Thee, from time immemorial, and in the presence of the congregation of Our well-favored ones, for this very purpose. Be not impatient if the blind in heart hurl down the shafts of their idle fancies upon Thee. Leave them to themselves, for they follow the promptings of the evil ones.

Cry out before the gaze of the dwellers of heaven and of earth: I am the Maid of Heaven, the Offspring begotten by the Spirit of Bahá. My habitation is the Mansion of His Name, the All-Glorious. Before the Concourse on high I was adorned with the ornament of His names. I was wrapt within the veil of an inviolable security, and lay hidden from the eyes of men. Methinks that I heard a Voice of divine and incomparable sweetness, proceeding from the right hand of the God of Mercy, and lo, the whole Paradise stirred and trembled before Me, in its longing to hear its accents, and gaze on the beauty of Him that uttered them. Thus have We revealed in this luminous Tablet, and in the sweetest of languages, the verses which the Tongue of Eternity was moved to utter in the Qayyúmu'l-Asmá'.

Say: He ordaineth as He pleaseth, by virtue of His sovereignty, and doeth whatsoever He willeth at His own behest. He shall not be asked of the things it pleaseth Him to ordain. He, in truth, is the Unrestrained, the All-Powerful, the All-Wise.

They that have disbelieved in God and rebelled against His sovereignty are the helpless victims of their corrupt inclinations and desires. These shall return to their abode in the fire of hell: wretched is the abode of the deniers!

CXXX. Be generous in prosperity, and thankful in adversity. Be worthy of the trust of thy neighbor, and look upon him with a bright and friendly face. Be a treasure to the poor, an admonisher to the rich, an answerer of the cry of the needy, a preserver of the sanctity of thy pledge. Be fair in thy judgment, and guarded in thy speech. Be unjust to no man, and show all meekness to all men. Be as a lamp unto them that walk in darkness, a joy to the sorrowful, a sea for the thirsty, a haven for the distressed, an upholder and defender of the victim of oppression. Let integrity and uprightness distinguish all thine acts. Be a home for the stranger, a balm to the suffering, a tower of strength for the fugitive. Be eyes to the blind, and a guiding light unto the feet of the erring. Be an ornament to the countenance of truth, a crown to the brow of fidelity, a pillar of the temple of righteousness, a breath of life to the body of mankind, an ensign of the hosts of justice, a luminary above the horizon of virtue, a dew to the soil of the human heart, an ark on the ocean of knowledge, a sun in the heaven of bounty, a gem on the diadem of wisdom, a shining light in the firmament of thy generation, a fruit upon the tree of humility.

[285]

CXXXI. The Pen of the Ancient King hath never ceased to remember the loved ones of God. At one time, rivers of mercy have streamed from His Pen, at another, through its movement, God's perspicuous Book hath been revealed. He is the One to Whom none can compare, Whose utterance mortal man can never rival. He it is Who from everlasting hath been established upon the seat of ascendancy and might, He from Whose lips have gone out counsels that can satisfy the needs of the whole of mankind, and admonitions that can profit them.

The One true God beareth Me witness, and His creatures will testify, that not for a moment did I allow Myself to be hidden from the eyes of men, nor did I consent to shield My person from their injury. Before the face of all men I have arisen, and bidden them fulfil My pleasure. My object is none other than the betterment of the world and the tranquillity of its peoples. The well-being of mankind, its peace and security, are unattainable unless and until its unity is firmly established. This unity can never be achieved so long as the counsels which the Pen of the Most High hath revealed are suffered to pass unheeded.

Through the power of the words He hath uttered the whole of the human race can be illumined with the light of unity, and the remembrance of His Name is able to set on fire the hearts of all men, and burn away the veils that intervene between them and

His glory. One righteous act is endowed with a potency that can so elevate the dust as to cause it to pass beyond the heaven of heavens. It can tear every bond asunder, and hath the power to restore the force that hath spent itself and vanished. . . .

Be pure, O people of God, be pure; be righteous, be righteous. . . . Say: O people of God! That which can ensure the victory of Him Who is the Eternal Truth, His hosts and helpers on earth, have been set down in the sacred Books and Scriptures, and are as clear and manifest as the sun. These hosts are such righteous deeds, such conduct and character, as are acceptable in His sight. Whoso ariseth, in this Day, to aid Our Cause, and summoneth to his assistance the hosts of a praiseworthy character and upright conduct, the influence flowing from such an action will, most certainly, be diffused throughout the whole world.

CXXXII. The Purpose of the one true God, exalted be His glory, in revealing Himself unto men is to lay bare those gems that lie hidden within the mine of their true and inmost selves. That the divers communions of the earth, and the manifold systems of religious belief, should never be allowed to foster the feelings of animosity among men, is, in this Day, of the essence of the Faith of God and His Religion. These principles and laws, these firmly-established and mighty systems, have proceeded from one Source, and are the rays of one Light. That they differ one from another is to be attributed to the varying requirements of the ages in which they were promulgated.

Gird up the loins of your endeavor, O people of Bahá, that haply the tumult of religious dissension and strife that agitateth the peoples of the earth may be stilled, that every trace of it may be completely obliterated. For the love of God, and them that serve Him, arise to aid this most sublime and momentous Revelation. Religious fanaticism and hatred are a world-devouring fire, whose violence none can quench. The Hand of Divine power can, alone, deliver mankind from this desolating affliction. . . .

The utterance of God is a lamp, whose light is these words: Ye are the fruits of one tree, and the leaves of one branch. Deal ye one with another with the utmost love and harmony, with friendliness and fellowship. He Who is the Day Star of Truth beareth Me witness! So powerful is the light of unity that it can illuminate the whole earth. The one true God, He Who knoweth all things, Himself testifieth to the truth of these words.

Exert yourselves that ye may attain this transcendent and most sublime station, the station that can ensure the protection and security of all mankind. This goal excelleth every other goal, and this aspiration is the monarch of all aspirations. So long, however, as the thick clouds of oppression, which obscure the day star of justice, remain undispelled, it would be difficult for the glory of this station to be unveiled to men's eyes. . . .

Consort with all men, O people of Bahá, in a spirit of friendliness and fellowship. If ye be aware of a certain truth, if ye possess a jewel, of which others are deprived, share it with them in a language of utmost kindliness and good-will. If it be accepted, if it fulfil its purpose, your object is attained. If any one should refuse it, leave him unto himself, and beseech God to guide him. Beware lest ye deal unkindly with him. A kindly tongue is the lodestone of the hearts of men. It is the bread of the spirit, it clotheth the words with meaning, it is the fountain of the light of wisdom and understanding. . . .

CXXXIII. The ordinances of God have been sent down from the heaven of His most august Revelation. All must diligently observe them. Man's supreme distinction, his real advancement, his final victory, have always depended, and will continue to depend, upon them. Whoso keepeth the commandments of God shall attain everlasting felicity.

A twofold obligation resteth upon him who hath recognized the Day Spring of the Unity of God, and acknowledged the truth of Him Who is the Manifestation of His oneness. The first is steadfastness in His love, such steadfastness that neither the clamor of the enemy nor the claims of the idle pretender can deter him from cleaving unto Him Who is the Eternal Truth, a steadfastness that taketh no account of them whatever. The second is strict observance of the laws He hath prescribed—laws which He hath always ordained, and will continue to ordain, unto men, and through which the truth may be distinguished and separated from falsehood.

CXXXIV. The first and foremost duty prescribed unto men, next to the recognition of Him Who is the Eternal Truth, is the duty of steadfastness in His Cause. Cleave thou unto it, and be of them whose minds are firmly fixed and grounded in God. No act, however meritorious, did or can ever compare unto it. It is the king of all acts, and to this thy Lord, the All-Highest, the Most Powerful, will testify. . . .

The virtues and attributes pertaining unto God are all evident and manifest, and have been mentioned and described in all the heavenly Books. Among them are trustworthiness, truthfulness, purity of heart while communing with God, forbearance, resignation to whatever the Almighty hath decreed, contentment with the things His Will hath provided, patience, nay, thankfulness in the midst of tribulation, and complete reliance, in all circumstances, upon Him. These rank, according to the estimate of God, among the highest and most laudable of all acts. All other acts are, and will ever remain, secondary and subordinate unto them. . . .

The spirit that animateth the human heart is the knowledge of God, and its truest adorning is the recognition of the truth that "He doeth whatsoever He willeth, and ordaineth that which He pleaseth." Its raiment is the fear of God, and its perfection steadfastness in His Faith. Thus God instructeth whosoever seeketh Him. He, verily, loveth the one that turneth towards Him. There is none other God but Him, the Forgiving, the Most Bountiful. All praise be to God, the Lord of all worlds.

cxxxv.   O Letter of the Living! The ear of God hath heard thy cry, and His eyes have beheld thy written supplication. He is calling thee from His seat of glory, and is revealing unto thee the verses that have been sent down by Him Who is the Help in Peril, the Self-Subsisting.

Blessed art thou for having utterly abolished the idol of self and of vain imagination, and for having rent asunder the veil of idle fancy, through the power of the might of thy Lord, the Supreme Protector, the Almighty, the one Beloved. Thou art indeed to be numbered with those Letters that have excelled every other Letter. Wherefore thou hast been singled out by God through the tongue of thy Lord, the Báb, the brightness of Whose countenance hath enveloped, and will continue to envelop, the whole of creation. Render thanks unto the Almighty, and magnify His name, inasmuch as He hath aided thee to recognize a Cause that hath made the hearts of the inhabitants of the heavens and of the earth to tremble, that hath caused the denizens of the Kingdoms of creation and of Revelation to cry out, and through which the hidden secrets of men's breasts have been searched out and tested.

Thy Lord, the Most High (the Báb), addresseth thee, from His Realm of glory, these words: Great is the blessedness that awaiteth thee, O Letter of the Living, for thou hast truly believed in Me, hast refused to shame Me before the Concourse on high, hast fulfilled thy pledge, hast cast away the veil of vain imaginings, and hast fixed thy gaze upon the Lord, thy God, the Lord of the unseen and the seen, the Lord of the Frequented Fane. I am well pleased with thee, inasmuch as I have found thy face beaming with light on the Day when faces have been made dismal and turned black.

Say: O people of the Bayán! Did We not admonish you, in all Our Tablets and in all Our hidden Scriptures, not to follow your evil passions and corrupt inclinations, but to keep your eyes directed towards the Scene of transcendent glory, on the Day when the Most Mighty Balance shall be set, the Day when the sweet melodies of the Spirit of God shall be poured out from the right hand of the throne of your Lord, the omnipotent Protector, the All-Powerful, the Holy of Holies? Did We not forbid you to cleave to the things that would shut you out from the Manifestation of our Beauty, in its subsequent Revelation, be they the embodiments of the names of God and all their glory, or the revealers of His attributes and their dominion? Behold, how, as soon as I revealed Myself, ye have rejected My truth and turned away from Me, and been of them that have regarded the signs of God as a play and pastime!

By My Beauty! Nothing whatsoever shall, in this Day, be accepted from you, though ye continue to worship and prostrate yourselves before God throughout the eternity of His dominion. For all things are dependent upon His Will, and the worth of all acts is conditioned upon His acceptance and pleasure. The whole universe is but a handful of clay in His grasp. Unless one recognize God and love Him, his cry shall not be heard by God in this Day. This is of the essence of His Faith, did ye but know it.

Will ye be content with that which is like the vapor in a plain, and be willing to forgo the Ocean Whose waters refresh, by virtue of the Will of God, the souls of men? Woe unto you, for having repaid the bounty of God with so vain and contemptible a thing! Ye are, indeed, of them that have rejected Me in My previous Revelation. Would that your hearts could comprehend!

Arise, and, under the eyes of God, atone for your failures in duty towards Him. This is My commandment unto you, were ye to incline your ears unto My commandment. By Mine own Self! Neither the people of the Qur'án, nor the followers of either the Torah or the Evangel, nor those of any other Book, have committed that which your hands have wrought. I, Myself, have dedicated My whole life to the vindication of the truth of this Faith. I, Myself, have announced, in all My Tablets, the advent of His Revelation. And yet, no sooner did He manifest Himself, in His subsequent Revelation, clothed in the glory of Bahá and arrayed in the robe of His grandeur, than ye rebelled against Him Who is the supreme Protector, the Self-Subsisting. Beware, O people! Be ye ashamed of that which hath befallen Me at your hands in the path of God. Take heed that ye be not of them that have rejected that which hath been sent down unto them from the Heaven of God's transcendent glory.

Such, O Letter of the Living, are the words which thy Lord hath spoken, and addressed unto thee from the realms above. Proclaim the words of thy Lord unto His servants, that perchance they may shake off their slumber, and ask pardon of God, Who hath formed and fashioned them, and sent down unto them this most effulgent, this most holy, and manifest Revelation of His Beauty.

cxxxvi.   Say: Deliver your souls, O people, from the bondage of self, and purify them from all attachment to anything besides Me. Remembrance of Me cleanseth all things from defilement, could ye but perceive it. Say: Were all created things to be entirely divested of the veil of worldly vanity and desire, the Hand of God would in this Day clothe them, one and all, with the robe "He doeth whatsoever He willeth in the kingdom of creation," that thereby the sign of His sovereignty might be manifested in all things. Exalted then be He, the Sovereign Lord of all, the Almighty, the Supreme Protector, the All-Glorious, the Most Powerful.

Intone, O My servant, the verses of God that have been received by thee, as intoned by them who have drawn nigh unto Him, that the sweetness of thy melody may kindle thine own soul, and attract the hearts of all men. Whoso reciteth, in the privacy of his chamber, the verses revealed by God, the scattering angels of the Almighty shall scatter abroad the fragrance of the words uttered by his mouth, and shall cause the heart of every righteous man to throb. Though he may, at first, remain unaware of its effect, yet the virtue of the grace vouchsafed unto him must needs sooner or later exercise its influence upon his soul. Thus have the mysteries of the Revelation of God been decreed by virtue of the Will of Him Who is the Source of power and wisdom.

O Khalíl! God beareth Me witness. Though My Pen be still moving on My Tablet, yet, in its very heart, it weepeth and is sore distressed. The lamp burning before the Throne, likewise, weepeth and groaneth by reason of the things which the Ancient

Beauty hath suffered at the hands of them who are but a creation of His Will. God, Himself, knoweth and testifieth to the truth of My words. No man that hath purged his ear from the loud clamor of the infidels, and inclined it to all created things, can fail to hear the voice of their lamentation and weeping over the trouble that hath befallen Us at the hands of those of Our servants that have disbelieved in, and rebelled against, Us. Thus have We disclosed to thee a glimmer of the woes that have come upon us, that thou mayest be made aware of Our sufferings, and patiently endure thy sorrows.

Arise to aid thy Lord at all times and in all circumstances, and be thou one of His helpers. Admonish, then, the people to lend a hearing ear to the words which the Spirit of God hath uttered in this irradiant and resplendent Tablet. Say: Sow not, O people, the seeds of dissension amongst men, and contend not with your neighbor. Be patient under all conditions, and place your whole trust and confidence in God. Aid ye your Lord with the sword of wisdom and of utterance. This indeed well becometh the station of man. To depart from it would be unworthy of God, the Sovereign Lord of all, the Glorified. The people, however, have been led astray, and are truly of the heedless.

Unlock, O people, the gates of the hearts of men with the keys of the remembrance of Him Who is the Remembrance of God and the Source of wisdom amongst you. He hath chosen out of the whole world the hearts of His servants, and made them each a seat for the revelation of His glory. Wherefore, sanctify them from every defilement, that the things for which they were created may be engraven upon them. This indeed is a token of God's bountiful favor.

Beautify your tongues, O people, with truthfulness, and adorn your souls with the ornament of honesty. Beware, O people, that ye deal not treacherously with any one. Be ye the trustees of God amongst His creatures, and the emblems of His generosity amidst His people. They that follow their lusts and corrupt inclinations have erred and dissipated their efforts. They, indeed, are of the lost. Strive, O people, that your eyes may be directed towards the mercy of God, that your hearts may be attuned to His wondrous remembrance, that your souls may rest confidently upon His grace and bounty, that your feet may tread the path of His good-pleasure. Such are the counsels which I bequeath unto you. Would that ye might follow My counsels!

CXXXVII. Some have regarded it as lawful to infringe on the integrity of the substance of their neighbor, and have made light of the injunction of God as prescribed in His Book. Evil fall upon them, and the chastisement of God, the All-Powerful, the Almighty, afflict them! By Him Who shineth above the Day Spring of sanctity! If the whole earth were to be converted into silver and gold, no man who can be said to have truly ascended into the heaven of faith and certitude would deign to regard it, much less to seize and keep it. We have formerly referred to this subject in passages revealed in the Arabic tongue, in a language of exquisite beauty. God is Our witness! Whoever hath tasted the sweetness of those words will never consent to transgress the bounds which God hath fixed, neither will he turn his gaze towards any one except his Well-Beloved. Such a man will, with his inner eye, readily recognize how altogether vain and fleeting are the things of this world, and will set his affections on things above.

Say: Be ashamed, O ye that call yourselves the lovers of the Ancient Beauty! Be ye admonished by the tribulation He hath suffered, by the burden of anguish He hath carried for the sake of God. Let your eyes be opened. To what purpose hath He labored, if the manifold trials He hath endured are, in the end, to result in such contemptible professions, and such wretched conduct? Every robber, every worker of iniquity, hath, in the days prior to My Revelation, uttered these same words, and performed these same deeds.

Verily I say: Incline your ears to My sweet voice, and sanctify yourselves from the defilement of your evil passions and corrupt desires. They who dwell within the tabernacle of God, and are established upon the seats of everlasting glory, will refuse, though they be dying of hunger, to stretch their hands and seize unlawfully the property of their neighbor, however vile and worthless he may be.

The purpose of the one true God in manifesting Himself is to summon all mankind to truthfulness and sincerity, to piety and trustworthiness, to resignation and submissiveness to the Will of God, to forbearance and kindliness, to uprightness and wisdom. His object is to array every man with the mantle of a saintly character, and to adorn him with the ornament of holy and goodly deeds.

Say: Have mercy on yourselves and on your fellowmen, and suffer not the Cause of God—a Cause which is immeasurably exalted above the inmost essence of sanctity—to be sullied with the stain of your idle fancies, your unseemly and corrupt imaginations.

CXXXVIII. Thou seest, O God of Mercy, Thou Whose power pervadeth all created things, these servants of Thine, Thy thralls, who, according to the good-pleasure of Thy Will, observe in the daytime the fast prescribed by Thee, who arise, at the earliest dawn of day, to make mention of Thy Name, and to celebrate Thy praise, in the hope of obtaining their share of the goodly things that are treasured up within the treasuries of Thy grace and bounty. I beseech Thee, O Thou that holdest in Thine hands the reins of the entire creation, in Whose grasp is the whole kingdom of Thy names and of Thine attributes, not to deprive, in Thy Day, Thy servants from the showers pouring from the clouds of Thy mercy, nor to hinder them from taking their portion of the ocean of Thy good-pleasure.

All the atoms of the earth bear witness, O my Lord, to the greatness of Thy power and of Thy sovereignty; and all the signs of the universe attest the glory of Thy majesty and of Thy might. Have mercy, then, O Thou Who art the sovereign Lord of all, Who art the King of everlasting days, and Ruler of all nations, upon these Thy servants, who have clung to the cord of Thy commandments, who have bowed their necks to the revelations of Thy laws which have been sent down from the heaven of Thy Will.

Behold, O my Lord, how their eyes are lifted up towards the dawning-place of Thy loving-kindness, how their hearts are set upon the oceans of Thy favors, how their voices are lowered before the accents of Thy most sweet Voice, calling, from the most sublime Station, in Thy name the All-Glorious. Help Thou Thy loved ones, O my Lord, them that have forsaken their all, that they may obtain the things Thou dost possess, whom trials and tribulations have encompassed for having renounced the world and set their affections on Thy realm of glory. Shield them, I entreat Thee, O my Lord, from the assaults of their evil passions and desires, and aid them to obtain the things that shall profit them in this present world and in the next.

I pray Thee, O my Lord, by Thy hidden, Thy treasured Name, that calleth aloud in the kingdom of creation, and summoneth all peoples to the Tree beyond which there is no passing, the seat of transcendent glory, to rain down upon us, and upon Thy servants, the overflowing rain of Thy mercy, that it may cleanse us from the remembrance of all else but Thee, and draw us nigh unto the shores of the ocean of Thy grace. Ordain, O Lord, through Thy most exalted Pen, that which will immortalize our souls in the Realm of glory, will perpetuate our names in Thy Kingdom, and safeguard our lives in the treasuries of Thy protection and our bodies in the stronghold of Thy inviolable fastness. Powerful art Thou over all things, be they of the past or of the future. No God is there but Thee, the omnipotent Protector, the Self-Subsisting.

Thou seest, O Lord, our suppliant hands lifted up towards the heaven of Thy favor and bounty. Grant that they may be filled with the treasures of Thy munificence and bountiful favor. Forgive us, and our fathers, and our mothers, and fulfil whatsoever we have desired from the ocean of Thy grace and Divine generosity. Accept, O Beloved of our hearts, all our works in Thy path. Thou art, verily, the Most

Powerful, the Most Exalted, the Incomparable, the One, the Forgiving, the Gracious.

cxxxix. Let thine ear be attentive, O Nabíl-i-A'ẓam, to the Voice of the Ancient of Days, crying to thee from the Kingdom of His all-glorious Name. He it is Who is now proclaiming from the realms above, and within the inmost essence of all created things: "I truly am God, there is none other God but Me. I am He Who, from everlasting, hath been the Source of all sovereignty and power, He Who shall continue, throughout eternity, to exercise His kingship and to extend His protection unto all created things. My proof is the greatness of My might and My sovereignty that embraceth the whole of creation." . . .

Blessed art thou, O My name, inasmuch as thou hast entered Mine Ark, and art speeding, through the power of My sovereign and most exalted might, on the ocean of grandeur, and art numbered with My favored ones whose names the Finger of God hath inscribed. Thou hast quaffed the cup which is life indeed from the hands of this Youth, around Whom revolve the Manifestations of the All-Glorious, and the brightness of Whose presence they Who are the Day Springs of Mercy extol in the day time and in the night season.

His glory be with thee, inasmuch as thou hast journeyed from God unto God, and entered within the borders of the Court of unfading splendor—the Spot which mortal man can never describe. Therein hath the breeze of holiness, laden with the love of thy Lord, stirred thy spirit within thee, and the waters of understanding have washed from thee the stains of remoteness and ungodliness. Thou hast gained admittance into the Paradise of God's Remembrance, through thy recognition of Him Who is the Embodiment of that Remembrance amongst men.

Wherefore, be thankful to God, for having strengthened thee to aid His Cause, for having made the flowers of knowledge and understanding to spring forth in the garden of thine heart. Thus hath His grace encompassed thee, and encompassed the whole of creation. Beware, lest thou allow anything whatsoever to grieve thee. Rid thyself of all attachment to the vain allusions of men, and cast behind thy back the idle and subtle disputations of them that are veiled from God. Proclaim, then, that which the Most Great Spirit will inspire thee to utter in the service of the Cause of thy Lord, that thou mayest stir up the souls of all men and incline their hearts unto this most blessed and all-glorious Court. . . .

Know thou that We have annulled the rule of the sword, as an aid to Our Cause, and substituted for it the power born of the utterance of men. Thus have We irrevocably decreed, by virtue of Our grace. Say: O people! Sow not the seeds of discord among men, and refrain from contending with your neighbor, for your Lord hath committed the world and the cities thereof to the care of the kings of the earth, and made them the emblems of His own power, by virtue of the sovereignty He hath chosen to bestow upon them. He hath refused to reserve for Himself any share whatever of this world's dominion. To this He Who is Himself the Eternal Truth will testify. The things He hath reserved for Himself are the cities of men's hearts, that He may cleanse them from all earthly defilements, and enable them to draw nigh unto the hallowed Spot which the hands of the infidel can never profane. Open, O people, the city of the human heart with the key of your utterance. Thus have We, according to a pre-ordained measure, prescribed unto you your duty.

By the righteousness of God! The world and its vanities, and its glory, and whatever delights it can offer, are all, in the sight of God, as worthless as, nay, even more contemptible than, dust and ashes. Would that the hearts of men could comprehend it! Cleanse yourselves thoroughly, O people of Bahá, from the defilement of the world, and of all that pertaineth unto it. God Himself beareth Me witness. The things of the earth ill beseem you. Cast them away unto such as may desire them, and fasten your eyes upon this most holy and effulgent Vision.

That which beseemeth you is the love of God, and the love of Him Who is the Manifestation of His

Essence, and the observance of whatsoever He chooseth to prescribe unto you, did ye but know it.

Say: Let truthfulness and courtesy be your adorning. Suffer not yourselves to be deprived of the robe of forbearance and justice, that the sweet savors of holiness may be wafted from your hearts upon all created things. Say: Beware, O people of Bahá, lest ye walk in the ways of them whose words differ from their deeds. Strive that ye may be enabled to manifest to the peoples of the earth the signs of God, and to mirror forth His commandments. Let your acts be a guide unto all mankind, for the professions of most men, be they high or low, differ from their conduct. It is through your deeds that ye can distinguish yourselves from others. Through them the brightness of your light can be shed upon the whole earth. Happy is the man that heedeth My counsel, and keepeth the precepts prescribed by Him Who is the All-Knowing, the All-Wise.

CXL. O Muḥammad-'Alí! Great is the blessedness awaiting thee, inasmuch as thou hast adorned thine heart with the ornament of the love of thy Lord, the All-Glorious, the All-Praised. He that hath attained this station in this day, all good shall be his.

Pay thou no heed to the humiliation to which the loved ones of God have in this Day been subjected. This humiliation is the pride and glory of all temporal honor and worldly elevation. What greater honor can be imagined than the honor conferred by the Tongue of the Ancient of Days when He calleth to remembrance His loved ones in His Most Great Prison? The day is approaching when the intervening clouds will have been completely dissipated, when the light of the words, "All honor belongeth unto God and unto them that love Him," will have appeared, as manifest as the sun, above the horizon of the Will of the Almighty.

All men, be they high or low, have sought and are still seeking so great an honor. All, however, have, as soon as the Sun of Truth shed its radiance upon the world, been deprived of its benefits, and have been shut out as by a veil from its glory, except them that have clung to the cord of the unfailing providence of the one true God, and have with complete detachment from all else but Him turned their faces towards His holy court.

Render thanks unto Him Who is the Desire of all worlds for having invested thee with such high honor. Ere long the world and all that is therein shall be as a thing forgotten, and all honor shall belong to the loved ones of thy Lord, the All-Glorious, the Most Bountiful.

CXLI. A Book sent down in truth unto men of insight! It biddeth the people to observe justice and to work righteousness, and forbiddeth them to follow their corrupt inclinations and carnal desires, if perchance the children of men might be roused from their slumber.

Say: Follow, O people, what hath been prescribed unto you in Our Tablets, and walk not after the imaginations which the sowers of mischief have devised, they that commit wickedness and impute it to God, the Most Holy, the All-Glorious, the Most Exalted. Say: We have accepted to be tried by ills and troubles, that ye may sanctify yourselves from all earthly defilements. Why, then, refuse ye to ponder Our purpose in your hearts? By the righteousness of God! Whoso will reflect upon the tribulations We have suffered, his soul will assuredly melt away with sorrow. Thy Lord Himself beareth witness to the truth of My words. We have sustained the weight of all calamities to sanctify you from all earthly corruption, and ye are yet indifferent.

Say: It behoveth every one that holdeth fast to the hem of Our Robe to be untainted by anything from which the Concourse on high may be averse. Thus hath it been decreed by thy Lord, the All-Glorious, in this His perspicuous Tablet. Say: Set ye aside My love, and commit what grieveth Mine heart? What is it that hindereth you from comprehending what hath been revealed unto you by Him Who is the All-Knowing, the All-Wise?

We verily behold your actions. If We perceive from them the sweet smelling savor of purity and holiness, We will most certainly bless you. Then will

[307]

the tongues of the inmates of Paradise utter your praise and magnify your names amidst them who have drawn nigh unto God.

Cling thou to the hem of the Robe of God, and take thou firm hold on His Cord, a Cord which none can sever. Beware that the clamor of them that have repudiated this Most Great Announcement shall not deter thee from achieving thy purpose. Proclaim what hath been prescribed unto thee in this Tablet, though all the peoples arise and oppose thee. Thy Lord is, verily, the All-Compelling, the Unfailing Protector.

My glory be with thee and with those of My loved ones that associate with thee. These indeed are they with whom it shall be well.

CXLII. I swear by the beauty of the Well-Beloved! This is the Mercy that hath encompassed the entire creation, the Day whereon the grace of God hath permeated and pervaded all things. The living waters of My mercy, O 'Alí, are fast pouring down, and Mine heart is melting with the heat of My tenderness and love. At no time have I been able to reconcile Myself to the afflictions befalling My loved ones, or to any trouble that could becloud the joy of their hearts.

Every time My name "the All-Merciful" was told that one of My lovers had breathed a word that runneth counter to My wish, it repaired, grief-stricken and disconsolate to its abode; and whenever My name "the Concealer" discovered that one of My followers had inflicted any shame or humiliation on his neighbor, it, likewise, turned back chagrined and sorrowful to its retreats of glory, and there wept and mourned with a sore lamentation. And whenever My name "the Ever-Forgiving" perceived that any one of My friends had committed any transgression, it cried out in its great distress, and, overcome with anguish, fell upon the dust, and was borne away by a company of the invisible angels to its habitation in the realms above.

By Myself, the True One, O 'Alí! The fire that hath inflamed the heart of Bahá is fiercer than the fire that gloweth in thine heart, and His lamentation louder than thy lamentation. Every time the sin committed by any one amongst them was breathed in the Court of His Presence, the Ancient Beauty would be so filled with shame as to wish He could hide the glory of His countenance from the eyes of all men, for He hath, at all times, fixed His gaze on their fidelity, and observed its essential requisites.

The words thou hadst written have, as soon as they were read in My Presence, caused the ocean of My fidelity to surge within Me, and the breeze of My forgiveness to be wafted over thy soul, and the tree of My loving-kindness to overshadow thee, and the clouds of My bounty to rain down upon thee their gifts. I swear by the Day Star that shineth above the horizon of eternity, I sorrow for thee in thy grief, and lament with thee in thy tribulation. . . . I bear witness to the services thou hast rendered Me, and testify to the various troubles thou hast sustained for My sake. All the atoms of the earth declare My love for thee.

The call thou didst raise, O 'Alí, is highly acceptable in My sight. Proclaim with both thy pen and tongue My Cause. Cry out and summon the people to Him Who is the Sovereign Lord of all worlds, with such zeal and fervor that all men may be set on fire by thee.

Say: O my Lord, my Best-Beloved, the Mover of my actions, the Lode Star of my soul, the Voice that crieth in mine inmost being, the Object of mine heart's adoration! Praise be to Thee for having enabled me to turn my face towards Thee, for having set my soul ablaze through remembrance of Thee, for having aided Me to proclaim Thy Name and to sing Thy praises.

My God, my God! If none be found to stray from Thy path, how, then, can the ensign of Thy mercy be unfurled, or the banner of Thy bountiful favor be hoisted? And if iniquity be not committed, what is it that can proclaim Thee to be the Concealer of men's sins, the Ever-Forgiving, the Omniscient, the All-Wise? May my soul be a sacrifice to the trespasses of them that trespass against Thee, for upon such trespasses are wafted the sweet savors of the tender mercies of Thy Name, the Compassionate, the All-Merciful. May my life be laid down for the transgressions of such as transgress against Thee, for through them the breath of Thy grace and the fragrance of Thy loving-kindness are made known and diffused amongst men. May my inmost being be offered up for the sins of them that have sinned against Thee, for it is as a result of such sins that the Day Star of Thy manifold favors revealeth itself above the horizon of Thy bounty, and the clouds of Thy never-failing providence rain down their gifts upon the realities of all created things.

I am he, O my Lord, that hath confessed to Thee the multitude of his evil doings, that hath acknowledged what no man hath acknowledged. I have made haste to attain unto the ocean of Thy forgiveness, and have sought shelter beneath the shadow of Thy most gracious favor. Grant, I beseech Thee, O Thou Who art the Everlasting King and the Sovereign Protector of all men, that I may be enabled to manifest that which shall cause the hearts and souls of men to soar in the limitless immensity of Thy love, and to commune with Thy Spirit. Strengthen me through the power of Thy sovereignty, that I may turn all created things towards the Day Spring of Thy Manifestation and the Source of Thy Revelation. Aid me, O my Lord, to surrender myself wholly to Thy Will, and to arise and serve Thee, for I cherish this earthly life for no other purpose than to compass the Tabernacle of Thy Revelation and the Seat of Thy Glory. Thou seest me, O my God, detached from all else but Thee, and humble and subservient to Thy Will. Deal with me as it beseemeth Thee, and as it befitteth Thy highness and great glory.

O 'Alí! The bounty of Him Who is the Lord of all worlds hath been, and is still being, vouchsafed unto thee. Arm thyself with His strength and power, and arise to aid His Cause and to magnify His holy name. Let not thine ignorance in human learning and thy inability to read or write grieve thine heart. The doors of His manifold grace are within the mighty grasp of the power of the one true God. He hath opened, and will continue to open, them in the face of all them that serve Him. I fain would hope that this breeze of Divine sweetness will, at all times, continue to be wafted from the meadow of thine heart upon the whole world, in such wise that its effects may be manifested in every land. He it is that hath power over all things. He, verily, is the Most Powerful, the All-Glorious, the Almighty.

CXLIII. Blessed art thou, O My servant, inasmuch as thou hast recognized the Truth, and withdrawn from him who repudiated the All-Merciful, and was condemned as wicked in the Mother Tablet. Walk thou steadfastly in the love of God, and keep straight on in His Faith, and aid Him through the power of thine utterance. Thus biddeth thee the All-Merciful

Who is suffering imprisonment at the hands of His oppressors.

If tribulation touch thee for My sake, call thou to mind My ills and troubles, and remember My banishment and imprisonment. Thus do We devolve on thee what hath descended upon Us from Him Who is the All-Glorious, the All-Wise.

By My Self! The day is approaching when We will have rolled up the world and all that is therein, and spread out a new order in its stead. He, verily, is powerful over all things.

Sanctify thine heart, that thou mayest remember Me; and purge thine ear, that thou mayest hearken unto My words. Set then thy face towards the Spot wherein the throne of thy Lord, the God of Mercy, hath been established, and say: Praise be to Thee, O my Lord, for having enabled me to recognize the Manifestation of Thine own Self, and aided me to fix mine heart on the court of Thy presence, the object of my soul's adoration. I beseech Thee, by Thy name that caused the heavens to be rent and the earth to be cleft asunder, to ordain for me what Thou didst ordain for them that have turned away from all else but Thee, and rested their hearts firmly upon Thee. Grant that I may be seated in Thy presence on the seat of truth, within the Tabernacle of Glory. Powerful art Thou to do what Thou willest. There is none other God but Thee, the All-Glorious, the All-Wise.

CXLIV. The Pen of the Most High hath decreed and imposed upon every one the obligation to teach this Cause. . . . God will, no doubt, inspire whosoever detacheth himself from all else but Him, and will cause the pure waters of wisdom and utterance to gush out and flow copiously from his heart. Verily, thy Lord, the All-Merciful, is powerful to do as He willeth, and ordaineth whatsoever He pleaseth.

Wert thou to consider this world, and realize how fleeting are the things that pertain unto it, thou wouldst choose to tread no path except the path of service to the Cause of thy Lord. None would have the power to deter thee from celebrating His praise, though all men should arise to oppose thee.

Go thou straight on and persevere in His service. Say: O people! The Day, promised unto you in all the Scriptures, is now come. Fear ye God, and withhold not yourselves from recognizing the One Who is the Object of your creation. Hasten ye unto Him. Better is this for you than the world and all that is therein. Would that ye could perceive it!

CXLV. If ye meet the abased or the down-trodden, turn not away disdainfully from them, for the King of Glory ever watcheth over them and surroundeth them with such tenderness as none can fathom except them that have suffered their wishes and desires to be merged in the Will of your Lord, the Gracious, the All-Wise. O ye rich ones of the earth! Flee not from the face of the poor that lieth in the dust, nay rather befriend him and suffer him to recount the tale of the woes with which God's inscrutable Decree hath caused him to be afflicted. By the righteousness of God! Whilst ye consort with him, the Concourse on high will be looking upon you, will be interceding for you, will be extolling your names and glorifying your action. Blessed are the learned that pride not themselves on their attainments; and well is it with the righteous that mock not the sinful, but rather conceal their misdeeds, so that their own shortcomings may remain veiled to men's eyes.

CXLVI. It is Our wish and desire that every one of you may become a source of all goodness unto men, and an example of uprightness to mankind. Beware lest ye prefer yourselves above your neighbors. Fix your gaze upon Him Who is the Temple of God amongst men. He, in truth, hath offered up His life as a ransom for the redemption of the world. He, verily, is the All-Bountiful, the Gracious, the Most High. If any differences arise amongst you, behold Me standing before your face, and overlook the faults of one another for My name's sake and as a token of your love for My manifest and resplendent Cause. We love to see you at all times consorting in amity and concord within the paradise of My good-pleasure, and to inhale from your acts the fragrance of friendliness and unity, of loving-kindness and fellowship.

Thus counselleth you the All-Knowing, the Faithful. We shall always be with you; if We inhale the perfume of your fellowship, Our heart will assuredly rejoice, for naught else can satisfy Us. To this beareth witness every man of true understanding.

CXLVII. The Most Great Name beareth Me witness! How sad if any man were, in this Day, to rest his heart on the transitory things of this world! Arise, and cling firmly to the Cause of God. Be most loving one to another. Burn away, wholly for the sake of the Well-Beloved, the veil of self with the flame of the undying Fire, and with faces joyous and beaming with light, associate with your neighbor. Ye have well observed, in all its aspects, the behavior of Him Who is the Word of Truth amidst you. Ye know full well how hard it is for this Youth to allow, though it be for one night, the heart of any one of the beloved of God to be saddened by Him.

The Word of God hath set the heart of the world afire; how regrettable if ye fail to be enkindled with its flame! Please God, ye will regard this blessed night as the night of unity, will knit your souls together, and resolve to adorn yourselves with the ornament of a goodly and praiseworthy character. Let your principal concern be to rescue the fallen from the slough of impending extinction, and to help him embrace the ancient Faith of God. Your behavior towards your neighbor should be such as to manifest clearly the signs of the one true God, for ye are the first among men to be re-created by His Spirit, the first to adore and bow the knee before Him, the first to circle round His throne of glory. I swear by Him Who hath caused Me to reveal whatever hath pleased Him! Ye are better known to the inmates of the Kingdom on high than ye are known to your own selves. Think ye these words to be vain and empty? Would that ye had the power to perceive the things your Lord, the All-Merciful, doth see—things that attest the excellence of your rank, that bear witness to the greatness of your worth, that proclaim the sublimity of your station! God grant that your desires and unmortified passions may not hinder you from that which hath been ordained for you.

CXLVIII. O Salmán! All that the sages and mystics have said or written have never exceeded, nor can they ever hope to exceed, the limitations to which man's finite mind hath been strictly subjected. To whatever heights the mind of the most exalted of men may soar, however great the depths which the detached and understanding heart can penetrate, such mind and heart can never transcend that which is the creature of their own conceptions and the product of their own thoughts. The meditations of the profoundest thinker, the devotions of the holiest of saints, the highest expressions of praise from either human pen or tongue, are but a reflection of that which hath been created within themselves, through the revelation of the Lord, their God. Whoever pondereth this truth in his heart will readily admit that there are certain limits which no human being can possibly transgress. Every attempt which, from the beginning that hath no beginning, hath been made to visualize and know God is limited by the exigencies of His own creation—a creation which He, through the operation of His own Will and for the purposes of none other but His own Self, hath called into being. Immeasurably exalted is He above the strivings of human mind to grasp His Essence, or of human tongue to describe His mystery. No tie of direct intercourse can ever bind Him to the things He hath created, nor can the most abstruse and most remote allusions of His creatures do justice to His being. Through His world-pervading Will He hath brought into being all created things. He is and hath ever been veiled in the ancient eternity of His own exalted and indivisible Essence, and will everlastingly continue to remain concealed in His inaccessible majesty and glory. All that is in heaven and all that is in the earth have come to exist at His bidding, and by His Will all have stepped out of utter nothingness into the realm of being. How can, therefore, the creature which the Word of God hath fashioned comprehend the nature of Him Who is the Ancient of Days?

CXLIX. Should any man, in this Day, arise and, with absolute detachment from all that is in the heavens and all that is on the earth, set his affections on Him Who is the Day Spring of God's holy Revelation, he will, verily, be empowered to subdue all created things, through the potency of one of the Names of the Lord, his God, the All-Knowing, the All-Wise. Know thou of a certainty that the Day Star of Truth hath, in this Day, shed upon the world a radiance, the like of which bygone ages have never witnessed. Let the light of His glory, O people, shine upon you, and be not of the negligent.

CL. When the victory arriveth, every man shall profess himself as believer and shall hasten to the shelter of God's Faith. Happy are they who in the days of world-encompassing trials have stood fast in the Cause and refused to swerve from its truth.

CLI. Release yourselves, O nightingales of God, from the thorns and brambles of wretchedness and misery, and wing your flight to the rose-garden of unfading splendor. O My friends that dwell upon the dust! Haste forth unto your celestial habitation. Announce unto yourselves the joyful tidings: "He Who is the Best-Beloved is come! He hath crowned Himself with the glory of God's Revelation, and hath unlocked to the face of men the doors of His ancient Paradise." Let all eyes rejoice, and let every ear be gladdened, for now is the time to gaze on His beauty, now is the fit time to hearken to His voice. Proclaim unto every longing lover: "Behold, your Well-Beloved hath come among men!" and to the messengers of the Monarch of love impart the tidings: "Lo, the Adored One hath appeared arrayed in the fullness of His glory!" O lovers of His beauty! Turn the anguish of your separation from Him into the joy of an everlasting reunion, and let the sweetness of His presence dissolve the bitterness of your remoteness from His court.

Behold how the manifold grace of God, which is being showered from the clouds of Divine glory, hath, in this day, encompassed the world. For whereas in days past every lover besought and searched after his Beloved, it is the Beloved Himself Who now is calling His lovers and is inviting them to attain His presence. Take heed lest ye forfeit so precious a favor; beware lest ye belittle so remarkable a token of His grace. Abandon not the incorruptible benefits, and be not content with that which perisheth. Lift up the veil that obscureth your vision, and dispel the darkness with which it is enveloped, that ye may gaze on the naked beauty of the Beloved's face, may behold that which no eye hath beheld, and hear that which no ear hath heard.

Hear Me, ye mortal birds! In the Rose Garden of changeless splendor a Flower hath begun to bloom, compared to which every other flower is but a thorn, and before the brightness of Whose glory the very essence of beauty must pale and wither. Arise, therefore, and, with the whole enthusiasm of your hearts, with all the eagerness of your souls, the full fervor of your will, and the concentrated efforts of your entire being, strive to attain the paradise of His presence, and endeavor to inhale the fragrance of the incorruptible Flower, to breathe the sweet savors of holiness, and to obtain a portion of this perfume of celestial glory. Whoso followeth this counsel will break his chains asunder, will taste the abandonment of enraptured love, will attain unto his heart's desire, and will surrender his soul into the hands of his Beloved. Bursting through his cage, he will, even as the bird of the spirit, wing his flight to his holy and everlasting nest.

Night hath succeeded day, and day hath succeeded night, and the hours and moments of your lives have come and gone, and yet none of you hath, for one instant, consented to detach himself from that which perisheth. Bestir yourselves, that the brief moments that are still yours may not be dissipated and lost. Even as the swiftness of lightning your days shall pass, and your bodies shall be laid to rest beneath a canopy of dust. What can ye then achieve? How can ye atone for your past failure?

The everlasting Candle shineth in its naked glory. Behold how it hath consumed every mortal veil. O ye moth-like lovers of His light! Brave every danger, and consecrate your souls to its consuming flame. O ye that thirst after Him! Strip yourselves of every earthly affection, and hasten to embrace your Beloved. With a zest that none can equal make haste to attain unto Him. The Flower, thus far hidden from the sight of men, is unveiled to your eyes. In the open radiance of His glory He standeth before you. His voice summoneth all the holy and sanctified beings to come and be united with Him. Happy is he that turneth thereunto; well is it with him that hath attained, and gazed on the light of so wondrous a countenance.

CLII. Thine eye is My trust, suffer not the dust of vain desires to becloud its luster. Thine ear is a sign of My bounty, let not the tumult of unseemly motives turn it away from My Word that encompasseth all creation. Thine heart is My treasury, allow not the treacherous hand of self to rob thee of the pearls which I have treasured therein. Thine hand is a symbol of My loving-kindness, hinder it not from holding fast unto My guarded and hidden Tablets. . . . Unasked, I have showered upon thee My grace. Unpetitioned, I have fulfilled thy wish. In spite of thy undeserving, I have singled thee out for My richest, My incalculable favors. . . . O My servants! Be as resigned and submissive as the earth, that from the soil of your being there may blossom the fragrant, the holy and multicolored hyacinths of My knowledge. Be ablaze as the fire, that ye may burn away the veils of heedlessness and set aglow, through the quickening energies of the love of God, the chilled and wayward heart. Be light and untrammeled as the breeze, that ye may obtain admittance into the precincts of My court, My inviolable Sanctuary.

CLIII. O banished and faithful friend! Quench the thirst of heedlessness with the sanctified waters of My grace, and chase the gloom of remoteness through the morning-light of My Divine presence. Suffer not the habitation wherein dwelleth My undying love for thee to be destroyed through the tyranny of covetous desires, and overcloud not the beauty of the heavenly Youth with the dust of self and passion. Clothe thyself with the essence of righteousness, and let thine heart be afraid of none except God. Obstruct not the luminous spring of thy soul with the thorns and brambles of vain and inordinate affections, and impede not the flow of the living waters that stream from the fountain of thine heart. Set all thy hope in God, and cleave tenaciously to His unfailing mercy. Who else but Him can enrich the destitute, and deliver the fallen from his abasement?

O My servants! Were ye to discover the hidden, the shoreless oceans of My incorruptible wealth, ye would, of a certainty, esteem as nothing the world, nay, the entire creation. Let the flame of search burn with such fierceness within your hearts as to enable you to attain your supreme and most exalted goal—the station at which ye can draw nigh unto, and be united with, your Best-Beloved. . . .

O My servants! Let not your vain hopes and idle fancies sap the foundations of your belief in the All-Glorious God, inasmuch as such imaginings have been wholly unprofitable unto men, and failed to direct their steps unto the straight Path. Think ye, O My servants, that the Hand of My all-encompassing, My overshadowing, and transcendent sovereignty is chained up, that the flow of Mine ancient, My ceaseless, and all-pervasive mercy is checked, or that the clouds of My sublime and unsurpassed favors have ceased to rain their gifts upon men? Can ye imagine that the wondrous works that have proclaimed My divine and resistless power are withdrawn, or that the potency of My will and purpose hath been deterred from directing the destinies of mankind? If it be not so, wherefore, then, have ye striven to prevent the deathless Beauty of My sacred and gracious Countenance from being unveiled to men's eyes? Why have ye struggled to hinder the Manifestation of the Almighty and All-Glorious Being from shedding the radiance of His Revelation upon the earth? Were ye to be fair in your judgment, ye would readily recognize how the realities of all created things are inebriated with the joy of this new and wondrous Revelation, how all the atoms of the earth have been illuminated through the brightness of its glory. Vain and wretched is that which ye have imagined and still imagine!

Retrace your steps, O My servants, and incline your hearts to Him Who is the Source of your creation. Deliver yourselves from your evil and corrupt affections, and hasten to embrace the light of the undying Fire that gloweth on the Sinai of this mysterious and transcendent Revelation. Corrupt not the holy, the all-embracing, and primal Word of God, and seek not to profane its sanctity or to debase its exalted character. O heedless ones! Though the wonders of My mercy have encompassed all created things, both visible and invisible, and though the revelations of My grace and bounty have permeated every atom of the universe, yet the rod with which I can chastise the wicked is grievous, and the fierceness of Mine anger against them terrible. With ears that are sanctified from vain-glory and worldly desires hearken unto the counsels which I, in My merciful kindness, have revealed unto you, and with your inner and outer eyes contemplate the evidences of My marvelous Revelation. . . .

O My servants! Deprive not yourselves of the unfading and resplendent Light that shineth within the Lamp of Divine glory. Let the flame of the love of God burn brightly within your radiant hearts. Feed it with the oil of Divine guidance, and protect it within the shelter of your constancy. Guard it within the globe of trust and detachment from all else but

God, so that the evil whisperings of the ungodly may not extinguish its light. O My servants! My holy, My divinely ordained Revelation may be likened unto an ocean in whose depths are concealed innumerable pearls of great price, of surpassing luster. It is the duty of every seeker to bestir himself and strive to attain the shores of this ocean, so that he may, in proportion to the eagerness of his search and the efforts he hath exerted, partake of such benefits as have been pre-ordained in God's irrevocable and hidden Tablets. If no one be willing to direct his steps towards its shores, if every one should fail to arise and find Him, can such a failure be said to have robbed this ocean of its power or to have lessened, to any degree, its treasures? How vain, how contemptible, are the imaginations which your hearts have devised, and are still devising! O My servants! The one true God is My witness! This most great, this fathomless and surging Ocean is near, astonishingly near, unto you. Behold it is closer to you than your life-vein! Swift as the twinkling of an eye ye can, if ye but wish it, reach and partake of this imperishable favor, this God-given grace, this incorruptible gift, this most potent and unspeakably glorious bounty.

O My servants! Could ye apprehend with what wonders of My munificence and bounty I have willed to entrust your souls, ye would, of a truth, rid yourselves of attachment to all created things, and would gain a true knowledge of your own selves—a knowledge which is the same as the comprehension of Mine own Being. Ye would find yourselves independent of all else but Me, and would perceive, with your inner and outer eye, and as manifest as the revelation of My effulgent Name, the seas of My loving-kindness and bounty moving within you. Suffer not your idle fancies, your evil passions, your insincerity and blindness of heart to dim the luster, or stain the sanctity, of so lofty a station. Ye are even as the bird which soareth, with the full force of its mighty wings and with complete and joyous confidence, through the immensity of the heavens, until, impelled to satisfy its hunger, it turneth longingly to the water and clay of the earth below it, and, having been entrapped in the mesh of its desire, findeth itself impotent to resume its flight to the realms whence it came. Powerless to shake off the burden weighing on its sullied wings, that bird, hitherto an inmate of the heavens, is now forced to seek a dwelling-place upon the dust. Wherefore, O My servants, defile not your wings with the clay of waywardness and vain desires, and suffer them not to be stained with the dust of envy and hate, that ye may not be hindered from soaring in the heavens of My divine knowledge.

O My servants! Through the might of God and His power, and out of the treasury of His knowledge and wisdom, I have brought forth and revealed unto you the pearls that lay concealed in the depths of His everlasting ocean. I have summoned the Maids of

Heaven to emerge from behind the veil of concealment, and have clothed them with these words of
Mine—words of consummate power and wisdom. I
have, moreover, with the hand of divine power, unsealed the choice wine of My Revelation, and have
wafted its holy, its hidden, and musk-laden fragrance
upon all created things. Who else but yourselves is to
be blamed if ye choose to remain unendowed with so
great an outpouring of God's transcendent and all-
encompassing grace, with so bright a revelation of
His resplendent mercy? . . .

O My servants! There shineth nothing else in Mine
heart except the unfading light of the Morn of
Divine guidance, and out of My mouth proceedeth
naught but the essence of truth, which the Lord
your God hath revealed. Follow not, therefore, your
earthly desires, and violate not the Covenant of God,
nor break your pledge to Him. With firm determination, with the whole affection of your heart, and
with the full force of your words, turn ye unto Him,
and walk not in the ways of the foolish. The world
is but a show, vain and empty, a mere nothing, bearing the semblance of reality. Set not your affections
upon it. Break not the bond that uniteth you with
your Creator, and be not of those that have erred and
strayed from His ways. Verily I say, the world is like
the vapor in a desert, which the thirsty dreameth to
be water and striveth after it with all his might, until
when he cometh unto it, he findeth it to be mere

illusion. It may, moreover, be likened unto the life-less image of the beloved whom the lover hath sought and found, in the end, after long search and to his utmost regret, to be such as cannot "fatten nor appease his hunger."

O My servants! Sorrow not if, in these days and on this earthly plane, things contrary to your wishes have been ordained and manifested by God, for days of blissful joy, of heavenly delight, are assuredly in store for you. Worlds, holy and spiritually glorious, will be unveiled to your eyes. You are destined by Him, in this world and hereafter, to partake of their benefits, to share in their joys, and to obtain a portion of their sustaining grace. To each and every one of them you will, no doubt, attain.

CLIV. Warn, O Salmán, the beloved of the one true God, not to view with too critical an eye the sayings and writings of men. Let them rather approach such sayings and writings in a spirit of open-mindedness and loving sympathy. Those men, however, who, in this Day, have been led to assail, in their inflammatory writings, the tenets of the Cause of God, are to be treated differently. It is incumbent upon all men, each according to his ability, to refute the arguments of those that have attacked the Faith of God. Thus hath it been decreed by Him Who is the All-Powerful, the Almighty. He that wisheth to promote the Cause of the one true God, let him promote it through his pen and tongue, rather than have recourse to sword or violence. We have, on a previous occasion, revealed this injunction, and We now confirm it, if ye be of them that comprehend. By the righteousness of Him Who, in this Day, crieth within the inmost heart of all created things: "God, there is none other God besides Me!" If any man were to arise to defend, in his writings, the Cause of God against its assailants, such a man, however inconsiderable his share, shall be so honored in the world to come that the Concourse on high would envy his glory. No pen can depict the loftiness of his station, neither can any tongue describe its splendor. For whosoever standeth firm and steadfast in this holy, this glorious, and exalted Revelation, such power shall be given him as to enable him to face and withstand all that is in heaven and on earth. Of this God is Himself a witness.

O ye beloved of God! Repose not yourselves on your couches, nay bestir yourselves as soon as ye recognize your Lord, the Creator, and hear of the things which have befallen Him, and hasten to His assistance. Unloose your tongues, and proclaim unceasingly His Cause. This shall be better for you than all the treasures of the past and of the future, if ye be of them that comprehend this truth.

CLV. The first duty prescribed by God for His servants is the recognition of Him Who is the Day Spring of His Revelation and the Fountain of His laws, Who representeth the Godhead in both the Kingdom of His Cause and the world of creation. Whoso achieveth this duty hath attained unto all good; and whoso is deprived thereof, hath gone astray, though he be the author of every righteous deed. It behoveth every one who reacheth this most sublime station, this summit of transcendent glory, to observe every ordinance of Him Who is the Desire of the world. These twin duties are inseparable. Neither is acceptable without the other. Thus hath it been decreed by Him Who is the Source of Divine inspiration.

They whom God hath endued with insight will readily recognize that the precepts laid down by God constitute the highest means for the maintenance of order in the world and the security of its peoples. He that turneth away from them is accounted among the abject and foolish. We, verily, have commanded you to refuse the dictates of your evil passions and corrupt desires, and not to transgress the bounds which the Pen of the Most High hath fixed, for these are the breath of life unto all created things. The seas of Divine wisdom and divine utterance have risen under the breath of the breeze of the All-Merciful. Hasten to drink your fill, O men of understanding! They that have violated the Covenant of God by breaking His commandments, and have turned back on their heels, these have erred grievously in the sight of God, the All-Possessing, the Most High.

O ye peoples of the world! Know assuredly that My commandments are the lamps of My loving providence among My servants, and the keys of My mercy for My creatures. Thus hath it been sent down from the heaven of the Will of your Lord, the Lord of Revelation. Were any man to taste the sweetness of the words which the lips of the All-Merciful have willed to utter, he would, though the treasures of the earth be in his possession, renounce them one and all, that he might vindicate the truth of even one of His commandments, shining above the dayspring of His bountiful care and loving-kindness.

Say: From My laws the sweet smelling savor of My garment can be smelled, and by their aid the standards of victory will be planted upon the highest peaks. The Tongue of My power hath, from the heaven of My omnipotent glory, addressed to My creation these words: "Observe My commandments, for the love of My beauty." Happy is the lover that hath inhaled the divine fragrance of his Best-Beloved from these words, laden with the perfume of a grace which no tongue can describe. By My life! He who hath drunk the choice wine of fairness from the hands of My bountiful favor will circle around My commandments that shine above the dayspring of My creation.

Think not that We have revealed unto you a mere code of laws. Nay, rather, We have unsealed the choice Wine with the fingers of might and power. To this beareth witness that which the Pen of Revelation hath revealed. Meditate upon this, O men of insight! . . .

Whenever My laws appear like the sun in the heaven of Mine utterance, they must be faithfully obeyed by all, though My decree be such as to cause the heaven of every religion to be cleft asunder. He doth what He pleaseth. He chooseth; and none may question His choice. Whatsoever He, the Well-Beloved, ordaineth, the same is, verily, beloved. To this He Who is the Lord of all creation beareth Me witness. Whoso hath inhaled the sweet fragrance of the All-Merciful, and recognized the Source of this utterance, will welcome with his own eyes the shafts of the enemy, that he may establish the truth of the laws of God amongst men. Well is it with him that hath turned thereunto, and apprehended the meaning of His decisive decree.

CLVI. He Who is the Eternal Truth hath, from the Day Spring of Glory, directed His eyes towards the people of Bahá, and is addressing them in these words: "Address yourselves to the promotion of the well-being and tranquillity of the children of men. Bend your minds and wills to the education of the peoples and kindreds of the earth, that haply the dissensions that divide it may, through the power of the Most Great Name, be blotted out from its face, and all mankind become the upholders of one Order, and the inhabitants of one City. Illumine and hallow your hearts; let them not be profaned by the thorns of hate or the thistles of malice. Ye dwell in one world, and have been created through the operation of one Will. Blessed is he who mingleth with all men in a spirit of utmost kindliness and love."

CLVII. They that have forsaken their country for the purpose of teaching Our Cause—these shall the Faithful Spirit strengthen through its power. A company of Our chosen angels shall go forth with them, as bidden by Him Who is the Almighty, the All-Wise. How great the blessedness that awaiteth him that hath attained the honor of serving the Almighty! By My life! No act, however great, can compare with it, except such deeds as have been ordained by God, the All-Powerful, the Most Mighty. Such a service is, indeed, the prince of all goodly deeds, and the ornament of every goodly act. Thus hath it been ordained by Him Who is the Sovereign Revealer, the Ancient of Days.

Whoso ariseth to teach Our Cause must needs detach himself from all earthly things, and regard, at all times, the triumph of Our Faith as his supreme objective. This hath, verily, been decreed in the Guarded Tablet. And when he determineth to leave his home, for the sake of the Cause of his Lord, let him put his whole trust in God, as the best provision for his journey, and array himself with the robe of virtue. Thus hath it been decreed by God, the Almighty, the All-Praised.

If he be kindled with the fire of His love, if he forgoeth all created things, the words he uttereth shall set on fire them that hear him. Verily, thy Lord is the Omniscient, the All-Informed. Happy is the man that hath heard Our voice, and answered Our call. He, in truth, is of them that shall be brought nigh unto Us.

CLVIII.   God hath prescribed unto every one the duty of teaching His Cause. Whoever ariseth to discharge this duty, must needs, ere he proclaimeth His Message, adorn himself with the ornament of an upright and praiseworthy character, so that his words may attract the hearts of such as are receptive to his call. Without it, he can never hope to influence his hearers.

CLIX.   Consider the pettiness of men's minds. They ask for that which injureth them, and cast away the thing that profiteth them. They are, indeed, of those that are far astray. We find some men desiring liberty, and priding themselves therein. Such men are in the depths of ignorance.

Liberty must, in the end, lead to sedition, whose flames none can quench. Thus warneth you He Who is the Reckoner, the All-Knowing. Know ye that the embodiment of liberty and its symbol is the animal.

That which beseemeth man is submission unto such restraints as will protect him from his own ignorance, and guard him against the harm of the mischief-maker. Liberty causeth man to overstep the bounds of propriety, and to infringe on the dignity of his station. It debaseth him to the level of extreme depravity and wickedness.

Regard men as a flock of sheep that need a shepherd for their protection. This, verily, is the truth, the certain truth. We approve of liberty in certain circumstances, and refuse to sanction it in others. We, verily, are the All-Knowing.

Say: True liberty consisteth in man's submission unto My commandments, little as ye know it. Were men to observe that which We have sent down unto them from the Heaven of Revelation, they would, of a certainty, attain unto perfect liberty. Happy is the man that hath apprehended the Purpose of God in whatever He hath revealed from the Heaven of His Will that pervadeth all created things. Say: The liberty that profiteth you is to be found nowhere except in complete servitude unto God, the Eternal Truth. Whoso hath tasted of its sweetness will refuse to barter it for all the dominion of earth and heaven.

CLX. He is indeed a true believer in the unity of God who, in this Day, will regard Him as One immeasurably exalted above all the comparisons and likenesses with which men have compared Him. He hath erred grievously who hath mistaken these comparisons and likenesses for God Himself. Consider the relation between the craftsman and his handiwork, between the painter and his painting. Can it ever be maintained that the work their hands have produced is the same as themselves? By Him Who is the Lord of the Throne above and of earth below! They can be regarded in no other light except as evidences that proclaim the excellence and perfection of their author.

O Shaykh, O thou who hast surrendered thy will to God! By self-surrender and perpetual union with God is meant that men should merge their will wholly in the Will of God, and regard their desires as utter nothingness beside His Purpose. Whatsoever the Creator commandeth His creatures to observe, the same must they diligently, and with the utmost joy and eagerness, arise and fulfil. They should in no wise allow their fancy to obscure their judgment, neither should they regard their own imaginings as the voice of the Eternal. In the Prayer of Fasting We have revealed: "Should Thy Will decree that out of Thy mouth these words proceed and be addressed unto them, 'Observe, for My Beauty's sake, the fast, O people, and set no limit to its duration,' I swear by the majesty of Thy glory, that every one of them will faithfully observe it, will abstain from whatsoever will violate Thy law, and will continue to do so until they yield up their souls unto Thee." In this con-

[337]

sisteth the complete surrender of one's will to the Will of God. Meditate on this, that thou mayest drink in the waters of everlasting life which flow through the words of the Lord of all mankind, and mayest testify that the one true God hath ever been immeasurably exalted above His creatures. He, verily, is the Incomparable, the Ever-Abiding, the Omniscient, the All-Wise. The station of absolute self-surrender transcendeth, and will ever remain exalted above, every other station.

It behoveth thee to consecrate thyself to the Will of God. Whatsoever hath been revealed in His Tablets is but a reflection of His Will. So complete must be thy consecration, that every trace of worldly desire will be washed from thine heart. This is the meaning of true unity.

Do thou beseech God to enable thee to remain steadfast in this path, and to aid thee to guide the peoples of the world to Him Who is the manifest and sovereign Ruler, Who hath revealed Himself in a distinct attire, Who giveth utterance to a Divine and specific Message. This is the essence of faith and certitude. They that are the worshipers of the idol which their imaginations have carved, and who call it Inner Reality, such men are in truth accounted among the heathen. To this hath the All-Merciful borne witness in His Tablets. He, verily, is the All-Knowing, the All-Wise.

CLXI. Gird up the loins of thine endeavor, that haply thou mayest guide thy neighbor to the law of God, the Most Merciful. Such an act, verily, excelleth all other acts in the sight of God, the All-Possessing, the Most High. Such must be thy steadfastness in the Cause of God, that no earthly thing whatsoever will have the power to deter thee from thy duty. Though the powers of earth be leagued against thee, though all men dispute with thee, thou must remain unshaken.

Be unrestrained as the wind, while carrying the Message of Him Who hath caused the Dawn of Divine Guidance to break. Consider, how the wind, faithful to that which God hath ordained, bloweth upon all the regions of the earth, be they inhabited or desolate. Neither the sight of desolation, nor the evidences of prosperity, can either pain or please it. It bloweth in every direction, as bidden by its Creator. So should be every one that claimeth to be a lover of the one true God. It behoveth him to fix his gaze upon the fundamentals of His Faith, and to labor diligently for its propagation. Wholly for the sake of God he should proclaim His Message, and with that same spirit accept whatever response his words may evoke in his hearer. He who shall accept and believe, shall receive his reward; and he who shall turn away, shall receive none other than his own punishment.

On the eve of Our departure from 'Iráq, We have

warned the faithful to anticipate the appearance of the Birds of Darkness. There can be no doubt whatever that the croaking of the Raven shall be raised in certain lands, as it hath been heard in recent years. Whatever may betide, seek refuge in the one true God, that He may shield you from the wiles of the impostor.

Verily I say, in this most mighty Revelation, all the Dispensations of the past have attained their highest, their final consummation. Thus counselleth you your Lord, the All-Knowing, the All-Wise. Praise be to God, the Lord of all worlds.

CLXII. The All-Merciful hath conferred upon man the faculty of vision, and endowed him with the power of hearing. Some have described him as the "lesser world," when, in reality, he should be regarded as the "greater world." The potentialities inherent in the station of man, the full measure of his destiny on earth, the innate excellence of his reality, must all be manifested in this promised Day of God.

The Pen of the Most High hath, at all times and under all conditions, remembered, with joy and tenderness, His loved ones, and hath counselled them to follow in His way. Well is it with him whom the changes and chances of this world have failed to deter from recognizing the Day Spring of the Unity of God, who hath quaffed, with unswerving resolve, and in the name of the Self-Subsisting, the sealed wine of

His Revelation. Such a man shall be numbered with the inmates of Paradise, in the Book of God, the Lord of all worlds.

CLXIII. All praise be to God Who hath adorned the world with an ornament, and arrayed it with a vesture, of which it can be despoiled by no earthly power, however mighty its battalions, however vast its wealth, however profound its influence. Say: the essence of all power is God's, the highest and the last End of all creation. The source of all majesty is God's, the Object of the adoration of all that is in the heavens and all that is on the earth. Such forces as have their origin in this world of dust are, by their very nature, unworthy of consideration.

Say: The springs that sustain the life of these birds are not of this world. Their source is far above the reach and ken of human apprehension. Who is there that can put out the light which the snow-white Hand of God hath lit? Where is he to be found that hath the power to quench the fire which hath been kindled through the might of thy Lord, the All-Powerful, the All-Compelling, the Almighty? It is the Hand of Divine might that hath extinguished the flames of dissension. Powerful is He to do that which He pleaseth. He saith: Be; and it is. Say: The fierce gales and whirlwinds of the world and its peoples can never shake the foundation upon which the rock-like stability of My chosen ones is based. Gracious God! What could have prompted these people to enslave and imprison the loved ones of Him Who is the Eternal Truth? . . . The day, however, is approaching when the faithful will behold the Day Star of justice shining in its full splendor from the Day Spring of glory. Thus instructeth thee the Lord of all being in this, His grievous Prison.

CLXIV. Members of the human race! Hold ye fast by the Cord which no man can sever. This will, indeed, profit you all the days of your life, for its strength is of God, the Lord of all worlds. Cleave ye to justice and fairness, and turn away from the whisperings of the foolish, them that are estranged from God, that have decked their heads with the ornament of the learned, and have condemned to death Him Who is the Fountain of wisdom. My name hath uplifted them to lofty grades, and yet, no sooner did I reveal Myself to their eyes than they, with manifest injustice, pronounced the sentence of My death. Thus hath Our Pen revealed the truth, and yet the people are sunk in heedlessness.

Whoso cleaveth to justice, can, under no circumstances, transgress the limits of moderation. He discerneth the truth in all things, through the guidance of Him Who is the All-Seeing. The civilization, so often vaunted by the learned exponents of arts and sciences, will, if allowed to overleap the bounds of moderation, bring great evil upon men. Thus warneth you He Who is the All-Knowing. If carried to excess, civilization will prove as prolific a source of evil as it had been of goodness when kept within the restraints of moderation. Meditate on this, O people, and be not of them that wander distraught in the wilderness of error. The day is approaching when its flame will devour the cities, when the Tongue of Grandeur will proclaim: "The Kingdom is God's, the Almighty, the All-Praised!"

All other things are subject to this same principle of moderation. Render thanks unto thy Lord Who hath remembered thee in this wondrous Tablet. All-Praise be to God, the Lord of the glorious throne.

Were any man to ponder in his heart that which the Pen of the Most High hath revealed and to taste of its sweetness, he would, of a certainty, find himself emptied and delivered from his own desires, and utterly subservient to the Will of the Almighty. Happy is the man that hath attained so high a station, and hath not deprived himself of so bountiful a grace.

In this Day, We can neither approve the conduct of the fearful that seeketh to dissemble his faith, nor sanction the behavior of the avowed believer that clamorously asserteth his allegiance to this Cause. Both should observe the dictates of wisdom, and strive diligently to serve the best interests of the Faith.

Let every man observe and meditate on the conduct of this wronged One. We have, ever since the dawn of this Revelation until the present time, refused either to hide Ourself from Our enemies, or to withdraw from the companionship of Our friends. Though encompassed with a myriad griefs and afflictions, We have, with mighty confidence, summoned the peoples of the earth to the Day Spring of Glory. The Pen of the Most High is disinclined to recount, in this connection, the woes it hath suffered. To reveal them would, no doubt, plunge into sorrow the favored among the faithful, they that truly uphold the unity of God and are wholly devoted to His Cause. He, verily, speaketh the truth, and is the All-Hearing, the All-Knowing. Our life hath, for the most part, been spent in the midst of Our enemies. Witness how We are, at present, living in a nest of serpents.

This Holy Land hath been mentioned and extolled in all the sacred Scriptures. In it have appeared the Prophets of God and His chosen Ones. This is the wilderness in which all the Messengers of God have wandered, from which their cry, "Here am I, here am I, O my God" was raised. This is the promised Land in which He Who is the Revelation of God was destined to be made manifest. This is the Vale of God's unsearchable decree, the snow-white Spot, the Land of unfading splendor. Whatever hath come to pass in this Day hath been foretold in the Scriptures of old. These same Scriptures, however, unanimously condemn the people that inhabit this land. They have, at one time, been stigmatized as the "generation of vipers." Behold how this wronged One is now, whilst surrounded by a "generation of vipers," calling aloud and summoning all men to Him Who is the world's Ultimate Desire, the Summit and Day Spring of Glory. Happy is the man that hath hearkened to the voice of Him Who is the Lord of the Kingdom of Utterance, and woe betide the heedless, they that have strayed far from His truth.

CLXV.   Know thou that every hearing ear, if kept pure and undefiled, must, at all times and from every direction, hearken to the voice that uttereth these holy words: "Verily, we are God's, and to Him shall we return." The mysteries of man's physical death and of his return have not been divulged, and still remain unread. By the righteousness of God! Were they to be revealed, they would evoke such fear and sorrow that some would perish, while others would be so filled with gladness as to wish for death, and beseech, with unceasing longing, the one true God—exalted be His glory—to hasten their end.

Death proffereth unto every confident believer the cup that is life indeed. It bestoweth joy, and is the bearer of gladness. It conferreth the gift of everlasting life.

As to those that have tasted of the fruit of man's earthly existence, which is the recognition of the one

true God, exalted be His glory, their life hereafter
is such as We are unable to describe. The knowledge
thereof is with God, alone, the Lord of all worlds.

CLXVI. Whoso layeth claim to a Revelation direct
from God, ere the expiration of a full thousand years,
such a man is assuredly a lying impostor. We pray
God that He may graciously assist him to retract and
repudiate such claim. Should he repent, God will, no
doubt, forgive him. If, however, he persisteth in his
error, God will, assuredly, send down one who will
deal mercilessly with him. Terrible, indeed, is God in
punishing! Whosoever interpreteth this verse otherwise than its obvious meaning is deprived of the Spirit
of God and of His mercy which encompasseth all
created things. Fear God, and follow not your idle
fancies. Nay, rather follow the bidding of your Lord,
the Almighty, the All-Wise.

GLOSSARY AND NOTES

'Abdu'l-'Azíz:
: The Sulṭán who decreed each of Bahá'u'lláh's three banishments.

'Abdu'l-Bahá:
: The appointed Successor of Bahá'u'lláh and Center of His Covenant. (1844-1921).

'Abdu'lláh-i-Ubayy:
: An opponent of Muḥammad.

Abhá:
: Bahá means "glory". Abhá is its superlative. Both are titles of Bahá'u'lláh and of His Kingdom.

Abú 'Ámir:
: An opponent of Muḥammad.

Afnán:
: Lit. "twigs". Denotes relatives of the Báb.

'Akká:
: The prison city in Palestine where Bahá'u'lláh was finally exiled. He arrived there on August 31, 1868.

'Alí:
: The first Imám; cousin and first disciple of Muḥammad and married to His daughter Fáṭimih.

'Alí Muḥammad:
: Siyyid 'Alí Muḥammad, born in Shíráz, Persia, on October 20, 1819; the "Point of the Bayán" and the "Báb" and precursor of Bahá'u'lláh.

Ancient of Days:
: A title of God, peculiar in the Bible to the Book of Daniel.

Annas:
: High Priest of the Jews and father-in-law to Caiaphas (John 18. V.13.).

Aqdas:
: The greatest of Bahá'u'lláh's works containing His laws and ordinances (1873).

Ashraf:
: Siyyid Ashraf, born in the Fort of Zanján during the siege.

Báb, The:
: The Herald of the Faith (1819-1850).

Bahá:
: A title given to Bahá'u'lláh by the Báb.

Bahá'u'lláh:
: The Founder of the Bahá'í Faith (1817-1892).

Balál:	An Ethiopian slave in Mecca, illiterate and despised, but transformed by his recognition of Muḥammad.
Bayán:	The greatest doctrinal work of the Founder of the Bábí Dispensation (lit. "Exposition").
Burning Bush:	See Exod. 3.V.2. Symbolic of God's presence in the heart of Moses.
Caiaphas:	High Priest and President of the Court that condemned Jesus.
Carmel, Mount:	One of the sacred spots in Bahá'í history, where are the shrines of the Báb and of 'Abdu'l-Bahá and memorials to other members of 'Abdu'l-Bahá's family.
City of Certitude:	A condition of high spiritual attainment.
Day Star of Muḥammad:	Symbol of the Prophet as enlightening the world.
Dhabíḥ:	Ishmael, famous Bahá'í and brother of Mírzá Jání of Káshán (see *The Dawn-Breakers*). Given this title (sacrifice) by Bahá'u'lláh.
Divine Elixir:	Symbol of the power of faith to confer eternal life upon man; from "elixir", an imaginary liquor supposed to prolong human life indefinitely.
Divine Messenger:	Prophet of God. The Great Soul, the All-Perfect One through whom such a Revelation is given.
Divine Messiah:	The Divine King and Deliverer expected by the Hebrews.
Gabriel:	Said to be the highest of the angels, and to hover over the throne of God and shelter it with his wings.
Ḥusayn:	The third Imám, the Martyr of Karbilá.
Imám 'Alí:	The first Imám, and son-in-law of the Prophet.
Isaiah, Book of:	See Isaiah 2.V.10.

Islám:	Lit. "Obedience to the will of God," the name given to the religion of Muḥammad.
Javád:	Ḥájí Siyyid Javád, one of the earliest Bábís, extolled by both the Báb and later by Bahá'u'lláh whom he met in Baghdád.
Kaaba:	The Shrine which holds the Black Stone in the Mosque at Mecca.
Ka'b-ibn-i-Ashraf:	An implaccable foe of Muḥammad whose life he sought.
Kamál:	Ḥájí Mírzá Kamál, a famous Bábí of high education who met and recognized the station of Bahá'u'lláh in Baghdád before His declaration. He wished to tell the News to everyone and was sent back to Persia.
Karbilá:	The city in 'Iráq where the Imám Ḥusayn was martyred and where he is buried. One of the two "supreme shrines," the other being Najaf.
Kawthar:	A river in Paradise, and the source of all other rivers.
Lamp of God, The:	The spiritual light shed by God's prophet.
Manifestation:	One who is the "express image" of the perfections and attributes of God.
Mecca:	The city where Muḥammad was born and where he declared Himself.
Medina:	The city which sheltered Muḥammad and where He is buried; esteemed as second only to Mecca in sanctity.
Mihdí:	Title of the Manifestation expected by Islám.
Most Great Name, The:	A title of Bahá'u'lláh.
Muḥammad:	Lit. "The Praised One." The Founder of Islám, the son of 'Abdu'lláh of the family of Háshim, born in Mecca in (it is said) the year 570 A.D.

Mustaghá<u>th</u>:	Lit. "He who is invoked." By reference to the numerical value of this word, the Báb reveals the ninth year of this Era (A.D. 1853) as the date of Bahá'u'lláh's manifestation.
Nabíl-i-A'ẓam:	The Bahá'í title of Muḥammad-i-Zarandí, a devoted follower of the Báb and Bahá'u'lláh, author of the historical work known as "Nabíl's Narrative."
Naḍr-ibn-i-Ḥári<u>th</u>:	An opponent of Muḥammad.
Nimrod:	The persecutor of Abraham.
Párán:	A mountain-range north of Sinai, used to typify a place of revelation.
Pentateuch:	The first five books of the Bible, attributed to Moses.
Qá'im:	The Promised One of Islám.
Qayyúmu'l-Asmá:	One of the chief works of the Báb.
Quintessence:	The last or highest essence of an object.
Qur'án:	The Scripture of the Muḥammadans, written in the Arabic language.
Revelation:	The Unveiling by God to men of something which hitherto He had hidden from them.
Riḍván:	The custodian of Paradise. Used to denote Paradise itself.
Sadratu'l-Muntahá:	The name of a tree planted at the end of a road to serve as a guide; a symbol of a Manifestation.
Salmán, or <u>Shaykh</u> Salmán:	Born in southern Persia, an illiterate, he became one of the most beloved and most devoted disciples of Bahá'u'lláh who entrusted him with many dangerous and important missions.
Salsabíl:	A fountain in Paradise.
Seal of the Prophets:	A title of Muḥammad, referring to the approaching close of the Prophetic Cycle.

S_h_áh:	Náṣiri'd-Dín S_h_áh.
S_h_ay_kh_:	Referring to S_h_ay_kh_ Salmán.
S_h_í'ih:	A Muḥammadan sect distinguished by its spiritual doctrine of the Imámate and represented by the S_h_áh.
Shoghi Effendi:	Grandson of 'Abdu'l-Bahá and Guardian of the Bahá'í Faith.
Sinai:	The Mountain where God gave the tables of the Law to Moses; sometimes an emblem of the human heart which is the place of God's descent.
Sulṭán:	Sultán 'Abdu'l-Azíz.
Sunní:	The larger and more powerful of the two great Islamic sects, represented by the Sulṭán, the outward and visible Defender of the Faith.
Súriy-i-Ra'ís:	Tablet of Bahá'u'lláh revealed in Adrianople.
Ṭá, Land of:	Meaning Ṭihrán, being the initial letter of the name.
Tablet to Ra'ís:	Epistle of Bahá'u'lláh to 'Álí Pás_h_á the Grand Vazír.
Talisman:	Lit. a charm which drew down the power of heaven to protect its wearer. A symbol of man protected by the power of God.
Ṭihrán:	The birthplace of Bahá'u'lláh (November 12, 1817) and capital of Irán.
Torah:	The Pentateuch of Moses.
Zá, Land of:	Meaning Zanján, being the initial letter of the name.
Zanján:	Capital of the district of K_h_amsih and scene of the martyrdom of some 1800 Bábís.
Zion:	A hill in Jerusalem, the site of the royal residence of David and his successors.

—Prepared by George Townshend

INDEX

INDEX

INDEX

INDEX

INDEX

INDEX

INDEX

INDEX

Manifestations
  sovereignty of, 26, 31, 47, 67, 72–73
  station, two-fold, 22, 48, 50–55, 66–67
  successive, 68, 73, 74, 91, 174, 269
  Voice of God, 50, 55, 66

Mankind
  call of Bahá'u'lláh to (see Bahá'u'lláh)
  condition of, today, 39–45, 81, 136, 137, 196, 213, 216, 218, 255
  creation of, 231
  dependent upon Manifestation, 66, 67, 179
  duties of, 4, 5, 8, 14, 94, 105, 261, 289, 290, 330–331
  in Day of God, 263
  inequality of, 149, 187–189
  maturity, 77
  oneness of, 81, 95, 140, 214, 217, 250, 255, 260, 288, 334
  regenerated by Word of God, 68, 84–85, 97, 136, 137, 141, 196, 313
  unity of
    enjoined, 6, 9, 11, 95, 96, 140, 196, 203, 215, 217, 218, 249, 254, 315, 334
    meaning of, 338
    power of, 288
    through Revelation of Bahá'u'lláh, 97, 243, 255, 286, 287–288, 316, 333

Martyrs, 109, 121, 135, 180–182
Material possessions (see Possessions)
Mecca and Medina, 83
Messiah still expected, 20
Metals, transmutation of, 197, 198, 200
Mihdí, 114
Mind (see Man)
Minister to Sháh, Tablet to, 219–231

Miracle requested from Bahá'u'lláh, 131
Moderation, 216, 235, 251, 342, 343
Moses, 20, 23, 51, 57, 62, 88, 221, 270
  opposition to, 19
Most Great Name, power of, 28, 34, 121, 189, 242, 286, 333
Most Great Peace, 249, 254
Mount Carmel, 14, 15, 16, 211
Muḥammad, 51, 67, 69, 76, 77, 83, 101, 102, 270
  afflictions of, 24, 25
  oneness with Christ, 21
  sovereignty established, 24, 26
  why opposed by Jews, 22, 23, 24, 57
  words of, 21, 25, 162
Muḥammad, Tablet to, 111
Muḥammad-'Alí, Tablet to, 305
Muṣṭafá, Tablet to, 119
Mustagháth, time of, 73
Mystics, 317

Nabíl-i-A'ẓam, Tablet to, 302
Naḍr-ibn-i-Ḥáriṯh, 25
Name, Most Great, 28, 121, 189, 190, 203, 242, 246, 316, 333
Names of God, 258, 274, 293, 319
Naṣír, Tablet to, 107
Nations, unity of, 95, 249
"Nearness" (see Presence of God)
Nimrod, 88
Noah, 51, 84
Non-believers
  afflictions of, 169, 209, 214, 339
  character of, 169, 181, 183, 232, 233
  condition of, 71, 87, 136, 145–148, 168, 190, 191, 284, 293, 331

Obedience
  to governments, 207, 229, 240, 241
  to Laws of God (see Laws)

INDEX

INDEX

INDEX

Teachers
influence of, 277, 334-335
preparation of, 201, 277, 334, 335, 339
success due to Word of God, 277
traveling, 334

Teaching
enjoined, 38, 196, 197, 205, 276, 278, 280, 281, 296, 303, 314, 330, 335
through words, not violence, 278, 303, 330
with kindness, 8, 279, 289

Tests and trials, 12, 27

Ṭihrán, 228
believers of, 122
blessing of pilgrimage to, 121, 122
future of, 111
martyrs of, 109, 121
station of, 120, 121
Tablet regarding visit to, 120
Tablet to, 109, 110, 121

Torah, 294

Traditions, meaning of, 171, 174

Tribulations assist Cause, 42, 72, 270, 333

Trustworthiness, 232, 233, 266, 278, 285, 290, 299

Truthfulness, 232, 271, 290, 297, 299, 305

Truths, beyond expression, 176

Turkish Ministers, Tablet to, 122-125

Unbelievers (see Non-believers)

Understanding, 132, 194 (see also Man, mind of)

Unity, Divine, meaning of, 59, 69, 70, 166, 167, 187, 191

Unity of God, 21, 59, 64, 143, 162, 167, 189-193, 231, 261, 336, 340, 344

Unity of Mankind (see Mankind)

Vain imaginations, 6, 12, 34, 42, 82, 83, 93, 156, 196, 203, 204, 219, 291, 307, 324, 326, 337, 338

Victory
dependent upon obedience, 289
of Cause, 43, 248, 287, 306, 332, 334, 341
over self, 93
through fear of God, 272
time of, 319

Violence, 277, 303

Violence prohibited in teaching, 278, 303, 330

Wealth (see Possessions)

Will, Divine, 5, 61, 65, 209, 211, 217, 318, 324, 329, 338

Will, Divine, known through Manifestations, 59, 167

Will, free, 71, 149, 164, 335-338

Will, surrender of, 336-338

Wind, 339

Word of God
compared to tree, 9,
everlasting, 175
known only by Manifestations, 158, 175
power from reciting, 295
power of, 29, 35 76, 86, 87, 104, 141, 142, 175, 200, 270, 277, 286, 316, 325

Words
limitations of, 176
vitalized by Bahá'u'lláh, 93

Work, a duty, 202

World, 162
animating power of, 93, 157
compared with body of man, 81, 254, 255
compared with mirage, 328
condition of, today, 97, 118, 136, 200, 213, 218, 255
of dreams, 152, 162

INDEX